Neelkanth Varni

Neelkanth Varni

The incredible true story of an eleven-year-old orphan boy's
seven-year journey of discovery and liberation

Nilesh Manani

www.whitefalconpublishing.com

Neelkanth Varni

Nilesh Manani

www.whitefalconpublishing.com

All rights reserved

First Edition, 2023

© Nilesh Manani, 2023

Cover design by White Falcon Publishing, 2023

Cover image of Neelkanth Varni © Swaminarayan Aksharpith

The contents of this book have been certified and timestamped on
the Gnosis blockchain as a permanent proof of existence. Scan the
QR code or visit the URL given on the back cover to
verify the blockchain certification for this book.

Requests for permission should be addressed to
neelkanthvarni1781@gmail.com

ISBN - 978-1-63640-781-4

Dedicated to our beloved

Bhagwan Swaminarayan

Contents

Introduction

"Non-violence is the highest ethical code."
Shikshapatri Verse 12
Bhagwan Swaminarayan

India in the eighteenth century was a land of deep divisions and contrasts. It saw the decline of the Mughal Empire during the war of succession after the death of Aurangzeb in 1707. Internally, there were the revolts from the Sikhs, Jats, and Marathas, and externally, the foreign invasion from Nadir Shah effectively ended the Mughal Empire. European countries like France, England, Portugal, and Spain started to fill the void by trading with India, creating political and economic instability, and ultimately, destroying India's economy.

Socially, men dominated the communities. The education of girls was neglected. Widow burning was common in some communities and female infanticide was practiced in others, driven largely by the abject poverty of the people. Deep social and cultural divisions existed between regions based on tribal differences, language, caste, and religion. Above it all were the rich and powerful nobles, steeped in luxury and comfort, who tried to protect their lifestyles at the expense of the peasants living at the bare subsistence level, bearing all sorts of injustices and inequities. Many were taxed off their lands. The severe famine of 1769-70 made the lives of the peasants even more desperate. Modern historians estimate that ten million people may have died due to the famine and the exploitative taxes and revenue policies of the British East India Company.

It was after this devastation that never allowed the poor to recover that an eleven-year-old Neelkanth started his seven-year journey from Ayodhya in the early hours of the morning of 29 June 1792. Barefoot and dressed only in a loincloth, he courageously entered the soaring wilderness of the Himalayas during its most hostile season. He emerged four years later, emaciated but alive, aware of what he must do to liberate the people of India from millennia of conquerors, whose exploitative policies had devastated India's ancient traditions of justice and support of the poor, the meek, and the holy. Neelkanth walked across the length and breadth of India to restore the justice of the ancient wisdom of India, founded on the highest ethical principle of *Ahimsa* – non-violence. In an age of violence and exploitation, he advocated non-violence. Neelkanth wanted to restore its value and made it the foundation of his philosophy. It formed the foundation of the Non-Violence Movement, which ultimately led to the independence of India. Neelkanth stopped the practice of female infanticide and the burning of widows. He improved the lives of the poor and helped set up almshouses. Neelkanth had a following of millions when the British Governor of Bombay, Sir John Malcolm, met him in Rajkot in February 1830.

Introduction

Neelkanth Varni's journey inspires me daily to try a little harder, to embrace the spirit of service in the age-old truth that a good and happy life is found not in the accumulation of power and wealth or materialism, but in having little, and, if we have a lot, by giving, in love and serving. May this incredible story of an eleven-year-old orphan Neelkanth Varni inspire you all, as it does me.

Nilesh Manani

Route Map of Neelkanth Varni's Journey

1

Leaving Home

After a long day of meditation under his favorite banyan tree by the banks of the holy Saryu River, on the edge of the ancient city of Ayodhya, Ghanshyam, the eleven-year-old orphan child of Brahmin parents, returned to the dung and mud house to meet his sister-in-law. Suhasini had gone to great lengths to arrange this visit of his future bride and was in no mood to accept any excuses. But watching Ghanshyam approach the house, his long hair drenched, his clothes soaked, and his head bowed, the love of a mother melted Suhasini's heart, and she rushed into the house to collect a towel and change of clothes. She took Ghanshyam's hand without saying a word, led him inside the house, bathed him in warm water, and sat him down to feed him. Suhasini watched Ghanshyam eat silently, lovingly adding spoonfuls of steaming hot foods to his plate.

Suhasini had married Ghanshyam's much older brother before Ghanshyam was born. She had bathed Ghanshyam, fed him, clothed him, and played with him. It was Suhasini Ghanshyam went to when he was hurt. It was in Suhasini's embrace Ghanshyam had toddled into when he took his first steps. She was the witness when Ghanshyam picked up a book when his parents tested him as a baby with a sword, a pile of gold jewelry, and a book. She was the witness with his parents when a renowned astrologer pronounced that Ghanshyam would become a great scholar and lift the miseries of countless people. Suhasini loved Ghanshyam like a son. Ghanshyam loved Suhasini like a mother.

Her love had grown since the passing of his parents six months ago.

Ghanshyam looked up when Suhasini sniffed and saw the tears trickling down her rosy cheeks. 'I am sorry, Bhabhi,' said Ghanshyam, wiping her tears with his fingers. 'It seems this will be the last meal I will eat from your hands.'

Suhasini pinched Ghanshyam's cheek, sensing his innocence. 'Today was only the meeting of the two families. There is still the engagement, then the wedding, before the arrival of your wife to the house. It will be months before she joins the family. I wish you had not gone away without meeting the girl. You would have liked her. She is very beautiful and from a good family.'

'But there is so much I still want to do and learn,' cried Ghanshyam with a passion Suhasini had not seen before, a passion that Ghanshyam had held in check for three years now because he did not want to cause grief to his parents, a passion that was about to be quashed by his family, but a passion Ghanshyam had vowed to fulfill no matter the obstacles.

The allure of silence, solitude, and meditation had always been too strong in Ghanshyam's heart. His soul craved for it. His mind thought about it. The daily toil of living did not appeal to Ghanshyam because he could never understand how, having once been born in this magnificence we called the human body, all we did was waste our lives enslaved to it, in the daily grind of sustenance, work, marriage, children, old age, and, inevitably, death. Everything that was born, everything that grew, eventually died and decayed. It was a notion he could not engage with no matter how hard he tried to convince himself otherwise. It tormented him daily. There surely had to be a greater reason, a greater purpose to this human birth.

It was this deep inner craving to find the true meaning of life, living, that excited his heart, a yearning greater than even love, a thirst that could not be quenched by all the sweet waters of the world nor by the ancient city with all its historic charms and heroic tales of chivalry, grief, and sacrifice, sung daily in the temples dotted around the city. Ghanshyam longed to be free.

There was sadness in Ghanshyam's heart when he got up in the middle of the night, the sadness of hurting the family and friends he would leave behind. But there was joy too, in finally beginning his journey. Above him, the monsoon rains pounded on the roof, occasionally disrupted by a crackle of the thunder as if to rebuke him for the inconsolable grief he was about to cause his family.

Ghanshyam thought about his daily lessons with his father, the wisdom of ages he had so meticulously written in a little booklet he was going to take with him. He bowed to his nephew and the younger brother, sleeping peacefully on a homemade mattress thrown on the dung and mud floor next to his much older brother. He knelt when his eyes fell on Suhasini and bowed his head on the ground. 'Please forgive me, Bhabhi,' he whispered, aware that she would miss him more than anyone else.

Lightening flashed in the night sky when Ghanshyam stepped on the veranda as if to dissuade him. He waited for the anger of the thunder to die down, sighed, and splashed on the puddle with bare feet, unperturbed by the gloomy portents.

Soon his bare body, clad only in a loincloth, shone under the light of the full moon as he made his way through the deserted dirt lane. The neatly tied bun on top of his head became loose and fell over his eyes. He pushed the soaked clumps to the side when he approached a temple, stopped, and bowed in the direction of the inner sanctum for blessings.

Tiny stones washed by the rain pricked his bare feet near the raging river in full flood. He had witnessed her anger the previous day and had nothing but respect for her. He looked back for one last time to see the dark silhouette of the spires and domes of the ancient city of Ayodhya against the sky before sitting down on the granite steps to watch the thrust of the surging waters. His heart willed him to take the plunge, but good sense told him to wait for a boat. He had waited for far too long to meet death at the start.

As lightning struck in the distance, someone's hands grabbed him from behind and threw him into the river. He could not see who it was as the fast currents caught him and carried him down the river. Unable to fight the surge, he opened his arms and splayed his legs to remain afloat. The waters held him in a bowl as if to shield him. In all the years of swimming in the river, he had never seen it so angry, and he knew he had little choice but to obey.

His heart warmed when he saw faint traces of light appear on the horizon. The rain gradually began to ease until only a soft shower remained. The clouds cleared by the time the white disk of the sun rose above the horizon. The mist over the river evaporated, but the surge of the water did not relent.

There was no relief, even at midday, when the bright rays of the sun dazzled his eyes. His heart skipped with joy when he met the spirited golden mahseer fish jumping bravely against the flow of the water, a few even jumping over him before swimming on their way upstream. He knew they would keep going until they reached the shallow bed of the river past Ayodhya to spawn amid the fine-leafy plants rising from the river.

The sun was behind him when he finally reached the widest part of the river. The surge of the water eased and the bowl of water that had carried him so far melted as if it had done its duty. As his feet touched the riverbed, he pushed hard to rise and swam to the shallow edge filled with fine stones, smoothed and polished by the waters over millennia and more. It felt good to stand again and walk on them with the rays of the sun on his bare back. Even the occasional sharp prick against the sole of his feet could not suppress the joy of surviving the longest water ride of his life.

The loincloth dripped with water as he stepped onto the bank. He unwrapped it and rinsed it before wrapping it again around his waist. His eyes closed in reverence as he faced the sun and opened his arms wide to absorb the healing rays to soothe the tiredness of his limbs. They warmed his heart as well as his body as he thought about his parents.

'You have been my teacher, my guru, father; all I am is because of you, mother. May you shield me during my journey,' whispered Ghanshyam as if to seek their blessings before stepping under the shade of a banyan tree. There he sat and brushed his hair with his fingers to release the knots before tying it into a bun on top of his head as a mark of his determination to find the truth. His belly groaned with hunger and he remembered the Shaligram – the fossilized shell he had tied around his neck as the representation of God to accompany him on the pilgrimage. He collected a few fresh leaves and placed the Shaligram on them.

A man in fine clothes approached him as he washed the Shaligram with water. He bowed. 'I am Prince Varun. I have been playing on the banks of the Saryu for as long as I can remember, but I have never seen you here. Please tell me who you are, from where you come, and who are the parents who have let you go at such a tender age?'

Ghanshyam gazed at the prince as he thought about his answer. It was still too close to Ayodhya to give his real name. He thought about the sacrifice of Lord Shiva, the ascetic of all the ascetics. It was the path he had chosen, and there seemed to be only one answer. 'I am Neelkanth,' he said. 'I come from a kingdom not known to man. Today is the first day of a pilgrimage I have held back for three years and broken the bond of a family that has nurtured me since birth. Yet, I feel free, free, and free of all the attachments that life brings.'

Intrigued by the response, the prince sat down on the bare ground, unwrapped a parcel of guava fruits, and gave them to Neelkanth. Neelkanth offered them to the Shaligram before sharing them with the prince.

'Your parents must be heartbroken,' said the prince.

'They are sadly no more. They bathed me when I could not, dressed me when I was unable, fed me when I was hungry, and held me in their embrace when I was sad. How can I then cause them grief? Is it not the duty of a child to honor and serve his parents in ill health and old age?'

'I am sorry that they have passed away when you are still only a child. How will you survive in the wild? What will you eat? Where will you shelter?'

Neelkanth looked up at the sky dotted with birds enjoying the warm air currents. 'The sky is my shelter, Mother Earth is my bed, and nature provides all the fruits I can eat.'

'What about growing up, learning a craft, marriage, love, children, and all the joys that a family brings? Will you not miss them?'

Neelkanth grinned. 'Oh, prince, did you decide the time of your birth?'

'No.'

'Did you have a choice about where you are born?'

7

'No.'

'Did you have a choice of parents, your gender, or your first name?'

'No,' the prince said.

'But we have a choice about the decisions we make for our life.'

'I am a prince and will one day have to assume the throne. I have no choice.'

'We all have a choice. It is good that not everyone chooses the path of renunciation because there is a need for a cobbler, a merchant, a farmer, and a prince too. It is a choice you will have to make when the time comes. Although you should know that this human birth is extremely rare and more precious than we can imagine. Do not waste it. Be a prince, but be a prince like none other, of service to those you will one day rule. You have the power of the sun in your Atman – the eternal soul, so use it wisely.'

The prince smiled. 'You are in the body of a child, but you speak with the wisdom of ages. It is my good fortune to have met you. I shall try to be as you say. I hope you find success on your journey.' The prince stood up. Neelkanth watched him paddle merrily along the shallow edge of the river until he disappeared behind some bushes. He laid down on the ground to rest for a while.

A light shower had shrouded the river in a mist when he got up. It was late afternoon, and the sun was still up, so he decided to follow the river north. The blades of the grass felt good on the soft sole of his bare feet. In the distance, a rainbow arched like a bridge over the width of the river. Neelkanth stopped and keenly studied the richness of the colors before moving on. When darkness settled around the river, he sat down under a tree and closed his eyes.

The chirping of crickets joined the soft ripples of the river, occasionally disturbed by the flutter of wings and tweets of the birds nestling in the trees. Neelkanth tried to meditate but was unable to concentrate as the grief of his family and friends in Ayodhya flooded his thoughts. He thought about the Hanuman of the Ayodhya temple.

A sudden rush of the wind forced him to open his eyes. They fell on a monkey, richly adorned in a red dhoti and a gold necklace and earrings.

Neelkanth bowed. 'How did you find me here?'

'You thought about me,' Hanuman said with a grin. 'You have spoilt me with your daily visits to the temple. When you did not come, I visited your house and only saw the tears of your family. I searched for you in the forest and heard the cries of your friends. I searched for you on the banks of the Saryu and saw your friend Veni lamenting. So, I sat down in meditation in the hope of seeing you.'

Neelkanth took his hand. 'I am glad you came. You are renowned for your wisdom, strength, courage, and devotion. Today is the first day of my journey, and I am honored to have your blessings at the start.'

'It is I who should be asking for your blessings,' Hanuman said. 'Will you not return to Ayodhya to comfort your mourning family and friends? Everyone thinks you had gone for your morning bath in the Saryu and drowned.'

Neelkanth gazed at Hanuman with kindness. 'It is not auspicious to return without completing what one has started.'

'I have watched and protected you since you were born. How will I survive without you? How will your family and friends survive?'

'It is true that I would not have survived without your vigilance,' grinned Neelkanth.

'There will be a lot of hardships on the journey. Who will protect you from the wild animals? What will you eat? You are a growing boy and will need all the nourishment.'

Neelkanth sensed the worry in Hanuman's gentle voice. 'Hanuman, if I was afraid, I would not have even contemplated the journey. You would be a good companion for any traveler, but I have vowed to travel alone.'

Hanuman's eyes dropped. Neelkanth sensed his disappointment. 'If you must serve me, come whenever I think of you. Return to Ayodhya for now to tell my family that I am safe. Tell them not to worry and that I shall contact them one day. It is unlikely to be any time soon, so tell them to be patient.'

Hanuman bowed and walked into the forest behind him. Neelkanth got up and collected a bunch of fallen leaves to sweep the ground. Joy and sadness clashed in his heart when he laid down. He wondered whether he had done the right thing by abandoning his family without telling them where he was going? Whether it would have been better to have left with their permission?

A loud crow of a rooster woke Neelkanth up early in the morning. The tiredness of the previous day had still not ebbed. Neelkanth stretched his arms and legs for a while to release the tension, then stepped into the shallow edge of the Saryu to bathe before facing east for meditation. His father had drummed the importance of facing east for as long as Neelkanth could remember, but he had never asked him the reason until one day when he bravely plucked the courage to question him.

Rather than brushing his question aside, his father raised his hands in the air with joy. 'A question, finally,' he had said with cheer. 'Always question and try to find out the how, where, when, and why. Accept nothing without questioning. It will strengthen your understanding and knowledge. East is the direction where the sun rises. The sun gives power, strength, and life to all the living things on earth. Facing east awakens the strength and power within us and allows us to achieve our goals. It gives us peace, happiness, wealth, and health.' His father cried from the top of his voice so that Neelkanth would remember the moment.

Neelkanth did not forget. He never forgot that first question because of his father's euphoric reaction to it. He inhaled deeply and exhaled gently from his mouth with a long 'Aum' until his breathing settled into a rhythm. When the sun crept up the horizon, he felt the soft warmth of the morning rays. It filled his heart with strength and vigor. The tiredness melted away until a peace embraced him, a peace that melted all his doubts about whether he had done the right thing by leaving his family without telling them, a peace that transcended all understanding, a peace that came from the core of his soul, the 'Atman'. There was joy on his face when he saw the Self. There was something familiar about it.

It was only disturbed when the residents of the nearby village came to bathe and fill their pots with fresh water. Neelkanth heard their voices but did not open his eyes until the call of loving mothers summoned him. He had never ignored the call of their selfless love.

'Who is he?'

'He is so young.'

'He looks so at peace.'

'Which mother would let go of a son who is so noble in appearance?'

Neelkanth opened his eyes. 'The love of a mother is indeed hard to ignore,' he said, bowing.

The mothers pressed their palms together. 'Are you lost, child? You should be at home and not out in the forest all alone.'

'Mother, I am at home. It is others who are lost.'

The mothers gazed at him in confusion. 'Who are you? Where is your home?'

'My name is Neelkanth. I have no home. I only have a journey.'

'Where are you going?'

'Wherever I can help the poor, the meek, and the holy.'

'Why don't you make your home here? We will look after you like our son.'

Neelkanth looked up at the clouds. 'Mother, my journey is like the monsoon clouds because there is thirst everywhere. I just cannot stop moving.'

One mother offered him a bunch of bananas. Neelkanth took one and returned the rest.

'Please keep them. The harvest has been good this year.'

'There is no point in renouncing home if one is constantly going to think about what to eat. A yogi should be detached like the sky, observing all but attached to none.'

A village elder came forward. 'Are you not afraid to travel alone?'

'What is there to fear? God resides in all; therefore, his Will prevails in all.'

A man stepped forward. 'If you do not take any fruits with you, will you not at least accept this gourd to keep water?'

Neelkanth glanced at a gourd beautifully decorated with floral patterns in flame orange. 'The colors of an ascetic,' he said and hugged the man. 'The water will help quench my thirst.'

'Be careful of the wild animals in the forests ahead,' the man warned.

Neelkanth bowed and left, fearful of the temptations in the village.

A gentle breeze blew the dry leaves as he stepped onto a wide path while sparrows swept up and down to pick up the thorns. Grey monsoon clouds released a light shower, cooling the soft blades of grass on the ground. The branches of the trees bowed and released the juiciest fruits and rolled them in front of him. Neelkanth smiled at the bounty of nature, ate a little, and left the rest for the birds that were chirping and tweeting their tunes merrily to keep him company.

He reached the edge of a small village of Bareli after a few hours but decided not to enter the village after his earlier experience with villagers. He followed the river to a jute bridge. He crossed it and reached a beautifully manicured garden, lined with trees, gentle streams, and flowers with colors he had not seen before. Birds tweeted and peacocks danced and sang as if to welcome him. Neelkanth stopped to enjoy the beauty and peace of the place. A butterfly flew near a rose bush. He reached out and watched the butterfly gently settle on the back of his hand. He was about to release it when a man greeted him from behind. Neelkanth turned. 'You have created a wonderful garden,' he said.

The man bowed. 'Years of hard work, care, and love, my child.'

'Yes, even nature needs some help to create such a fine garden.'

'I am only the caretaker. The master comes with his family to enjoy his summers.'

'To seek relief from the intense heat of our summers.'

'Yes, but he would not forgive me if I did not invite an ascetic of your aura to bless his home. Please, please do come.' The man bent low and waved Neelkanth forward.

'Meek,' whispered Neelkanth and followed the caretaker to the veranda in front of a grand red stone house where the caretaker offered him a plate full of flower petals. Neelkanth took some in his hand and sprinkled them on the wooden floor to bless the home. 'This is as far as I go,' he said when the man invited him to visit the inner rooms, ever alert to any temptations that could stall him on his journey.

'Please.' The caretaker pointed to a swing on the side.

Neelkanth placed the gourd of water on the floor and removed the rosary from around his neck. The caretaker sat down on the floor. Neelkanth invited him to sit with him.

The caretaker put his palms together and pulled the swing with a string. 'My child, over more than thirty years here, I have come across more ascetics than I can count, but I have yet to come across anyone who shines like our ancient rishis.'

'The ancient rishis had the wisdom of the Gods. I am only eleven and still have so much to learn.'

The caretakers smiled. 'Pralad was a child, but he knew the Vedas. Holy men have taught me enough to know that age is not a barrier to knowledge nor does it define the wisdom of a person. Is the soul not eternal? Is it not born and reborn? Is wisdom not an accumulation of a soul's many births and experiences through the cycle of births and deaths?'

'You have listened well,' said Neelkanth. He raised his legs and crossed them. Birds flew in and out of the trees in front of them, whistling and tweeting. Neelkanth felt at peace, caressed by the beauty and serenity of the place. His attention was distracted when a peacock appeared on the ground below the veranda and opened the tail feathers like a fan. Neelkanth stood up and watched the peacock from the top of the stairs. He sat down when the caretaker went inside the house, closed his eyes, and started to sing.

Pray to the Lord, the merciful,
Who extinguishes life's fearful dangers.
He possesses eyes like a new-born lotus,
Moreover, a lotus-like face with hands of pink lotus...

Trees swayed in the breeze, peacocks twirled and sang, dogs barked, and birds tweeted. In the distance, wild cats roared and elephants blew their trumpets. Neelkanth clapped and swayed from side to side in tune with the song. Soon, the garden was no more. The birds and animals were no more. The tweets, roars, and trumpets were no more. There was only joy in his heart while a growing crowd gathered in front of him.

The crowd burst into applause when Neelkanth stopped. Stunned by their presence, Neelkanth bowed. They put their palms together and pressed him to continue. The caretaker came out with a plate full of fruits and water. While Neelkanth drank the water, the crowd stepped forward and gathered around him. Some sat down on the steps.

Neelkanth sang the first verse of a song he was sure they would know. *'Ram Krishna Govinda, Jai, Jai Govinda.'* He stood up as they sang and swayed to the rhythm of the beat and then raised his hands above his head and clapped to signal them to follow. The boys joined him on the top and mimicked his steps. Encouraged by their mothers, the girls twirled and spun with grace with each clap. Neelkanth laughed and encouraged the men until everyone clapped in tune with him, mesmerized by the divine atmosphere.

They cheered and clapped when they stopped. Neelkanth waved to them to sit down. His eyes fell on a man in torn clothes, standing timidly at the back of the crowd. He waved him forward. The crowd opened a corridor for him. The man hesitated. Neelkanth waved to him to come forward. The man looked at the crowd without moving.

'He is from the untouchable caste of Dalits who live outside the village,' said a village elder.

'Untouchables,' Neelkanth frowned in a raised voice as if to rebuke. 'We are all children of God, so how can anyone be untouchable.' He stood up and walked to the man, took his hand, and sat him down next to him on the top of the stairs. 'Please, please do take some fruit.'

The man glanced at the village elder. Neelkanth saw the fear in his eyes. He picked up a slice of mango and fed him, then purposefully took another slice with the same hand and ate it just to set an example to the villagers. 'God does not discriminate between the rich and poor, between a prince or a pauper, a peasant or a merchant, whether we live in a grand house or a mud hut. He only looks at the purity of our hearts. Nor is the quality of a person determined by their birth family but by the quality of their character, just as the strength of a warrior is not determined by the weapons he wields but by the strength of his courage.'

The village elder stepped forward and pressed his trembling hands together. 'Child, we have displeased you.

Please forgive us. Thank you for reminding us that we are all children of God.'

Over a lifetime of living in the village, the elder had seen many ascetics but none like Neelkanth, none so young and yet fearless in putting a wrong right. He sensed a divine aura around Neelkanth. He felt love, the love of a grandfather, and felt compelled to do as Neelkanth said like a dotting grandfather.

Neelkanth sensed the sincerity in the elder's voice and wrapped his hands in his palms. Their eyes met, their hearts melted, and their souls touched. 'The true character of this village is visible in how it treats the poor, the meek, and the holy. You are a village elder, respected by all. You must lead the way by showing compassion for everyone. The prosperity of the village will depend on it,' said Neelkanth.

The village elder bowed as Neelkanth gave the plate of fruits to him. He took a slice of fruit and asked a boy to take it around. Neelkanth watched to check if everyone had taken a slice of fruit. His work done, Neelkanth got up, thanked the caretaker, bowed to the crowd, and made his way through the path the crowd created. 'Who are you?' Neelkanth heard the village elder ask from behind, but Neelkanth kept on walking without looking back as the voice inside him repeated the same words he had uttered many times before: I am a servant of the poor, the meek, and the holy.

Tall conifers stood like an army of soldiers in the dense woods as if to warn Neelkanth not to enter. He intently stared deep into the darkness of the forest and listened to the roars of the wild animals before bowing to the ancient sage Naradji who had done penance in the forest as a child and had the vision of Lord Vishnu when he had told him that he would not see him again until his death. Though sad and disappointed, the desire to see Vishnu again fueled Naradji's devotion for the rest of his life. Neelkanth had heard the story from his father and he wanted to fuel his desire for silence and solitude in the same way.

Though he knew he would not be able to spot the exact tree under which the child sage had done penance, he hoped to feel the energy from the tree under which he had sat. He was sure the sage's sacrifice would have fueled the lucky tree with his aura. He touched the trees to feel their vibrations. He listened to the rustle of their leaves to touch his heart. He looked for the rays of the sun to direct him. Ever alert, Neelkanth followed a faint dirt path as far as he could until dense foliage blocked all sunlight. Around him, pythons hung from leaning branches and hissed as he passed, while lions and tigers roared as if to challenge each other for the kingship of the forest. Neelkanth felt their presence in the vicinity, but neither his heart nor his eyes wavered in their resolve. He was one with nature and nature was one with him as he marched on, pushing through the vegetation. He only stopped when night fell and plunged the forest into pitch darkness. He laid down on the ground and soon fell asleep, listening to the echoes of the wild, thinking about the courage of the child sage Naradji, the same courage that embraced him now.

A roar woke him up in the morning. He was surprised he had not jumped. Faint rays of light had broken through the foliage. Then he saw, a little ahead, a wide beam of sunlight wrapped around a giant tree, its trunk as wide as the belly of an elephant. Neelkanth instantly knew it was an ancient tree with memories as long as millennia. He stepped closer, touched it, and felt the vibrations, the remnants of the energy and the sacrifice of the child sage. There was a quietness in its voice, a calm, a joy that evolved from its ancient wisdom, from being a witness to the vision of Lord Vishnu experienced by the child sage. He was sure this was the tree that had protected the child sage. He bowed his head in reverence and whispered a blessing before moving on.

On the way ahead, bushes gave way to a soft crush of dry leaves on the ground. When birds began to fly freely between branches, Neelkanth felt the edge of the forest was close, if not near. His pace quickened when he heard the chanting of hymns in the distance. He followed it and soon saw a group of ascetics. They jumped to their feet when they saw him approaching. Neelkanth had entered the forest to find solitude and was disappointed that he could not be alone.

Neelkanth stopped and bowed respectfully as they surrounded him. They led him to a banyan tree, where they sat down in a circle. The same questions that had reminded him of his home surfaced again. He dismissed them as best as he could, wanting to leave that life behind in pursuit of the greater dream, a greater purpose he had imprinted on his mind. He learned that the ascetics were on their way to the Himalayas to perform penance. He learned that they had been on a pilgrimage for years without finding any peace. The journey to the Himalayas was their final attempt to seek what had eluded them.

'The peace you seek is within you,' said Neelkanth. 'Meditate, still the mind, and touch the soul because therein sits what you all seek.'

'To still the mind is very hard,' the ascetics confessed.

Neelkanth liked their honesty and felt compelled to help. 'Yes, it is very hard because the soul and the mind are close friends. Their friendship is like the friendship between milk and water.'

'Like milk and water?' asked the ascetics in surprise.

'Yes, like milk and water,' said Neelkanth. 'When milk and water are mixed and heated, water settles below the milk and itself burns, but it does not allow the milk to burn. To save the water, the milk overflows and extinguishes the fire. Such is their friendship. Our soul and the mind have a similar close friendship. The problem is we allow the mind to rule like a king, forgetting that it is part of the body. It will die with the death of the body. On the other hand, the soul has accumulated the wisdom of the ages over many, many lives. It is the real king of the body.'

'Oh, please tell us about the soul. What is it like?' the ascetics asked together.

Neelkanth closed his eyes. 'The soul has no caste. It is no one's daughter or son, no one's mother or father. It belongs to no community and to no class. When we have mastered the art of looking at the soul, one will see the soul as extremely luminous, like the sun and fire. It is, therefore, very powerful. The soul is our true self. It is smaller than the smallest particle. It resides in the heart, it is sentient, and through its sense of feeling pervades our entire body and allows us to feel. It is conscious, and therefore, it is fully aware of everything that happens.'

'You are an ancient soul in a child's body,' said the ascetics in admiration.

Neelkanth thought about his many lessons from his father, his many debates with the most learned of Brahmins in Varanasi that had honed his answers. 'My father taught me penance alone is not enough. We must learn to serve the poor and the vulnerable to find our inner self.'

'Yogiraj, tell us how we may find God in human form?'

Neelkanth grinned. 'Find God,' he whispered and touched the chest of one of the ascetics with his fingers. 'Look at your hearts and ask yourself if your desire to see him is pure.'

'Oh, it is, it is!' the ascetics said together.

'Then you will not have to find him. He will find you.'

Neelkanth stood up. 'I must go. I am keen to reach Badrinath before the end of the month. As you are aware, it closes at the start of winter.'

'Yogiraj, can we follow you? Oh, please,' one ascetic asked.

'I like to travel alone, but you can join me for a while if you want.'

The ascetics quickly gathered their belongings and stood ready like obedient students. Neelkanth smiled at their eagerness, how they hung onto his every word. It spoke of their humble nature, and as a servant of the poor, the meek, and the holy, he led them forward with a rosary in one hand. The ascetics followed quietly to make sure they did not disturb him with their talk.

Neelkanth only stopped when twilight engulfed the forest and the way ahead was not clear. He found a clearing below a tree and decided to rest for the night. Without thinking twice, he laid down on the ground, rested his head on his arm, and closed his eyes.

The ascetics joined him on the ground, but as darkness descended around them and the chirping of the crickets filled the air, occasionally disturbed by the hooting of the owls and the roars of the cats, Neelkanth saw the ascetics pick up their belongings and tie their hammocks to the branches to sleep. He smiled, thinking they had not grasped the essence of what he had told them earlier. He turned to his side and fell asleep.

In the morning, Neelkanth's eyes fell on a hyena sleeping nearby. The hyena leaped to its feet when Neelkanth sat up. It walked around Neelkanth and went on its way. The ascetics came down and fell at his feet.

'What is the matter?' asked Neelkanth.

'You are a great yogi. Even the hyena sensed it.'

Neelkanth bowed. 'Animals sense our fear and respond accordingly. Did I not tell you not to be afraid?'

'We just couldn't help it.'

Neelkanth placed his palms together. 'You allowed the mind to win. I know it is very hard, but you must persevere, learn to overcome your fears, and become one with the soul. Find some silence and sit in meditation. It will be hard at first because you will be overwhelmed with your countless thoughts, but be brave and concentrate on Para-Brahman – the Supreme Self. If you practice it long enough and regularly, you will certainly become better.' With this, Neelkanth bid his farewell.

2

Ganga's Cradle

After his many unexpected brushes with people, Neelkanth longed to be alone, so he made his way north, towards the wilderness of the Himalayas. Ancient broadleaf and conifers closed in around him along the way. Neelkanth touched the trees as if to sense the secrets of the ancient sages the trees would have witnessed as they passed. He was sure many would have taken the same route on their way north. Farther up, the dense vegetation replaced the trees, making it harder to cut through. Neelkanth knelt on his hands and knees, and, at times, even crawled through small gaps between the bushes, smarting his legs and upper body.

He reappeared in the sunlight in the afternoon. His body glistened with perspiration. Inflamed fine cuts crisscrossed his legs, back, and hands. The ripples of flowing water brought him to the banks of a river. He guessed it to be the holy Ganga and placed the gourd on the sandy bank before stepping into the clear water, shimmering under the rays of the sun. The gentle hands of mother Ganga massaged his muscles as he stepped into her womb. Neelkanth took some water into the bowl of his palms and paid his respects.

As he sat down to meditate, his eyes fell on a woman, dressed in white, walking toward him. Curious to discover her identity, he waited until she came near. The woman bowed and placed a tray full of a variety of cooked foods and flowers in front of him. 'I am Ganga,' she said.

'Ganga? Mother Ganga in person?' asked Neelkanth in surprise.

'Yes. Are not all mothers like Ganga in spirit?' the woman asked without hesitation.

Neelkanth took joy in the meeting with the holy mother, unable to believe his luck.

'I have yearned for your visit for what seems like an eternity,' Ganga said.

Neelkanth frowned as Ganga picked up a garland from the tray and placed it around his neck, then took a golden bowl of sandalwood pulp, dipped her fingers in it, and marked his forehead with it. She shook her head when her eyes fell on the fine red lines of his brushes in the woods. 'You must be more careful of the thorns,' she said and rubbed the pulp on the cuts.

Neelkanth felt the soothing coolness of the pulp and thanked her.

'You look like you have not eaten in days. A growing boy needs his nourishment.' Ganga placed the tray on her lap.

Neelkanth glanced at the steaming hot foods beautifully arranged on the tray. He inhaled the spices. 'Mother, wherever I go, all people want to do is feed me.'

'Well, is it surprising?' Ganga scolded. 'Have you looked at yourself in the mirror recently? You are as thin as a stick.' She picked up a morsel and fed Neelkanth.

Neelkanth absorbed the juices from the spices as he chewed. 'The food is delicious,' he said. 'Will you take some food from my hands, mother?' He reached for a sweet before Ganga had a chance to reply and raised his hand to her lips. Ganga smiled as she ate. She fed him until all the bowls were empty. Neelkanth rubbed his stomach with satisfaction, having not eaten a fuller meal since leaving Ayodhya.

Ganga gazed at him seriously. 'I am a woman and a mother and know of the hardships women suffer,' she said, welling up. 'The women work the land with their husbands. They clean their homes. They cook for the family. They give birth, care, nurture, and raise fine children without ever complaining. Do you know that many baby girls die – no – killed by drowning in milk because their poor families do not have the means to raise the dowries for their marriage? Did you know that some widows are forced to burn alive on the funeral pyre of their husbands? It is always women who suffer the most. What type of society are we creating through such callous actions? What message are we giving young men? That women are a burden to be cast aside when they have performed their duty of giving birth to children?'

Neelkanth saw the tears on Ganga's cheeks and tenderly wiped them with his hand. 'It is a heinous crime to kill a helpless child,' he said. 'To kill a helpless baby girl is to destroy the heart of a society. To kill a mother is to destroy all that is good. People have forgotten the true essence of our ancient value of *Ahimsa* – non-violence in speech, action, and thought.'

'The world is warped in greed and violence,' Ganga said. 'We have been ravaged by ruthless dictators who have killed without any regard for life, tiny principalities whose monarchs have only served to fill their treasury at the expense of the masses. Farmers toil on the land, only for the landowners to claim the harvest, leaving little for them. They are helpless, at the mercy of their landlords.'

Neelkanth stared at the pain on Ganga's face. 'I promise you I will do whatever I can to put the injustice right wherever I see it, although I am not sure whether they will listen to a child.'

'If they see what I see, they will listen,' Ganga said without hesitating. Neelkanth sensed her confidence. Ganga put the tray on the sand. 'The sun will soon retire. You must be tired after your long walk through the forest.' She stood up and brushed the pebbles from the sand nearby. 'You will be comfortable here. The sand is soft and dry.'

Neelkanth laid down and rested his head on his hand. Ganga massaged his feet until he fell asleep. She watched him for a long time before collecting her things, her maternal instincts unable to hold the tears of what he was about to do as she walked towards the river.

Neelkanth left early in the morning and followed the Ganga north, stopping every so often to dip his feet in the cool water to wash the tiredness. It was slow progress, but he enjoyed the solitude after several unexpected encounters, a chance to reflect on what everyone had said. He promised himself he would intervene whenever he saw injustice, although he wasn't sure if anyone would listen to an eleven-year-old boy.

His pace picked up at first sight of the stunning snow-capped peaks of the Himalayas hugged by an occasional passing cloud. The Ganga basin grew wider higher up, curved, and broke up into several tributaries as if to slow the flow of the river for the farmers and pilgrims on the plains. Neelkanth followed on the edge, paddling in the river whenever he could.

The top crest of the sun had just sunk below the western horizon when Neelkanth reached the edge of the ancient city of Haridwar at the foothills of the Himalayas. Temple bells tolled, hymns echoed over the valley, and an orange glow of the many burning fires bathed the Ghats around the river. Neelkanth ran his eyes across the Ghats dotted with temples before navigating his way through the stairs packed with people. A coolness embraced him as he immersed his body in the water and took some water into the bowl of his palms. He poured it back into the river in prayer to help his ascent into the Himalayas. He was under no illusion that it would be the hardest thing he would do, especially when he was planning to enter the mountains at the start of the deadliest season.

A priest tapped his shoulder when he picked up some more water into the bowl of his palms and slowly poured it back into the river in reverence. Neelkanth looked up and saw a man in white clothes look down at him.

'Please, please come with me. It is crowded here because of the year of the Khumb Mela. They will trample you in the crush to bathe in the river if you are not careful.'

Neelkanth hesitated but picked up his gourd and stepped out. 'Why me? There are many here who would need your help?' he asked as the priest took his hand like a father.

'They are ascetics, but you are a yogi,' said the priest, smiling. He waved his hand at the crowd.

Neelkanth did not understand what he was trying to say. He ran his eyes across the length and breadth of the steps and saw a mass of men and women reciting verses. 'There are many worthy souls seeking enlightenment,' he said.

'Indeed, but none who shine like the sun. I am the priest of the Mahadev temple. I would be honored if you would grace us with your visit.' The priest took the gourd of water from Neelkanth's hand and led him up the steps, crisscrossing the crowd engrossed in prayer. Neelkanth softly touched their heads as he followed.

They crossed a crowded road and entered a temple as old as time, with withered stones stained with the hands of pilgrims. 'It has survived only because of the love and care,' said the priest.

'Of devoted priests,' said Neelkanth as they entered the temple. The cleanliness of the inner sanctum impressed him as he prostrated in front of the deities.

The priest offered him a soft cushion to sit on while he sat on the bare stone floor. 'Who are you?' he asked.

'I am Neelkanth and I am on a journey to help people. I want to visit Rishi Narayan, who resides in the Himalayas. Sri Krishna, who resides in Dwarka, is the same as the Narayan in the Himalayas. I wish to imbibe his virtues so that I may have his blessings before starting my work.'

The priest put his palms together. 'So sure at such a tender age, but my child, I hope you know that the mountains are cold and dangerous. You wish to go up in the deep of winter with only the loincloth and nothing on your feet. Have you ever seen snow? Do you know how cold it is? What will you eat? How will you keep warm? Where will you shelter in such an unforgiving environment? You are no ordinary soul, for you would not embark on this bold and brave journey otherwise at such a tender age. If you are to complete the journey and return safely, you will need to look after your body. Already you look frail and thin due to your travels. We will be honored if you will accept some food.'

Neelkanth grinned, unperturbed by the adversity. 'If food were a daily worry, I would not have left home, but since it is a daily necessity, I will take some if you will bring some.'

The priest got up and went to the kitchen. Neelkanth closed his eyes in meditation but opened them soon after when he felt the presence of someone near. His eyes fell on a woman sitting in front of him. 'Mother,' he said as if to ask her if there was anything he could do.

'Child, rarely does my husband show such eagerness to cook a meal. If you wish, I will prepare a delicious meal for you.'

Neelkanth smiled, sensing a mischievous motive. 'I do not understand what you are trying to say. The best thing to do would be to prepare it together. A husband and wife should be like Parvati and Shiva, like Radha and Krishna. I will eat whatever you two prepare.'

The woman looked down in embarrassment, bowed, and left. Neelkanth closed his eyes.

The priest came to call Neelkanth a while later to take him to the kitchen. He sat him down on a soft cushion. They served him a variety of foods. 'The food is indeed delicious, made as it has been with love by both of you. Tell me, who are you? Only if you tell me the truth will I stay here for a few days.'

The woman smiled. 'This city is named after my beloved husband, Har, and I am Parvati.' Neelkanth knew from his many lessons with his father that Har's other name was Shiva, the King of the Yogis, whose life determined the birth and dissolution of the universe. Parvati was his wife, a powerful Goddess revered in temples all over India. He was aware that as Gods, who had control over all the elements, they could secretly live amongst the people and help.

'If you are who you say you are, it is I who should be bowing to ask for your blessings as I enter the Himalayas in search of the ashram of Rishi Narayan.' Neelkanth knelt and bowed his head on the floor.

'You will always have our blessings,' said Har, placing his hand on Neelkanth's head.

'Today, you have rewarded us for many years of sacrifice and service to the pilgrims,' Parvati said. 'Please allow us to introduce our family.' She summoned all the children to meet Neelkanth. If there was any doubt in Neelkanth's mind about staying in the temple for a few days, the children quashed it with their instant rapport with him. They reminded him of his friends in Ayodhya, their games in the forests around the city, and the play in the Saryu in the scorching summer months. He thought about his friend Veni and hoped he was fine.

The couple pampered Neelkanth. They woke up early every day to prepare a cooked breakfast of rice cakes, lentil soup, and yogurt. Neelkanth ate with their children before they sat down together with their father, who recited stories from the Mahabharat and Ramayan. Neelkanth observed the devotion of the couple to the many pilgrims visiting the temple and knew he would get too attached to them if he spent any more time with the family.

He woke up in the middle of the night on the fifth day and quietly slipped out. It was a full moon night, but there was not a single person on the steps that were full of people reciting sacred verses during the day. He was tempted to bathe in the river but thought it was better higher up where no one would be able to find him. He stopped briefly at the start of a winding dirt road and observed the dark waters of the Ganga cascading over large boulders. His eyes fell on a fire in the distance on the edge of the river, and for some odd reason, felt compelled to find out the reason for the fire so early in the morning.

As he approached, he saw a group of men chanting Sanskrit verses, sitting around a pile of wood on top of which lay a body. A man held a flame on a wooden pole, and a group of women sat not far away comforting a woman. Neelkanth watched, curious to discover the reason for the funeral at such an odd hour.

As the men circled the body, the women got up. Two men approached them and pulled a crying woman. She screamed as she resisted. Neelkanth knew what was happening and rushed forward. The men saw him and stopped.

'*Ahimsa* is the pillar of our faith,' said Neelkanth. 'No good will come by burning a helpless widow on a funeral pyre of her husband.'

'We are doing what has been practiced for centuries,' a man said. 'A widow burning on the funeral pyre of her husband will attain liberation and become a Sati.'

'Nothing good will come from killing an innocent woman, but you will surely suffer the consequences of your cruelty, either in this life or the next. There is nothing more precious than a human birth, acquired after many millennia of births and deaths in lower life forms. God is the giver of life, and therefore, he alone can take the life that he has given.'

'What do you know? You are only a child,' a man shouted.

'He may only be a child, but there is no one more courageous at present than this child,' Parvati said from behind.

Neelkanth looked back and saw the priest and his wife standing with folded hands. He stepped aside.

'You should be protecting the wife when her husband is not there to protect her. Instead, you want to kill her in the name of Sati.'

'Or you want to kill her because you do not wish to take on the burden of looking after her,' Parvati said. She reached out with her hand to the widow. 'Come. We will look after you.'

The men stepped back as the woman approached Parvati, who took her hand and hugged her.

'Thank you,' Neelkanth said.

'And you thought you could sneak out in the middle of the night,' Har said, smiling.

'Please spend a few more days with us?' Parvati said, bowing.

Neelkanth put his palms together. 'Mother, I have vowed to reach Badrinath before the end of the month. As you are aware, the Badrinath temple closes for winter. I did not want to upset the children. They have become very attached to me, and I to them, so please allow me to leave now.' He walked away without looking back.

Neelkanth followed a winding dirt path up a hill and reached a plateau at the top just as the sun started to peer above the white mountains, bathing the land in a pink haze. He liked mornings as the land woke up from the stillness of the night, the mist lifted, flowers opened their petals, and birds sang their tunes. He listened to the call of the birds and the groans and the crackle of the mountains for a while before stepping onto the edge of a lake.

He broke the thin film of ice with his foot and stepped in slowly to allow his body to get used to the icy chill of the water. His heart raced and his body shivered as the chill entered his core. He inhaled deeply before finally immersing his head in the water. There, he remained for a while before rising to a most refreshing feeling of warmth, the likes of which he had not experienced before. Although Neelkanth was used to cold water from his daily early morning dips in the Saryu, he had never bathed in ice-cold water. A warm glow embraced him as he sat in meditation.

He stood up when the soft rays of the morning sun shone on his face, stood on one leg, and raised his arms above his head. As the rays warmed his body, he felt energized for another long walk up the mountains.

Yellow and blue autumn poppies swept across the meadows and a burst of musk roses ran wild, clothing pine trees, hedges, and hugging boulders. The air was heady with their scent. Neelkanth occasionally stopped to absorb the banquet of colors and watched the honeybees feast on the nectar. With not a person in sight, he had never felt so at peace. Solitude was what he had sought and solitude was what he finally found. It was liberating.

It was evening when Neelkanth reached the beautiful grove of Tapovan where many ascetics had gathered to perform penance. He knew from the stories he had heard from his father that the great sage Dhruvji had performed penance there for many years, and Mother Ganga had appeared in person and cried when he left. Over the centuries since, many had sought to follow in Dhruvji's experience, but none had been able to perform penance with the same commitment. Neelkanth was not one of them. His sights were set higher. He had come to Tapovan to pay his respects to Dhruvji and seek his blessings for a higher purpose he had in mind.

A pink flush of cranesbills filled the retreat, interspersed with balls of white primula and wild strawberries. Neelkanth collected a handful, washed them in a stream, and offered them to the Shaligram. As he sat in prayers, a group of ascetics gathered around him, keen to discover why someone so young wanted to take up the ascetic life. Neelkanth sensed their interest.

'Child, you remind us of young Dhruvji,' the leader of the ascetic said, an elderly monk with long white hair tied in a ponytail and a beard that stretched down to his chest. 'Please tell us your story. Why have you chosen the path of a wandering ascetic at such a tender age?'

Neelkanth looked down to reflect. 'I am a servant of the poor, the meek, and the holy,' he said. 'People of India are suffering. I want to help them to rediscover our ancient wisdom. I have come to Tapovan to seek the blessings of the good and holy. I am on my way to the ashram of Rishi Narayan.'

'Child, it is hardly surprising that people have lost their way. They have been ruled and oppressed by foreign invaders for centuries. Our land is stained with the blood of our people. When generations are harassed, killed, and forced to live a life of submission and little, it is inevitable that people will lose hope and acquiesce to find peace.'

'At the cost of the soul of our country,' said Neelkanth. 'For so long, bathed in non-violence, we are now drenched in violence. I cannot watch our people suffer and stand idle.'

'You have been taught well. Who is the teacher who taught you all this?'

'My parents are my teachers. They have taught me all I know. They are sadly no more.'

'Is Badrinath not the ashram of Rishi Narayan?'

'So the legend says. I shall visit and find out if it is, but I will not rest until Rishi Narayan stands in front of me in person.'

'We wish you success, but please stay with us for a while.'

'Yes, please stay.' The other ascetics echoed their leader's wish.

Neelkanth glanced at their expectant faces and sensed the sincerity of their plea. His heart felt compelled to accept the invitation.

'It will be good for all of us to gain the wisdom of your knowledge,' the leader said. 'It is clear from the radiant aura of your face that you are an ancient soul in a child's body.'

'I will stay a few days. I am the one who should listen to the wisdom of your experiences. I am only eleven with so much still to learn.'

The leader brushed his silver beard and grinned brightly. 'Is age a barrier to wisdom? Is true knowledge not a progressive accumulation of wisdom through the cycle of birth and death?'

Neelkanth put his palms together to accept the wisdom of the ascetic's words. His eyes fell on a spider weaving a web between two branches of a shrub. He studied it for a while. 'Look at that spider,' he said, pointing at it. All the ascetics watched it for some time as the spider weaved a web between the branches. 'See how it stretches its web between the two branches. Sometimes, it goes to one branch, then to the other, and at other times, it just sits on the web between the two branches. Our soul is like a spider.'

Everyone turned to him. 'Like a spider?' the leader asked.

'Yes. Suppose we consider God to be one branch, the mind, our intellect and the senses the other branch, and our sight as the web. When we sit down to meditate, we sometimes get absorbed in God. At other times, we stay with the mind, intellect, and senses when all sorts of thoughts engulf our mind.'

'It is not always possible to concentrate,' the leader admitted.

'Because the mind is fickle like a flame, which bends in the direction of the breeze,' said an ascetic.

'Yes,' said Neelkanth grinning. 'Sometimes, we just sit in the middle of the web, aimlessly drifting while we try to concentrate. At other times, there are no distractions and we are fully engaged in meditation, lost to all around us.'

The leader laughed. 'My dear child, I have led these humble souls for years but have never been able to explain it so succinctly. It is as if Dhruvji has returned in a different form to bless us.'

Neelkanth bowed. 'It would be such a waste of my visit to Tapovan if I did not learn from sage Dhruvji and did as he did.' He placed his hands on the knees as if to hint at what he wanted to do.

'It is the reason why we are all here. We will all join you.'

Neelkanth closed his eyes and inhaled deeply before releasing a long 'Aum' from his mouth as he exhaled. Soon, the air resonated with the energy of the Aum. A peace embraced the hearts of the ascetics. Birds gathered on branches and added their tunes to their Aum.

They sat down in quiet meditation every day for long periods. Neelkanth enjoyed their peaceful nature for nine days and quietly left before dawn on the tenth day when all the ascetics were fast asleep. He followed the Ganga north, paddling on the shallow edge of the river whenever he could.

It was late afternoon when he saw the spires of the temples in the distance. Ganga rushed down from the hills in her madness to greet him. Neelkanth bathed in her cold water at one of the Ghats before entering a temple. He fell to his feet in prostration when his eyes fell on the stone statue of Laxman. His mind raced back to Ayodhya, to the temple of Ram, where he had spent many happy hours listening to the story of the Ram, Sita, and Laxman.

Observing an image of his brother Ram in Neelkanth, Laxman emerged from the statue in princely robes and raised him. 'It is I who should be prostrating before you, brother,' he said, his eyes blurring with tears. He knelt and tried to place his head on Neelkanth's feet, but Neelkanth held his hands and raised him before his head touched the ground. He realized Laxman saw the image of Ram in him and felt compelled to honor the vision he saw.

'If you believe me to be your brother, then know that there is no higher or lower amongst brothers,' said Neelkanth and hugged Laxman. 'There has never been a brother who has so selflessly served his elder brother in all ages. In day or night, in hunger or fatigue, in grief and illness, you stood by me when I needed you the most. You lived a life of a nomadic monk when you could have enjoyed the carefree joys of a prince. Truly, there has never been a brother or a friend like you. Our exile was happy and flew by because of your presence by my side.'

Laxman took Neelkanth's hand and led him to a cushion. 'Look at you! It has only been a few months since you left Ayodhya and already you look so thin. You are neglecting your body. It will not last if you don't look after it. Take me with you. I will look after you. It will be good to reminisce of our adventures during the exile, of Sita, of your selfless disciple Hanuman, who flew thousands of miles to save me from certain death.'

'Nothing would please me more than to have a devoted companion such as you on my journey. Sadly, I have vowed to travel alone but know that you will always be in my thoughts.'

Laxman's head dropped. Neelkanth placed his hand on his chin and raised it. 'Will you at least share a meal with me, brother,' he said.

They glanced at the entrance to the temple and saw a woman enter with a tray. She came to them and placed a tray with a variety of steaming hot foods on the floor between them. Neelkanth looked at the rich variety. 'I was hoping to share the food that was cooked with your hands,' he said to Laxman.

'I don't think brother Laxman will be able to cook such a delicious meal.' The woman gazed at Laxman with a smirk.

Laxman inhaled the aroma of the spices. 'No,' he said, shaking his head. 'Not such rich food.'

Neelkanth laughed. He knew who she was. 'It appears Mother Ganga is determined to fatten me up.'

'Mother Ganga!' Laxman stared at the woman.

'I was hoping you would not recognize my disguise,' Ganga said. 'Forgive me, but the opportunity to feed the two brothers together on my banks after thousands of years was too difficult to resist.'

Neelkanth and Laxman took a piece each of a sweet and placed it in each other's mouths. They ate from the same plate, reminiscing their time in exile.

'Sita would have made this meeting perfect,' Ganga said.

'She lives in both our hearts,' Laxman said.

'A model of a perfect wife and mother for all women,' said Neelkanth.

'And as her father, wise Janak, would remind us, a perfect daughter,' Ganga said.

'A part of her lives in all the women of the world, inspiring them daily,' said Neelkanth.

Ganga raised her hand and pointed at her heart.

'Your delicious food is worthy of the many flavors I remember,' Laxman said to Ganga.

They wiped the plate clean. Neelkanth patted his stomach with joy and yawned.

Ganga smiled. Laxman took the hint, got up, and went to a room on the side of the temple to prepare a mattress before returning to call Neelkanth. Laxman massaged Neelkanth's feet until he fell asleep, then laid down on the floor near him. He woke up early in the morning, bathed, and got ready to serve Neelkanth.

Neelkanth's eyes fell on him when he got up and stretched his arms. 'Have you been awake all night?' he asked.

'I woke up early,' Laxman said.

They walked to the river to bathe. Ganga was waiting. She directed them to a hot pond near the temple. Neelkanth glanced at the mist rising from the pond. 'Mother, how will I ever get used to the cold if you keep spoiling me like this?'

'That is for you to worry about in the future. I will not allow you to bathe in cold water while you are near me,' Ganga said and disappeared as they washed.

She reappeared with a bowl of cut fruits a little later. Neelkanth served the fruits to the Shaligram before taking a little. Laxman asked the priest to distribute the rest to everyone in the temple.

The soft rays of the sun fell on Neelkanth's face as he exited the temple with Laxman. 'Please take me with you,' Laxman pleaded again, tears streaming down his cheeks.

Neelkanth wiped them with his hands. 'Though I have no doubt you will sacrifice your whole world and more for me, I have vowed to travel alone this time. You know I am never far away from you. Think of me, and I shall appear when you wish.'

Laxman picked up the gourd and walked with Neelkanth to the jute bridge. Neelkanth hugged him before making his way across the bridge. He looked back when he reached the other end and saw that Laxman was still standing there. He waved, breaking his vow never to look back for the first time since he left home.

3

Meeting with Rishi Narayan

Neelkanth trekked north, walking straight rather than following well-trodden trails that curved around steep hills with dark pine forests. As he entered deeper, the scent of pine needles filled his lungs, the streams grew louder, the bees hummed, and the birds chirped and tweeted. Occasionally, an angry roar resonated in the distance to disturb the calm. Neelkanth stopped every so often to catch his breath in the thinning mountain air and rest his aching muscles.

He reached Sripur in the evening, tucked away on top of a plateau near a waterfall. He liked the calm ambiance of the place and was not surprised that Uddhavji, a staunch disciple of Sri Krishna, had chosen the place to perform austerities after separation from him. It reminded him of Laxman's pain in the morning. His mind flashed back to the scene of their parting and his head bowed. He bathed in the cool waters, then found a mango tree on the edge of the village and sat in meditation, reflecting upon the deep devotion of Uddhavji.

The clanging of bells forced him to open his eyes. They fell on a group of monks standing in front of him with folded hands. Neelkanth reciprocated.

'Child, who are you? Who are your parents and from where do you come?' a monk asked.

Neelkanth gazed at his white robe. 'I am Neelkanth. I am the servant of the poor, the meek, and the holy. I am on my way to meet Rishi Narayan in the Himalayas.'

The monk raised his hand in awe. 'It would please us greatly if you would come inside our ashram for food. You look as if you haven't eaten in days.'

Neelkanth raised his hand. 'I am not hungry.'

'Then please come and spend the night in our ashram.'

'I do not stay in houses or ashrams.'

'We have all the facilities you will need.'

'We are blessed with the earth as our bed and the sky as the roof.'

'But there are wild animals in the area; many people have been killed by lions. Please spend the night in the ashram or go into the village.'

'I only live in the woods and have met many wild animals along the way. I do not fear death. If I die, it will be this body that will die, not my soul.'

'My dear child, please do not be so stubborn,' the monk pleaded with pressed palms, 'the wild animals do not discriminate. They will surely kill you.'

Neelkanth was in no mood to listen to the pleas. He had traveled through the woods for many days, slept in them, and lived under the constant threat of being attacked by them but had yet to feel fear. He closed his eyes in meditation to signal to the monk that there was nothing more he wanted to say. The monk took the hint, bowed, and went inside the ashram with his disciples.

Neelkanth remained in deep meditation, his body still as a stone statue until he heard a loud growl. He calmly opened his eyes and locked his gaze on a lion lazily ambling in his direction. The pine windows to the ashram flew open. The leader of the monk stared at Neelkanth, fearing the worst as the lion leaped forward. Neelkanth raised his right arm and instantly calmed the lion. It stepped near and sat down on the ground in front of him. Neelkanth ran his fingers through his golden-brown mane, got up, and rested his head on his belly. The lion rested his head on his front legs, and together they fell asleep. The monk stared at them in wonder and sighed.

Neelkanth and the lion woke up together when dawn broke. The lion followed Neelkanth to the river like a pet. Neelkanth patted him and sent him into the woods before stepping into the river. He inhaled deeply and sat down at the base of the river until he could hold his breath no longer. The monk and his disciples were waiting with folded hands when Neelkanth stepped out.

'Yogiraj, please forgive my ignorance. You are indeed worthy of commanding our respect. You are most certainly an ancient soul in a child's body with the wisdom of the universe. Please stay in the ashram. It has an annual income of more than a hundred thousand rupees. Please accept the leadership of the ashram. I shall serve you as a servant.'

Neelkanth gave him an icy glance. He had not set out with little only to be trapped by power, honor, and wealth. 'There would have been little point in leaving home had I wished to assume the leadership of an ashram,' he said, almost in rebuke. He picked up his gourd and resolutely walked away without looking back.

Up ahead, the grey and white of the soaring jagged Himalaya peaks stretched out like an impenetrable wall, foreboding. Neelkanth surveyed the peaks for a long time as he contemplated his journey ahead. A lifeless silence stared back as if to challenge the audacity of their young visitor in a loincloth and bare feet. Many far better prepared and equipped had tried to conquer its might, and not one had survived. Neelkanth stubbornly filled his lungs with the chilly air and deliberately stepped into the icy water of the Ganga to show that he was neither afraid nor unprepared; that there was no force of nature capable of subduing the iron will of his inner spirit.

The winds howled in ominous laughter and the glacier cracked to send an avalanche as if to warn him. Neelkanth stepped behind a boulder, crouched, and watched the snow cascade over him.

His heart thumped in determination as he felt the ashram of Rishi Narayan draw near. His steps quickened, as did the pricks of the glacial till under his bare feet. He only realized they had drawn blood when he stepped onto the thick film of snow higher up, leaving a trail of red footprints behind him.

Ascetics sat in deep meditation in hermitages in the valley behind the first peak. Keen to reach Badrinath,

Neelkanth blessed them as he passed and paid his respects at the temples along the way without stopping for too long. Ganga followed him like a doting mother as Neelkanth edged ever closer to her source. Dark pine forest bowed on either side to shield him from the chill.

He stopped at the mouth of a swinging rope bridge on his way to Gupta-Prayag and observed how effortlessly the villagers crossed the bridge by holding a rope above their heads while their feet stepped forward on loose wooden planks on the bridge. Neelkanth poured out the water from his gourd to lighten the load and tied it to the string around his waist before following them. Below him, the white waters of Ganga thrashed eagerly to catch him in her bosom, while behind him, regular users of the bridge drew near. Neelkanth ignored them, taking care not to step on the gaps between the planks. He was not surprised when they surrounded him at the other end and started asking the usual questions about him.

Overwhelmed and humbled by the attention, Neelkanth bowed without replying until an elderly man took his hand and led him to the temple at Triyuginarayan. 'Shiva and Parvati were married here,' he said.

'Yes.' Neelkanth's eye fell on the eternal flame, which had been burning since the wedding. He placed his hand on the flame for blessings before bowing to the silver images of Vishnu, Laxmi, and Saraswati. 'Yes, they are a very blessed couple to have married in the presence of Lords Vishnu and Brahma. Serve them well,' he said to the priest. The priest offered him some fruits. Neelkanth took some, thanked him, and moved on.

It was evening when Neelkanth reached the hot spring at Gaurikund. He remembered from the stories from his mother that it was at Gaurikund where Parvati had performed penance to win the love of Shiva. It was at Gaurikund that Parvati had sculpted her son Ganesh from the soap suds on her body, breathed life into him, and told him to guard the entrance to her house while she bathed. It was at Gaurikund that Shiva had cut off Ganesh's head after being barred from entering his own house. It was at Gaurikund that the inconsolable Parvati had forced Shiva to bring Ganesh back to life by replacing his head with the head of a wandering elephant. The love story of Shiva and Parvati reminded him of the affection between his parents, of a bond between Bhakti and Dharma, of devotion and duty, of a bond of love where one could not live without the other. Where there was Bhakti, there was Dharma. And where there was Dharma, there was Bhakti. Their passing away between six months of each other was a witness to their love.

Neelkanth honored his parents by bathing in the water before walking to the queue of people waiting to enter the temple. He was not surprised when the pilgrims in front of him stepped aside and allowed him to go forward. He had experienced the miracle of his sacrifice enough times to feel the reverence of the people for holy men, especially child yogis. His eyes downcast, Neelkanth bowed and went ahead.

'Welcome, child,' the temple priest greeted him as he reached the top of the stone stairway as if he had been waiting for the arrival of Neelkanth. 'Never in all the years of priesthood at the temple have I seen a yogi as young as you. With matted hair like Shiva and only a loincloth to cover your body in this cold, I feel like the child Shiva has come to see his dear Parvati.' He took a candle from near the feet of Parvati and offered it to Neelkanth. 'Goddess Parvati will be pleased that a yogi of your eminence visited the temple for her blessings.'

'The honor is mine,' Neelkanth said. 'May her blessings ease my journey ahead.'

The priest offered Neelkanth some cut fruits. Neelkanth took a slice and turned towards the exit. 'I am keen to reach Badrinath before the temple closes for winter,' he said.

The pilgrims parted to create a path for him. Several fell to the ground and bowed their heads as Neelkanth slowly made his way to the door. Whispers of Shiva resonated in the temple hall behind him. Neelkanth sensed their reverence and put his palms together as he exited.

He followed the well-trodden stone trek for a few miles, his bare feet feeling the sharp pricks of the stones cut through the soft skin of his child's sole even though the feet of countless pilgrims had crushed the stones to ease the pain. Neelkanth had hoped that walking hundreds of miles would have hardened his skin before reaching the Himalayas. Though he had never walked so high up, he had heard from the many pilgrims who had visited the mountains that they were unforgiving on the body. 'I am Atman, not the body,' he reminded himself with each step to forget the pain.

The soaring ranges stood like a white fortress wall in the distance, standing tall and formidable, yet beautiful and serene. Neelkanth stopped and ran his eyes through the valleys and peaks to soak up the beauty. Many pilgrims fell at his feet as he stopped. One ascetic stood in front of him. 'Please, please accept my blanket, child. I have two.' The ascetic took off the blanket from around his shoulders and tried to wrap it around Neelkanth.

Neelkanth raised his right arm and stopped him. 'Bless your kind heart, but I have vowed to brave all the conditions on my pilgrimage. Rishi Narayan has looked after me until now, and he will continue to do so,' he said and marched on.

Higher up, a white blanket of snow covered the stone pathway. Neelkanth curiously picked out a spot on the side untouched by the feet of pilgrims and tentatively stepped on it. The cool comfort of the soft snow instantly numbed the sting on his feet. He raised it to check the footprint and curiously stared at the dark red spots of his blood before moving on.

He saw the grey stone dome of the Kedarnath temple when the sun was just settling above the mountains in the west. He stared at the fiery glow of the peaks before bowing his head in the direction. A queue of pilgrims gave way as he stepped behind them, urging him to go forward. They formed a path for him right up to the entrance of the temple. Neelkanth bowed. The elderly priest greeted him at the door, bowed, took his hand, and led him to the statue of Shiva in the shrine.

Neelkanth paid his respects and took some fruit before taking his leave, eager to reach Badrinath temple.

The priest followed him to the foreground of the temple. He shook his head in disbelief and put his palms together. 'My child, it is already too cold. The Himalayan nights are very cold in winter and you don't have anything to protect you from the elements. It is better if you start in the morning. Stay in the temple for a few days and put on some fat. I will feed you well and look after you. It will be good to hear your story.'

Neelkanth looked up and thought for a moment. Snow-covered peaks towered behind the temple dome. Following the ancient route would require going back and double the time to reach Badrinath. It was getting far too close to the closure of the temple for winter. He did not like that option and decided he would go around Mount Kedarnath and cross whatever hurdles nature placed in front of him. After all, nothing of worth was achieved without trials and tribulations. 'Lord Narayan will look after me,' he said, bowed, and walked away behind the temple without looking back.

He walked towards the Chorabari glacier in the valley below Mount Kedarnath. On the right, the Gharwal range towered over him like a grey and white wall. Neelkanth walked on the edge to avoid the crevasses and seracs. The wind howled as if to dissuade him when night fell and the temperature dropped. He pushed on, one careful step at a time, glad that the glacial till was covered in snow. His tiny emaciated figure looked like a dark solitary dot amid the white colossus that surrounded him. Higher up, the snow became deeper, the air thinner, and the progress slow. Each step became a struggle as his bare feet dug into the snow and became numb. He sat down every so often to massage his feet to regain the feeling.

Dawn had just broken above the mountains when he reached the top of the glacier. The Gharwal range was covered in mist, so he could not see far, but there was a pleasurable stillness around him that he liked. He had expected to be dead, but he was not, nor did he feel the cold. He did not understand. Was his body adapting to the harsh environment of the Himalayas? Was there an inner source of energy, greater than even the sun, keeping him alive? Had his body merged with the icy chill of the mountains? Would he survive another night, another day, without food? He wondered as he sat down in meditation to merge with his inner strength, the spirit that was greater than anything imaginable. He would need it to survive the long track ahead.

He pushed on relentlessly for nine days, walking through the Gangotri glacier, through the valley of Bagirath mountain range to reach Nandanvan. Then, he crossed the Chaturangi glacier to arrive in the valley of River Avra. The river splashed through the shallow edge of the chilly water until it merged with River Alakananda at Ghastoli, a few miles ahead.

He followed the river valley to Alkapuri, where he bathed in the river to pay homage to Goddess Saraswati at the mouth of the river named after her before walking south. Despite not having eaten for days, Neelkanth's pace picked up when he saw the bright pinnacle of the Badrinath temple bathed in the late afternoon sun. He washed in the Alakananda before stepping into the hot spring nearby with other pilgrims. The tiredness of crossing the mountains lifted like rising vapor. He untied the bun of hair on the top of his head and dipped his head under water, holding his breath for a while before rising. Water poured from his hair and loincloth. Neelkanth rinsed the cloth and wiped his body and hair with it.

His eyes fell on the temple dome glowing in flame orange. There was no queue of people outside. Tears rolled down his cheeks as he entered the ancient temple, saw the statue of Lord Vishnu, and fell to the ground in prostration. The iron will that had allowed him to overcome the most inhospitable terrains gave way to a rare weakness. Neelkanth lay there for a long time until the temple priest reached for his hands and raised him from the ground.

The priest wiped Neelkanth's tears like a father wipes the pain of his son. He tenderly ran his hands over his emaciated body. 'Child, I have served in this temple for years, but I have never met a pilgrim such as you. Who are you? Where do you come from? Who are your parents?'

'I am the servant of the poor, the meek, and the holy,' Neelkanth said without adding any more as the priest led him to the inner shrine of the temple. He took off the garland from around the neck of Lord Vishnu and placed it around Neelkanth's neck.

'It is as if Lord Vishnu himself has come to bless me for all the years of service,' the priest said, his eyes tearing.

'He comes in disguise to serve all his devoted disciples,' Neelkanth said. 'Love is all the Lord seeks.'

'It will soon be Diwali. Please stay until then. I shall serve you as I have served Lord Vishnu.'

Neelkanth stared at his eyes and saw the deep desire of the priest to serve him. It was all he looked for in the heart to stay.

'It will be a triple celebration,' the priest said. 'The festival marks the end of Lord Vishnu's presence in the temple.'

Neelkanth nodded to signal that he would stay. He celebrated Diwali and the New Year with the large crowds at the temple. After the festival of New Year, the priest began to make preparations to leave. 'It gets very cold in Badrinath. The mountains will soon be covered in snow. It is time to take Lord Vishnu to Joshimath. Come with us.'

Neelkanth stared at the white peaks behind the temple. His heart was set on going higher, but for some odd reason that he could not fathom, he felt compelled to join the party.

The priest requested Neelkanth to sit on the golden stage on top of the second elephant. 'The first elephant will carry the statue of Lord Vishnu,' he said.

Neelkanth climbed the stage and was about to stand behind the seat. The priest insisted Neelkanth take the seat. He stood behind as the procession of pilgrims and elephants made its way down the gravel road, led by a party of musicians, drum players, and singers. Neelkanth took joy in the devotion of the pilgrims as they sang without tiring throughout the day-long journey. He stayed in the Jyotishvar temple for a few days before taking leave. The priest begged him to stay. He explained the hazards in the mountains during its harshest season.

'My heart is set on visiting the ashram of Rishi Narayan,' Neelkanth simply said.

'Child, Badrinath is the ashram of Rishi Narayan. We have just returned from there.'

Neelkanth glanced at the white peaks. 'My father says there is an ashram in the Himalayas where Rishi Narayan resides in person.'

'A myth propagated to keep the interest of the faithful alive. I have never met anyone who has found it.'

'I know it exists,' Neelkanth said. 'My father would not have told me otherwise.'

The priest sensed Neelkanth's determination. 'Badrinath will be covered in snow. The mountains will become impassable with thick snow. You have not walked on fresh snow. Your feet will dig in. They will become numb and ache. Every step will become a struggle.'

'Rishi Narayan will look after me,' Neelkanth said.

'The winds will pick up. How will you survive, clad only in a loincloth and with nothing to cover your feet or body? What will you eat? Everything dies in winter. You are already so thin.'

'Rishi Narayan will look after me,' Neelkanth said again, his faith in the ancient Rishi as fresh as the snow shower that began to fall over the temple like tiny soft lights.

'Child, look up.' The priest pointed at the peaks in front of them. 'The Himalayas do not spare anyone.'

Neelkanth inhaled the cold air. He tried to catch a few flakes in his palms. 'When was the path to God ever easy?' he asked, gazing at the mountains.

The priest shook his head in dismay. He wrapped his blanket around Neelkanth. 'Please take it with you. You are indeed an ancient soul in a child's body. Otherwise, you would not contemplate such a dangerous journey. Do be careful and return when you come down again. I shall serve you like a servant serves a king.'

Neelkanth sensed the purity of his love and humility. He bowed and took leave. He gave the blanket to a beggar on the way out of Joshimath.

Snow wrapped the hills that were only a few days ago singing with joy on the way down. Melting snow formed into tiny crystal spears on branches of trees and glistened in the sunlight. The soft green leaves became stiff with fear. Redstarts flew in and out of branches to catch the last rays of the sun. The joy of the New Year was wrapped in woolen blankets and hats. Neelkanth stopped and watched how quickly winter had sucked out the life from the Alakananda valley as he made his way north.

The progress was painfully slow, with his bare feet numb from walking in the snow, but it was better as long as he massaged his feet regularly than walking on glacial till and rubble that cut through his skin and drew blood and left his feet sore at the end of the day.

Neelkanth reached Alkapuri in the late afternoon of the third day. With the sky clear and the rays of the sun reflecting from the snow, there was a pleasant warmth in the air he had not felt before. He immersed his feet in the icy chill of the river to soothe the pain before visiting the cave where Ved Vyas had narrated the epic Mahabharat to Lord Ganesh. Neelkanth imagined the momentous scene.

Ved Vyas sat on a mat reciting the epic story to Lord Ganesh who sat opposite him, with a feather in hand, a pot of ink, and a pile of paper in front on a small pedestal. One the narrator, the other the writer, challenging the narrator that he would only write if his pen did not stop. Vyas put forward a counter stipulation that Ganesh can only write once he had understood the whole meaning of the verse and, by so doing, giving himself time to compose more verses. What would I have given to be present, he thought as he sat on the bank of the river to rest his tired and aching body.

A pink glow embraced the soaring white peaks in the morning when Neelkanth left Alkapuri to follow the valley of the Alakananda River west, which had transformed into an arctic desolation. He had heard from his father that the ashram of Rishi Narayan was somewhere between the peaks of Nar Narayan near Mount Satopanth. Neelkanth put his head down and marched forward, using the heat of his exertions to stay warm. As the snow deepened, his bare feet dug in, and every step strained his already depleted energy, made worse by the swirling snowflakes. His feet numb, the cold piercing like sharp arrows and icicles clinging to his long hair, Neelkanth struggled to breathe in the thinning air. Only the thought of meeting Rishi Narayan urged him to keep moving.

The sun cast a long shadow behind him when his eyes fell on an entourage of rishis in white and orange robes walking in his direction. Neelkanth rushed forward as one rishi ran towards him. He dropped the gourd and bowed at his feet.

The rishi raised him from the ground. 'I am Nar,' he said. 'It is I who should be falling at your feet for the sacrifices you have made to reach here.' He hugged Neelkanth. Nar's eyes misted when he felt the bones on Neelkanth's emaciated body. 'Oh, how have you withered your body to reach here,' he cried, then took a blanket from one of his companions and wrapped it around Neelkanth before offering a plateful of fruits.

Neelkanth sat down and offered the fruits to the Shaligram before taking some.

Nar then led Neelkanth into a tunnel. The sound of flowing water and singing birds and peacocks hurried Neelkanth's pace, the deep desire to meet Rishi Narayan washing away the tiredness from his limbs. His heart skipped a beat as he ran his eyes over the beauty of the place that the Himalayas had kept hidden from the touch of people.

'Only the pure of heart have ever been able to reach here.' Nar leaned forward and whispered in his ear. He took his hand and led him towards a river. They stopped at the edge. 'Human flesh cannot survive in these waters,' he said.

Neelkanth closed his eyes, held the image of Rishi Narayan in his heart, and took Nar's hand. They crossed the river together.

'I should have known,' Nar said when they reached the opposite bank.

Neelkanth laughed. 'Nothing of this world can hurt me when you are by my side and Narayan is in my heart!'

Nar bowed. 'I am only as powerful as our beloved Narayan wishes.'

Neelkanth's eyes fell on Rishi Narayan running towards them. He ran towards him like an excited child meeting his father after a long time. Neelkanth fell at his feet. 'I have craved for our meeting for years,' he said, looking up.

Rishi Narayan raised Neelkanth from the ground. He gazed at him as he held him by his shoulders. 'Only the pure of heart can reach Badrivan,' he said. 'You have sacrificed much. Your body is a pale reflection of the strong boy I saw in Ayodhya.' Rishi Narayan felt the bones on his ribs. 'You will not be able to do our work if you do not look after yourself.'

'Finding food when you are traveling in deserted forests and mountains is not always easy,' Neelkanth said.

Nar took his other hand. 'We will soon fatten you up,' he said, leading Neelkanth to a hut.

They sat Neelkanth down on a cushion on the steps of their mud hut. It was late evening and the light was fading. The other rishis lit torches and brought some cut fruits. Neelkanth ate a little.

Rishi Narayan took Neelkanth's hand. 'You have been very kind by visiting us. The mountains are difficult for people to endure. Badrivan can only be reached by years of penance and the grace of Shiva of Kedarnath.'

Neelkanth bowed. 'It is only through your grace that I have been able to visit Badrivan. The honor is mine. I have had a deep desire to visit you ever since my father spoke about you.'

'Your parents were the incarnation of Dharma and Bhakti,' Narayan said. 'Your father represented all that was virtuous. Your mother was a shining example of unfettered devotion to truth and all things holy.'

Neelkanth thought about his parents' selfless love for him. 'They taught me everything I know. You are the king of this world and rather than living like a king in a grand palace, with fine rich clothes, servants, and an army to protect your kingdom, you have chosen to live like a monk.'

'I have nothing to protect,' Narayan laughed, pointing at his mud hut.

'Our true greatness is not defined by how much wealth or power we possess but by the sacrifices we make for others,' Nar said.

Narayan smiled, looking at the growing assembly of rishis from different parts of Badrivan gathering around them. He welcomed them and requested them to come forward.

As the rishis sat down around them, Rishi Narayan sensed the buzz in the assembly. 'It seems the arrival of this child has created an interest I have not felt for a long time,' he said, glancing at the rishis.

'It is not often that we get visitors,' Nar said, speaking for everyone.

Neelkanth stood up, turned, and bowed to all the rishis. 'It is my honor to be in the presence of renowned rishis I have heard and read about ever since I was a little boy. Thank you for giving me a chance to meet you all.'

The rishis put their palms together and bowed.

Neelkanth turned to Rishi Narayan. 'You name has been on my lips with every bead of this rosary,' he said.

'Rather than speak about the journey, if you will permit me, I would like to speak about the people I met on the way. Listening to them, it seems to me that people have forgotten the basic tenet of living a good and selfless life. Violence and greed have replaced them. The poor, the meek, and the holy are suffering.'

Rishi Narayan nodded in agreement. He was aware of the rise of materialism at the expense of spirituality, peace, and harmony.

'According to Mother Ganga, a lethargy has crept into traditions that were once full of nobility, righteousness, and service.'

'You met Mother Ganga?' Nar asked in surprise.

Neelkanth smiled. 'Not only met her but tasted her delicious food.'

'She should know better than most, for her waters run deep and far, nourishing the farms and washing the sins of those who seek her sanctuary,' Narayan said.

'She nourishes the lands like no other,' Neelkanth said. 'Yet, those who toil are robbed of their harvest.'

'I have heard the landlords continue to rob the farmers of their crops; the monarchs continue to build their wealth at the expense of the poor, and the powerful try to control the weak,' Nar said.

'Nar, the forces of good and bad have been fighting for the rein of Mother Earth throughout the ages of man,' Narayan said.

'And you have taken birth to restore the balance.'

'We are living in the age of darkness, Nar. Deterioration of spirituality is an inevitable part of this age.'

'We must reach the bottom and suffer the consequences of our actions before we can realize the truth and rise to the top again,' Neelkanth said.

'Indeed, the road to truth has never been easy. Only in struggle, hardship, and pain do people turn to their inner self to find themselves.'

'Wealth, materialism, and power have made people blind,' Rishi Vasistha said from behind the assembly.

Neelkanth stood up as Rishi Vasistha stepped forward and tried to bow at his feet, but Rishi Vasistha took his foot away. 'You may be a child to all around you, but I know better,' he said, grinning. He knelt and bowed his head at Neelkanth's feet.

Rishi Narayan laughed. 'There is no deceiving Rishi Vasistha.'

'I do not wander the depths of this universe without learning something,' Vasistha said, chuckling. 'Rishi Narayan's austere life will eventually turn the tide in favor of the poor, the meek, the righteous, and the holy.'

'The age of darkness has only just begun. While progress will continue to be made in all areas of life, it will be at the expense of the equilibrium of nature that sustains life. Mother Earth is generous. She will continue to give, but like the Himalayas in winter, she also needs time to rest and recover. It is because of this long rest the plains sing in joy when spring comes.'

'There will be a time when even the Himalayas will become a game to humanity,' Vasistha said. 'Humanity does not know how to make sacrifices. Only through sacrifice can humanity realize its true potential. How can you remain so composed when there is so much pain in the world?'

'The spiritual amongst them will strive to keep the equilibrium,' Narayan said. He gazed at Neelkanth, listening with interest. Neelkanth yawned. Rishi Narayan took the hint. 'Hold on to that thought. We will talk more tomorrow. It has been a long and tiring journey for this child. We need to fatten him up in the time he is with us. There will be plenty of time for reflection and discussion. We mustn't forget why we are in Badrivan. While the world revels in having plenty, we must show the way with less, with sacrifices, by sharing, by helping the poor, the unfortunate, and the meek.'

All the rishis stood up, came forward, and bowed to Rishi Nar, Rishi Narayan, and Neelkanth before leaving. Neelkanth watched them with respect, his heart filled with hope. Rishi Narayan took his hand when they were all gone. 'You will carry the hope of everyone in Badrivan,' he said. 'Stay for a few months and recover because there is still so much work to do.'

Neelkanth felt at home after that first gathering of rishis. Over the next few days, Rishis Nar and Narayan took Neelkanth on a tour of Badrivan, its many orchards, flower gardens, streams, and hot springs. There was an unobtrusive calm in the ashram Neelkanth loved – an oasis of peace and plenty amid the rugged arctic desolation. He was not surprised so many rishis had chosen it to find their inner peace, the inner self. Their constant vigilance was an inspiration to Neelkanth.

He enjoyed the daily assemblies, the discussions about life, spirituality, and the joys and sorrows of humanity, amid the long spells of secluded meditation. It was what he had sought since leaving Ayodhya. In time, he forgot the world he had left behind, the struggles he had endured to reach Badrivan.

'The color has returned to your cheeks,' Rishi Narayan said after three months as if to remind him of his greater purpose.

Neelkanth glanced at him with disappointment. 'It is so peaceful here,' he said.

'Well, you are in Badrivan.' Rishi Narayan laughed and lovingly took his hand. 'Remember,' he simply said as he placed his hand on Neelkanth's head.

'I shall leave right away,' Neelkanth said.

'We will walk you to the edge of the ashram.' He told Nar to gather all the rishis. Nar closed his eyes, and within a short time, rishis started to come from all directions. He took Neelkanth's gourd. 'Are you sure you will not take something to keep you warm?'

'I have survived without it so far,' Neelkanth said, his faith in his body's resilience stronger than ever.

They crossed the river and gathered outside the mouth of the tunnel. The howling winds hit Neelkanth like a sharp blade. Neelkanth shivered for the first time in many months. Rishi Narayan embraced him. 'I know you will be fine. I would not have allowed you to leave otherwise.'

'I can withstand any pain with your blessings. I shall remember you in the temples I build,' Neelkanth promised, his eyes tearing.

Rishi Nar hugged him. Neelkanth put his palms together and bowed to all the rishis. They all watched the tiny emaciated figure of Neelkanth until it faded in the blizzard. Rishi Nar shook his head in dismay, feeling guilty that they had allowed Neelkanth to leave when winter had still not released its grip on the mountains.

Rishi Narayan read his mind. 'Neelkanth will be fine, Nar,' he said to reassure him. 'He has the power of his inner self to sustain him.'

4

Mansarovar

Neelkanth waded through the fresh snow towards Mana Ghat, crossing frozen glaciers that looked like transparent glass, often slipping and sliding on frozen mountainsides. His feet felt numb after a few hours. He stopped and massaged them every so often, got up, and moved forward.

As night fell, he slumped on the snow in exhaustion with a splitting headache, his legs sore from fighting through the frozen terrain. As snow swirled around him in the howling wind, Neelkanth forced himself to get up to build a snow cave for the night in the hope of retaining body heat. The inner heat of his soul tenderly rose from the depths of his heart and soothed and warmed his body until he fell asleep.

A quiet stillness gave relief when Neelkanth got up in the morning and dug himself out of the cave. The sky was clear and the sun was up. His body still ached, but he was glad that the splitting headache had gone. He stretched for a while before starting, one step at a time in tune with one deep breath, one bead, one name... Narayan. Another step as he exhaled. Maintaining the rhythm required concentration, but it allowed him to forget the cold.

Glistening white snow dazzled his eyes as he made his way to the edge of the glacier, blinding him. Neelkanth wrapped a cloth around his head and face to reduce the glare, leaving enough gap around his eyes to see where he was going.

He was glad to see the white disk of the sun drop behind him in the afternoon when he reached Mana Ghat and decided to carry on to take advantage of the rare good weather. It was evening when he reached the end of the glacier. The path ahead rose gently to a ridge of a mountain range, curving right. With the full moon bathing the mountains in a blue haze, Neelkanth decided to carry on. He followed the top of the range, one careful step at a time in rhythm with the turn of one bead of his rosary to prevent any strain on his bare feet, walking all night. It kept him warm. It drew him closer to Mount Kailash and Mansarovar.

He kept on walking when dawn broke until his eyes ached from the glare of the rising sun. He sat down, facing away from the sun. The long hours of walking on snow in bare feet left a deep throbbing pain in his feet. He massaged his feet. His stomach gnawed, but he ignored it. It had been begging for food every so often for two days now, but there was nothing to eat, no fruits trees to give any fruit. They would have lost their leaves anyway, he thought, as he looked at the lifeless white desolation around him. His eyes fell on a solitary golden eagle soaring high above the peaks. Neelkanth guessed that it, too, was looking for a quarry to kill. 'You will not find anything here,' he said loudly, 'but you are lucky and have good eyes that can see far.' He laid down and watched it soar above the mountains for a while, then closed his eyes and fell asleep.

Day after day and week after week, he continued to ride the mountain ridges like a lone survivor of a disaster. Each step taken with a deep breath, with a turn of a bead and the name of Narayan on his lips. Each step testing the resilience of his emaciated body and the power of the inner self over the might of the rugged mountains. Each step sealing his confidence in the will of his child's spirit, that 'yes, it can overcome all in its path.'

It was the end of February when he stepped onto the Tibetan plateau. Mount Kailash shone like a crystal pyramid in the distance, shining like a magical gateway to another land, its four sides perfectly aligned with the four sides of a compass, and its peak, a gateway to another world, heaven. He wondered whether the myth was true.

Six months had passed since he first sighted the soaring peaks of the Himalayas. He had seen them at their worst, desolate, and foreboding in the winter, but he had seen them at their best too, life-giving when spring opened its wings and the snow melted. The rivers came to life as they awoke from the deep slumber of winter, a calm, gentle meander as they stretched their arms to loosen the ice that, within weeks, turned into a flood that surged madly to the plains in its eagerness to serve.

Then, when the monsoons came, another world opened its doors. Rhododendrons bloomed and wild flowers peeped and painted the mountains with a medley of colors. It seemed to Neelkanth that when the Himalayas closed their wings in winter, they did so to recover from the onslaught of spring and summer. The snow, the blizzards, the winds, the roars, the crackle and the rumbles of winter were an expression of its joy of being left alone. In that solitude, it found its voice and its song, and within that song and joy, it found its silence and peace, all the answers it ever sought. The desolation of winter was the reason for the rich harvest of the plains, for plenty, and for life. It was the source of all that was good, for hope, for freedom, and for expression. 'No wonder they worship you like the gods,' Neelkanth said as he gazed at Mount Kailash, gleaming like a beacon of hope, glad that the heavens had given him a rare clear day to see Kailash without obstruction.

A loud rumble echoed over the mountain and an avalanche cascaded down its steep sides as if to welcome him. Neelkanth stopped as his eyes misted with tears of joy. He put his palms together and bowed. 'Only through your grace have I been able to reach here,' he whispered and stepped forward with renewed hope.

He had walked all night to witness Mount Kailash at sunrise. He had missed that, but he had seen the mountain with the sun behind it, and there was a purity about it that touched his heart and made the cold and the pain of his physical effort worthwhile.

It was mid-day when he stood at its hollowed white base, strewn with snow boulders brought down by frequent avalanches down its steep slopes. He had expected to be exhausted, but he was not. The sight of Kailash filled him with renewed vigor, a renewed purpose. He was keen to go around the mountain clockwise and set off without thinking twice.

The snow was deep and soft. His feet dug in with each step and it was an effort to dig them out again. In his keenness to finish the circumambulation, he set off at pace but fell in exhaustion after only a hundred yards. He lay in the snow for a while before forcing himself up, deciding that rhythm was what he needed and rhythm was what had allowed him to reach so far. He inhaled the thin altitude air and stepped forward gently rather than hard to stop the bare foot from digging into the snow before taking the next step. He felt good with the warmth of the sun on his back.

The sun had reached its highest point when he reached the top of the west face. His feet were numb, so he sat down and massaged them before forcing himself up to start the north face. A loud rumble echoed over him. Neelkanth looked up and saw a boulder hurtling down the mountainside. He dived to the edge and watched the boulder crush into a heap of snow in front of him.

He sighed, surveyed the crossing below the north face, and saw it strewn with heaps of snow from crushing snow boulders. He stepped away from the mountain to navigate a less arduous route, stopping every so often to massage his numb feet. The winds picked up as the temperature dropped and caught the loose snow into a swirl. It hit Neelkanth from the front to reduce his visibility. His eyes and nose leaked and the leaking fluid formed into ice.

Neelkanth leaned forward and fought his way through the storm, one measured step at a time in rhythm with his breath.

It was dark when he reached the end of the north face. The bun of hair on the top of his head had become loose. He collected the frozen strands of hair together and resolutely tied them into a bun in determination. With the winds working the snow into a blizzard, he knew he could not stop. He had to keep moving to stay warm. Kailash rumbled loudly around him as if in encouragement, or was it in warning? He did not know.

A quiet stillness embraced the mountains when the sun crept up the eastern horizon. Neelkanth faced the sun in welcome and bowed before thrusting himself forward to complete the circumambulation before sunset. His stomach gnawed, but he ignored its cries.

He reached the end of the eastern face at noon. A pool of water had collected from the melting snow. He stopped and washed the tiredness out of his limbs before starting the south face. With the end near, there was urgency in his pace, slowed only by the undulating terrain. He took joy in the warmth of the sun's rays as it accompanied him west.

The sun stood above the soaring peaks of the Himalayas when he stepped at the beginning again and fell to the ground as relief filled his legs with a sudden weakness. As nature displayed its daily spectacle of a sunset, he lay there for a long time, enjoying the cooling embrace of the snow after an exhausting circumambulation.

The clear sky was teeming with stars when he got up and dusted the snow from his bare body. His stomach gnawed again to remind him that his body needed food and nourishment. Neelkanth broke the ice in the river and filled the gourd with water. He slowly sipped the icy water to ease the gnawing cries before following the river through a valley to find Lake Mansarovar. When the mountains gave way to a plateau, he was sure he was on the right track. He walked in rhythm all night, stopping every so often to massage his feet.

The golden sun rose above the mountains to create a long orange and yellow path on the lake as if to show him the way. Neelkanth climbed a hill to inhale the calm of the morning before plunging forward in his determination to bathe in the waters of Mansarovar. He had once again not been able to meet his target of reaching the lake before sunrise. He did not mind because he had not gotten lost.

The chill of the night had left a thin film of ice on the lake. Neelkanth broke the ice when he sat down and thought about his parents while he filled the gourd with water. 'This is for you,' he whispered, almost gasping, eager to fulfill a wish they had spoken about for as long he could remember but had never been able to do so because of their devotion to him and his brothers. He washed the Shaligram with the second gourd of water.

A warm glow embraced him when he got up, rinsed the loincloth, and wiped his body. His eyes fell on his reflection in the water and he remembered the words of Mother Ganga. He stared at the emaciated figure for a while, the shrunken stomach, the bones of the ribcage without emotion before wrapping the loincloth around his waist. He had challenged every rule of survival in the arctic desolation of the Himalayas during its darkest months and broken every rule. He should be dead, but he was not. It was a triumph of his inner will, resilience, and fortitude – a triumph of his spirit over the frailties of the human body. 'Thank you for looking after me,' he bowed to Rishi Narayan.

As the sun crept up above the eastern ridge, he sat down in front of the Shaligram in meditation. More than sleep, meditating on the inner self, the soul, always seemed to ignite something in him like a fusion reaction in the inner core of the sun. It lifted the tiredness of his exertions like the sun evaporated the morning mist. He boldly decided he would go around the lake to find the source of River Saryu. When he opened his eyes, he was sure Mansarovar was the source of the holy river.

They fell on a flock of swans silently gathered around him like an assembly of eager pupils in front of the principal. Neelkanth gazed at them with joy and blessed them before standing up and starting his long walk around the lake in the clockwise direction. The swans rose in the air and accompanied him for a while until he waved them away.

Then he saw it, on the southern bank of the lake – a wide channel of water pouring out of the lake. He sat down in the water and poured two gourds of water over his head, thinking about his parents.

It took him four days to complete the circumambulation of Mansarovar. With spring coming close, fine, clear sunny days accompanied him all the way. He took joy in the easy walk, the beauty of the lake in different lights, the purity of its crystal clear waters, and the serenity in solitude. It gave him time to reflect on his journey, life, and the people he had met along the way. He remembered the promise he had made to the priest of Badrinath temple about returning to the temple if he survived the winter. There was a tenderness about his devotion he had liked, and without thinking twice, he started on the return journey to Badrinath.

Neelkanth saw that spring opened the wings of the Himalayas like a golden eagle discovering flight. The snow melted. Streams ran down narrow channels like eager children to their mothers, filling the rivers with their voices. Buds blossomed on fruit and flowering trees. The slopes of the mountains glowed with vibrant green as new leaves pointed up to soak up the sun. Monkeys jumped between branches of trees in joy at the abundance of fruits. Migrating birds returned, filling the woods with song. Mushrooms sprouted on the ground and flowers bloomed and painted the grass with color. Vines magically appeared from surfaces, gaining inches in days. Neelkanth inhaled the burst of aromas and took joy on his journey down the mountains, which, only months ago, was a desert of snow.

The bells of the temple of Badrinath tolled over the mountains long before Neelkanth reached its entrance. Devotees bowed and stared at him as he entered and fell to the ground in prostration in front of Lord Vishnu. They saw what he had seen in the reflection of Lake Mansarovar, and cried.

The priest rushed out when he heard and raised Neelkanth from the ground. His eyes, too, were filled with tears as he gazed at Neelkanth's emaciated body, the bones of his skeleton covered by a thin film of his skin. 'Not a day has gone by when I have not worried about you, my child,' he said. He ran his fingers over the ribs. 'How did you survive?'

'On water and air,' Neelkanth said, without hesitation.

The priest took his hand. 'Come,' he simply said and led Neelkanth to the kitchen. 'When was the last time you ate a proper meal?'

'I have not eaten since leaving the temple,' Neelkanth replied without emotion.

The priest raised his hands in the air. 'You are a miracle of God, my child.'

'The grace of Rishi Narayan,' Neelkanth said. He washed his hands while the priest prepared a plate of dal, curry, rice, sweets, and chapattis. Neelkanth offered it to the Shaligram before taking some in a bowl.

'Stay in the temple until you have put on some weight,' the priest said. 'The weather is good. So rest, regain your strength.'

Neelkanth liked the gentle nature of the priest. He reminded him of his father. 'I will stay,' he said, bowing.

Neelkanth did not remain idle despite protestations from the priest. He swept the temple every day, cooked, and helped the priest. When he was free, he sat in meditation in the corner, turning the rosary. Visitors came and went. Many bowed with respect. Neelkanth blessed them.

One morning when Neelkanth was sitting in meditation, a man sat down in front of him. Neelkanth opened his eyes and saw a man in rich clothes decorated with intricately carved diamonds and gold jewelry kneeling before him.

'I am Maharaja Ranjit Singh,' he bowed. 'I have traveled far and wide, met many wise men, but I have never felt so at peace in my heart as I do now.'

'You are in one of the four ashrams of God,' Neelkanth said, dismissing any thought in the Maharaja's mind that it was because of him.

The Maharaja bowed his head at Neelkanth's feet. 'The peace is due to the purity of your devotion. You are divine. I am your servant. Visit my palace. I will shower upon you all the riches of my kingdom. Ask for anything you like and it shall be yours.'

Neelkanth smiled. 'I am a Yogi. You are a Maharaja. How can the two meet? You travel on elephants. I travel on foot. You travel with your entourage. I travel alone. I find joy in God. You find joy in women, wealth, and luxury. I only see the sorrow in it.'

'I will bow to your every wish,' the Maharaja said.

'This life is like a dream. It is temporary. When our eyes close, this dream will be forgotten in a moment and we will leave everything behind. You will not remember that you were a king, nor who your wife was or your children were. You will not remember whether you were a man or a woman. An ant sees joy in a pile of dung. That is the way of the world. I have no love for that. A large lake may think it is big, but it fades into a tiny pond in comparison with the ocean. Even a king is not greater than God. You only eat what he grants you. All you have has been given to you by His grace. Abandon the ego of the position you hold to God, of wealth, and, like Maharaja Janak, learn to take joy in the glory of God.'

'Come with us,' the Maharaja said again.

'I walk due to the grace of Sri Krishna. If he wishes, I will come, and if he doesn't, I will not come. I have yet to visit Gangotri. If your desire is pure, I will meet you again in Haridwar.'

'Your wish is my desire. You are a yogi and can surely see the purity of my desire.'

'If it is as you say, we will surely meet in Haridwar.' Neelkanth stared into his eyes and saw his deep desire to please him.

The Maharaja bowed his head at the feet of Neelkanth.

Neelkanth made his way to Gangotri after a few days' rest. There he paid a visit to the Gangaji temple before arriving in Haridwar. As he sat in meditation at the Ghat of Har Ki Pauri, he felt the presence of someone at his feet. His eyes fell on the back of the head of Maharaja Ranjit Singh. He gently touched his head.

The Maharaja looked up, tears streaming down his cheeks. Neelkanth wiped them with his hands. 'Your desire was indeed pure,' he said.

'I have a deep desire to serve you,' the Maharaja said.

'I feel it,' Neelkanth said and looked at him with kindness. 'I wish to eat.'

The Maharaja immediately ordered his attendants to prepare a rich variety of dishes. He returned within an hour with dishes fit for a monarch, beautifully laid on a gold plate.

Neelkanth gazed at the gold plate. 'I am a yogi and can only eat in a wooden bowl.'

'Will you not honor me just once and eat from the gold plate?'

'I honor you by eating your food.'

The Maharaja's attendant presented a wooden bowl. Neelkanth took some in the bowl and asked the rest to be distributed. 'Do your duty as a Maharaja as well as you can,' he said.

The Maharaja pressed his palms together. 'I shall never forget our meeting. I shall always keep you in my heart and remember you.'

Neelkanth placed his hand on his head. 'The heart is weak,' he said, 'always weary of the attachments of life and its many associations. There are so many places I still want to visit.'

Neelkanth retraced the Ganga south. There was no haste in his steps now because the urgency of reaching Badrinath temple was no longer there. Yet, more than the Ganga, he looked forward to reaching the banks of River Saryu again. Having traced its source to Mansarovar, he looked forward to bathing in her again. The purity of its waters mirrored the turquoise purity of Mansarovar, so there was a reverence for the river that he had only reserved for Ganga. It had been a year since he had last swum in it. It had protected him like a mother from the relentless surge of the monsoons and saved him from certain drowning.

So when his eyes fell on the river, he rushed into the river, removed the Shaligram from around his neck, and washed it. Memories of his many games of fun and frolic with his friends flooded back like the time of a different life when he filled the gourd and poured it over his hair. He hoped they were fine and had got on with their life without him.

The wash in the Saryu refreshed his body and filled him with renewed vigor; it refreshed his mind and aroused a chain of thoughts he could not understand as he edged ever closer to the city. Why was he returning to Ayodhya? Why was he going back to a place where he would be so easily recognized? Did he have a secret desire to meet his family and friends again? Was the bond of the family too hard to break? Did his heart crave to find out that they were fine? Was his longing for silence and solitude a temporary mirage borne out of losing his parents?

The questions played on his mind when he entered the city and walked to all the familiar places he had made his own when the troubles of life were a distant dream. There was a timidity about the visit he had not known before, a fear of being recognized. He avoided the gaze of anyone who passed him on his way to his home. There, from a gully way, he listened to Suhasini singing while she cooked. The joy in her voice was apparent. It pleased him to know that she was happy. She appeared at the door when his elder brother left the house, passing his younger brother and nephew who were playing with their friends. He saw that life was normal again. It had found its rhythm without him. It comforted and reassured him. That really, he need not have worried. That life always found its rhythm after a change. That time healed all pain. It released him from the guilt that now and then surfaced to haunt him. It ignited the thought of Pulashram in the Himalayas. His father had spoken to him about King Bharatji, who had performed penance after abandoning the crown of his kingdom.

Early next morning, he swam to the opposite bank of the Saryu and trekked in the north-eastern direction, crossing dense forests and groves, before arriving outside a small town of Bansi on the foothills of the Himalayas. It had been a long trek, so he decided to rest in a garden near a river on the outskirts of the town. It was peaceful despite the constant tweets, chirps, and whistles of the many birds who nestled in the trees. They reminded him of the garden in Bareli. The joy of singing, the gentle village folk, and the patience of the caretaker. He prayed for them before closing his eyes in meditation. The solitude, the gentle rippling of the river, and the call of the birds made it an ideal place to close his mind to the world around him and merge with his inner self.

One day, a loud bang jolted Neelkanth's heart, which had, for days, enjoyed the peace and solitude of the garden. He jumped up when his eyes fell upon two birds, screaming and struggling on the ground. Soon they fell silent and still. Neelkanth wrapped them in his tiny hands to comfort them before digging a hole to bury them.

After bathing in the river, he sat down in meditation, but the thought of death was not easy to release. It slowly tightened around his neck like a noose. He jumped up, gasping for breath. After composing himself, he settled down in meditation until the gnaws of hunger cried for food. Sudden tiredness gripped him and he fell to the ground.

Moonlight shone from above when he opened his eyes. Delayed anger surfaced like thunder. 'Let the city burn!' he cried. A huge flash instantly rose from the hills. Orange flames engulfed the houses. Screams filled the air. Drums beat. Neelkanth realized what had happened and rebuked himself. 'No, it is unbecoming of a yogi,' he shouted as he watched the helpless crowds rush towards him. Women and children cried for help. Neelkanth ran to the river and plunged into the water until the flames subsided and died.

The power of his words hit him like a lightning bolt. A year of penance, prayers, and solitude had awakened something within him; it had filled him with the great power of ancient yogis, the Gods. He filled his palms with water. 'If I should ever think or utter impure words, let them fail to bear fruit,' he said, cursing his own words as he poured the water back into the river.

Cruelty filled Neelkanth's heart with sorrow as he watched the crowds gather on the bank of the river. He had vowed to wipe the stain of violence from the core of his heart. His eyes fell on two men engulfed in flame, rolling, screaming on the ground. He realized they were the king's men who had shot the birds. He immersed his head in water with a short prayer, his kind heart unable to forgive his harsh words.

While the crowds watched the flames die, Neelkanth emerged from the river, dried himself, picked up his few belongings, and quietly slipped out, unwilling to spend a moment longer near a village that had no reverence for life.

5

Penance at Pulashram

Thorns and piercing stones covered the ground through the forest, but Neelkanth ignored the pain, thinking when was the path to liberation ever easy. Tigers roared during the day, owls hooted at night, leaves rustled in the breeze, and wings fluttered. Neelkanth kept his gaze ahead, searching for some sign that the end of the forest was near. Without water and fruits – three days or four, he had lost count. He knew he could not go on for much longer when he began to struggle for breath and fell to the ground. He could not understand the weakness because he had lived on air and water for months in the Himalayas.

He got up when faint rays of light broke through the foliage and fell on his face. They gave him hope. He sat up, picked up his empty gourd, and stumbled forward with the help of branches. The sound of flowing water hurried his pace a little more. The river dazzled his eyes for the first time in four days as he stepped on its shallow edge and sat down to wash the Shaligram before entering the deeper water to bathe. There, he stood for a long time to wash the fatigue out of his body. Only then did he quench his thirst.

Climbing mountain after mountain, crossing valleys, Neelkanth reached the Kali Gandaki River flowing through a gorge. He followed her bank until the dark mountains folded in front of him, closing the way forward. It was evening and there was no other way to reach the other end. Neelkanth wondered whether there was another way when he saw a man in princely robes standing in the distance. The man bowed when Neelkanth approached him. 'You have been very kind to walk among my mountains barefoot,' the man said.

'My mountains?' Neelkanth gazed at him curiously.

'I am Himalaya,' the man said.

Neelkanth grinned but was not surprised after his many brushes with mythical people he had read and heard about. 'I want to go to Pulashram. It seems there is no other way but through the gorge.'

'It is the only way, I am afraid. The river is shallow and you can walk through, but there are crocodiles and snakes in the water. It is evening and soon it will be dark, so please rest and go in the morning. It will be safer.'

Neelkanth stared into the darkness through the mountains and started walking on the edge.

'I beg you not to enter,' the man shouted.

Neelkanth stopped. 'Don't worry. I will be fine. I am not afraid. I have been living with wild animals for months,' he said and plunged into the river.

Fear was one obstruction he had completely flushed out from his every being. The gorge echoed with the growls of the wild animals and occasionally splashed with abrupt turns of the crocodiles. Up ahead, the mountains closed in from above, creating a tunnel that grew ever smaller and darker. Neelkanth could not see how narrow it had become in the pitch darkness, but he felt it in the surge of the water pushing at him as he slowly edged forward by holding the side of the cave, resting on a narrow ledge every so often to catch his breath. Snakes slithered around him, but he knew he would be fine as long as he left them alone. He had seen enough snakes in the woods to know better.

His heart warmed when he saw a dim halo in the distance. The thrust of the water slowed as the cave grew wider, and the level of the water receded that had, at one stage, only left his head above water.

Outside, the black mountains wrapped around the valley of the river. He paddled on the shallow edge, enjoying the massage of the waters on his small feet. After many days of walking, he approached the temple at Muktinath.

He bowed to the golden statue of Vishnu with Lakshmi and Saraswati on either side. He thought about King Bharatji, who had renounced his crown to do penance in Pulashram. It was a story that filled his heart with sadness because, despite Bharatji's penance, his small indiscretion of falling in love with an orphaned deer while doing penance had led him to be born as a deer. 'I pray that I do not fall victim to the temptations around me,' he whispered before exiting.

He went to the back of the temple to walk under the 108 water fountains pouring out of the small bull heads before walking around the area nearby to search for a suitable place to perform his penance. His eyes fell on a tree nearby. He placed his gourd on the ground and bowed in the direction of the white disk of the sun before raising his right foot. He raised his hands above his head and recited:

I bow to the inner sun, the most splendid light in all the world.
Please illuminate my mind and intellect.

His eyes focused on the tip of his nose as he repeatedly recited the verse until he could no longer tolerate the pain in the legs and arms. He bathed in the river to ease the pain before starting again, prolonging the time he stood each time until he got into a rhythm of three long periods of penance per day, each broken with a dip in the river. He only ate some fruit in the evening.

Day after day and week after week, Neelkanth stood on one leg, his arms aloft above his head in a pinnacle. His muscles faded, stomach shrunk, cheeks sunk, and what little flesh was left on his bones disappeared. A prick on his skin drew water rather than blood. Mothers watched and begged him to stop. They cried when he did not. Fathers bowed and placed fruits at his feet. Ascetics prayed and prostrated before him. Birds flew to the trees around him and sang their sweet tunes. Neelkanth ignored them all in his determination to please the Sun-God, to experience what Bharatji had endured, and to flush out any association with his past.

After four months of austerity, a prince in full glory stood in front of him with folded hands, beseeching

Neelkanth to stop. Weak from the penance, Neelkanth fell at his feet. The prince picked him up. 'Enough, my child, enough,' he said and held Neelkanth in his embrace before sitting him down on the ground. 'I am Surya.'

Neelkanth gazed at him with tearful eyes. 'You give light to darkness, life to nature, sweetness to water, and food to humanity. The whole world enjoys your kindness, yet you ask for nothing in return. All that exists is through your grace. I am your humble servant. Grant me your blessings so that the characteristics like lust, greed, anger, envy, and ego are all wiped from my heart.'

The prince smiled. 'All I give is through your grace, my child. Should you wish, you can take it all back in one blink of an eye. The kindness is yours, not mine. I am serving the purpose for which you have created me. I am, therefore, compelled to grant whatever you ask, for that is my nature.' Surya placed his hand on Neelkanth's head and blessed him. 'May your travels be free of struggle.'

Neelkanth got up and bowed to the small crowd that had gathered around him. They parted and bowed as he walked to the river to bathe. There he sat for a long time to wash the tiredness from his limbs. He got up when the bells of the temple summoned him. Still weak, he slowly climbed the hill and entered the temple. The priest took his hand and sat him down on a cushion. He asked his companions to bring a plateful of food that had been offered to Lord Vishnu a little earlier and served Neelkanth.

'Young Yogi, I will never have a chance to serve a yogi of your capacity ever again.'

Neelkanth ate a little and asked the rest of the food to be served to everyone around him. He stood up, bowed, and left. He did not look back as the aura of the sun embraced him.

The terrain was difficult, with steep hills and dense vegetation covering the region. Eager to cover as much distance as possible, Neelkanth walked with haste despite months of austerities, eating what little fruit he found on the ground below the many wild fruit trees. He liked the solitude of the region, the scent of pine in the air, nature in full bloom, and the sound of rivers flowing again after the monsoon rains. His heart sang with joy the songs and poems taught by his parents, his sweet voice often attracting the tweets and whistles of birds. Some playfully swept high and low in front of him before settling on his shoulder like he was one with them and they were one with him.

He walked for weeks in their company, until one day he saw a man in white clothes rushing in his direction as if he was going to attack him. Neelkanth stopped and sensed that he was lost and was glad to see him. He saw the anxiety on his face when he came near.

'Child, I have been going round in circles for days and don't know where I am.'

'Don't worry,' Neelkanth calmed him. 'We travel in circles when we do not know any better.' He glanced at the monk's lost and tired expression and took pity on him. 'I am Neelkanth and I am on a pilgrimage to show the way to those who are lost. What is your name?'

'I am Mohandas and I am looking for someone to show me the way.'

'Then we have found what we are both looking for,' Neelkanth grinned and led the way. Mohandas followed quietly like an obedient student though he was so much older than Neelkanth. He keenly observed Neelkanth as he followed. The old loincloth, the bare feet, the effortless stride of each step, taken with the soft whisper of the Lord's name and a turn of a bead of a rosary that hung from his right hand. The purposeful steady gaze ahead of a person who knew exactly where he was going, what he was doing. The emaciated slender frame of a child that defied the strength of his every action. His eyes fell on the beautifully carved gourd. His heart pulled and his throat felt dry.

'That is a beautiful gourd you carry. Have you any water?' Mohandas asked.

Neelkanth stopped and shook the gourd before handing it to Mohandas. Mohandas drank what little water there was left. 'Shall I carry it?' he asked.

Neelkanth nodded.

Neelkanth told him about his travels in the Himalayas and Mohandas told him about his search for God. Neelkanth assured him that if his search was pure and true, he would find Him. 'God is always looking for the pure who have love in their hearts.'

They arrived on the bank of a river. Moss covered the many stones protruding from the river. Neelkanth stepped on a stone. 'Let me fill the gourd,' he said and took the gourd from Mohandas.

'Be careful,' Mohandas said. 'There is moss on the stones. You might slip and break the beautiful gourd.'

Neelkanth sensed that Mohandas was attracted to the gourd when he should be attracted to God. It was not worthy of someone who searched for God and decided to teach Mohandas a lesson. He deliberately stepped on the moss and slipped. The gourd struck a boulder and broke. Small pieces fell in the river. Some were washed away by the flowing water.

Mohandas rushed forward and picked up as many as he could. 'Now look, you have broken the gourd. I told you to be careful.'

'Mohandas, it is only a gourd,' Neelkanth said. He took the pieces from his hand and threw them in the river. 'Rather than concentrating your mind on God, you have become attached to the gourd. If you truly want to find God, you should shed all attachment to everything. Focus your mind on God alone and I promise you will find him.'

Mohandas bowed, sensing his weakness for beautiful and fine things. 'I have not learned the first lesson of sacrifice, have I?' he asked, mumbling, ashamed that a child should teach him this lesson.

Neelkanth liked his humble nature. 'Mohandas, the mind is very fickle. It is easily attracted to the beauty and the joys of this world. If one shows courage in the battle against its desires, one will certainly become a great yogi. If by trying, we lose this battle against the mind, our efforts will not be in vain. In time, in this birth or next, or even after many births, we will ultimately be liberated from the cycle of birth and death.'

Mohandas fell at Neelkanth's feet. 'Please forgive me. I am a fool. Your wisdom is faultless. You are clearly a great soul in a child's body.'

Neelkanth placed his hand on Mohandas' head and blessed him. Mohandas followed Neelkanth for many days, eating fruits that Neelkanth carefully selected for him.

They had been traveling for many days. The sun had settled behind the hills in the west. Neelkanth saw a fruit tree with violet fruits the size of mangoes fallen on the ground. 'We will rest here,' he said. He picked one fruit, peeled it, and started eating.

Mohandas followed.

'No, don't,' Neelkanth said. 'It is poisonous. It will kill you.'

'Why are you eating them?'

'I have been living on wild fruits for years and my body is used to them.'

Their eyes fell on a group of scantily clad men with metal spears walking toward them.

'Ah, food at last,' one man said. They collected a handful and started peeling the fruits.

'The fruits are poisonous and they will kill you,' Mohandas said.

The men looked at Neelkanth. 'Why is this boy eating them?'

'He is a great yogi,' Mohandas said.

'We too are great yogis,' the men said and ate the fruits until they were full.

They all slept under the tree that night. When Neelkanth woke up in the morning, Mohandas woke up with him. 'You said they would die if they ate the fruit, but they have been sleeping all night peacefully,' he said.

'Try and wake them up.' Neelkanth glanced at their still bodies.

Mohandas shook them to wake them up. He tried to wake all of them up, but none responded.

Neelkanth knelt and took the hand of one to check the pulse. He shook his head in dismay. 'There is no pulse.'

Mohandas placed his fingers on the neck of one man. 'You are right. They are dead.'

Neelkanth looked around and started collecting some fallen branches. 'We will need to cremate them.'

They piled the bodies on a heap of dry branches and set it alight. 'They will be born again in a family that will allow them to find God,' he said, trying to console the tearful Mohandas as they watched the flames engulf their bodies.

'The village is nearby. You will be fine from here.' Neelkanth pointed in the direction as if to give Mohandas a hint that he wished to travel alone.

Mohandas instantly fell to his feet. 'Allow me to travel with you. I will serve you with all my heart.' If there had been any doubt in Mohandas' mind about the divinity of Neelkanth, it was quashed by the death of the armed men.

Neelkanth looked down at him. 'Mohandas, you have a compassionate heart, but I have vowed to travel alone. Go to Gujarat in the west of India. I will meet you there in a few years.'

The thought of meeting Neelkanth again gave Mohandas hope because, for many years now, he had felt lost. It had made him sad, tired of life's endless challenges. It had sucked his will to live. Finally, he had found someone he could trust, open his heart and tell him how he felt. Though he was a teenage boy, he sensed his salvation and liberation lay in his hands. 'I feel it in my heart that we shall meet again,' Mohandas said.

'You feel it because it is true,' Neelkanth reassured him. He watched Mohandas until he disappeared amongst a cluster of huts. Neelkanth walked away with a heavy heart, having sent Mohandas away against his will.

A few minutes later, he stood on the edge of a hill. A dark green forest bathed in the sunlight of the midday sun stretched out in the valley below. There wasn't a cloud in the sky and he could see the wave of peaks surrounding the valley. His eyes fell on a small town with dark roofs in the middle of the valley. He sensed voices calling and felt compelled to answer their call.

A transformation was taking place within him that he could not explain. Penance, sacrifice, and meditation were awakening something within him that he could not understand. He could do things, hear voices, and read thoughts that he had never been able to do before. Then, he remembered the verse in the Bhagavad Gita that he had recited countless times: *This world is not for those who refuse to sacrifice, much less the other world.* It became clear to him that his sacrifices, penance, austerity, and fasting were all a necessary part – a preparation for what he wanted to accomplish. They were laying a foundation for the challenges ahead. Nothing of worth in this world was accomplished without sacrifice. It was the law of nature, of living, and of a fruitful, productive life. He thought about the sacrifices of Ram, Laxman, and Sita for each other; about the sacrifice of Laxmi for Vishnu and of Parvati for Shiva. They had all made sacrifices for a higher purpose. Life was about making sacrifices.

6

Rejects a Kingdom

Neelkanth entered a garden on the edge of the town of Bhutolpur with the thought of sacrifice at the forefront of his mind. The sun had reached the top of the peaks in the west, casting a long shadow of the trees around the garden. Neelkanth immediately felt at peace, glancing at the dirt path running towards a building. He stopped when he saw a man running towards him.

'Welcome, child yogi, welcome,' the man said, bowing.

Neelkanth introduced himself. 'I am looking for somewhere to stay for the night. My needs are simple and I will not bother anyone if you allow me to rest under a tree for the night.'

'Child yogi, I am the servant of King Mahadut. He is the ruler of all you see. He built this ashram just for yogis like you. So please stay for as long as you wish. Never have I felt such joy in welcoming a yogi to this ashram. Please come. There is no need for you to rest under a tree. You look as if you have not eaten for days.'

Neelkanth raised his hand. 'There is no need for a house for me to rest. I will be fine under a tree.' He pointed at a neem tree in the middle of the garden.

'As you wish, but will you at least take some fruit? His Majesty will not forgive me otherwise when he visits in the morning.'

'I will take some in the morning,' said Neelkanth. The man accompanied him to the tree and left after Neelkanth sat down and closed his eyes. He sat in meditation all night.

In the morning, Neelkanth bathed in the river nearby and again sat down in meditation. As the sun rose, he felt the warmth on his bare back. He would normally have got up to start on his journey, but he felt compelled to sit in meditation as the garden resonated with Sanskrit hymns. There was a scent of roses in the air. Neelkanth listened and absorbed the divine atmosphere in the garden. He only opened his eyes when he felt the presence of someone nearby. He put his palms together when his eyes fell on a man and a woman, kneeling before him with the gardener behind them.

'Welcome, child. I am King Mahadut and this is my sister Mayarani,' the man said. 'We are blessed that you should visit our humble kingdom. Who are you? Who are your parents? Where do you come from?'

They were all the familiar questions Neelkanth had been asked many times before, but he felt obliged to answer because of the sincerity of the king's welcome. 'I am Neelkanth. God is my father and my mother. The whole world is my home, so I come from nowhere and everywhere.'

It was not a response the king and his sister had expected because they had asked the same question to many visitors to the garden. They sensed a higher intellect, not of this world.

Mayarani's eyes misted as she stared at Neelkanth's emaciated body. She drew near and lovingly took Neelkanth's hand. 'Child, these are tears of a mother who sees a body famished by austerities when you should be enjoying life, eating, growing, and playing with your friends.'

Neelkanth gazed at Mayarani with kindness. 'Mother, do not worry about me. My body may be famished, but do my eyes not sparkle with joy and life?'

Mayarani looked into his eyes and felt a joy she had not felt before. 'There is a sparkle certainly that I have not seen in anyone. Forgive the foolishness of a mother's love. It is selfless. Please honor us with a visit to the palace?'

Neelkanth saw the love of his parents in their hearts and stood up. He realized why he had felt so compelled to visit the town as the king helped him on his horse. Mayarani followed behind him on her horse. Curious crowds gathered on either side of the dirt road as they entered the town and approached the palace gates. Many cheered, some stood with palms together, and others bowed their heads in reverence, mesmerized by the divine aura emanating from Neelkanth's body.

The remainder of the royal family greeted Neelkanth in the beautiful garden of the inner courtyard. The king helped Neelkanth down. Mayarani came forward and presented her nieces. 'Princesses Ila and Sushila,' she said.

They led Neelkanth to a room in the ascetic's bungalow. 'Stay here as long as you like. You will be looked after like a prince,' said the king.

Neelkanth ran his eyes through the room with drapes, a soft rug covering a marble floor, cushioned seats, and a large four-poster bed covered in a net. He had vowed to shun all luxury. 'Such luxury is inappropriate for a yogi,' he said.

'It is discourteous to refuse a gift from a king given in good faith and love,' Mayarani said.

'Mother, you will spoil me. I will not be able to live without them afterward. There are still many places I want to visit where I will have none of these luxuries.'

Mayarani stepped forward and took Neelkanth's hand. 'You will travel like a prince from now on,' she said, grinning.

Neelkanth looked down without saying anything. He was happiest when he was traveling light but allowed the indulgence of a mother's selfless love.

Mayarani ordered a scrumptious breakfast for Neelkanth and sat down with him when it arrived to make sure he ate, encouraging him again and again to take more.

'Mother, the food is delicious, but my little stomach will not be able to keep the food down if I eat too much,' Neelkanth said to seek relief.

Mayarani smiled. 'Then eat little, but frequently,' she said and made sure that he did. She visited Neelkanth with the princesses four more times with a different dish. Neelkanth ate a little each time and asked the rest to be served.

Ila and Sushila observed the envy of the other ascetics as they pandered to Neelkanth's every need. Once they left, Neelkanth returned to his preferred seat under the neem tree and sat in meditation.

The king posted a guard outside his room at night. Neelkanth closed the door and slept on the floor. The servants placed warm water for him in the bathroom in the morning. Neelkanth chose to bathe in the waters of the flowing river nearby. He had bathed in warm water before but had never felt as refreshed as he had done with cold water.

The Shaligram was sitting on a bed of white roses when Neelkanth returned to his room. Princesses Ila and Sushila sat on either side of the rug they had placed for Neelkanth in front of the Shaligram. Neelkanth glanced at them and bowed. His eyes fell on a variety of sweets and nuts beautifully arranged on a golden plate. 'Thank you,' he said as Sushila lit a wick in a bowl with a long handle decorated with gem stones.

'Shall we sing *Aum Jaya Jagadisha Hare*?' Ila asked. She picked up a small brass bell.

'Yes, let's,' Sushila said as the king and Mayarani appeared at the door, pleased that Ila and Sushila had found a purpose in life.

Neelkanth stood up and picked up the bowl. The king and his sister joined them on the side. '*Aum Jaya Jagadisha Hare...*' Neelkanth opened his pure voice and the royal family followed. Helped by the beautiful singing voices of the princesses and a bell in tune, the room echoed with a divine atmosphere not experienced in the palace before. Mayarani glanced at the king and grinned brightly.

Oh Lord of the Universe
Mighty Lord of the whole Universe
The troubles of devotees
The troubles of servants (of God)
In an instant, thou removest
Oh Lord of the Universe

He who's immersed in devotion
His mind's sadness ceases
Lord, his mind's sadness ceases
Joy, prosperity enter the home
Joy, prosperity enter the home
A body free of problems
Oh Lord of the Universe

Neelkanth served the sweets to the Shaligram and distributed them to the royal family.

'Will you not take some?' Mayarani asked with concern when Neelkanth put the plate down.

Neelkanth closed his eyes without saying a word and started to turn the rosary. Entranced by the devotion of their young visitor, the royal family sat in silence and watched Neelkanth turn one bead at a time in rhythm with his breathing. Time froze and a sense of peace like none before embraced their hearts.

They woke up from a divine trance when Neelkanth said 'Narayan' loudly.

Mayarani deliberately placed the plate of sweets in front of him as if to tell him that he had not taken any. Neelkanth smiled and took a piece.

'You must eat,' she said. 'A boy of your age should be bouncing with health.'

'All that exists is because of the Lord God,' said Neelkanth. 'All that we enjoy is because of the grace of God. It is only right that we serve him first for his infinite kindness in giving us this whole world without asking for anything in return.'

Mayarani curiously stared at him for a while as if she saw a purpose in the visit of Neelkanth. 'Child, who are you? Something must have prompted you to leave your home at such a tender age?' she asked.

'I am the servant of the poor, the meek, and the holy,' Neelkanth said softly.

'I can't imagine the pain of your parents to see you leave.'

'God had claimed them before I left.'

Mayarani grinned. 'I should have known. Your compassionate heart would never have hurt them.'

'What about the rest of your family?'

'They know I will find them again in the future.'

After that first experience of their child visitor, the royal family visited his morning prayers every day and shared in the sweets, nuts, fruits, and milk. Neelkanth enjoyed their company as he told them the stories of his travels in the Himalayas. One morning, the royal family arrived with rich clothes and jewelry and presented them to Neelkanth.

'Son, you know how much we love you,' Mayarani said. 'You are like a son the king never had and cannot have since the passing away of the queen.'

Neelkanth closed his eyes in prayer for the departed queen.

'It is not proper for a prince to dress in just an old loincloth,' the king said.

'Oh, please put them on,' Sushila cried. 'You would look so handsome in all these fine clothes with your long dark hair.'

'Like Krishna,' Ila said.

Neelkanth gazed at Mayarani. 'Mother, it is not proper for me to dress in these rich clothes. I have sacrificed all attachment to such things. Look at me. This is all I carry with me. Do I look like someone who would take joy in such rich clothes?'

Mayarani's heart sunk at the voice of rejection and her eyes misted with tears. 'Child, there is no son to rule after the king. The king would give this kingdom to you with Sushila and Ila in marriage,' she said.

'Our people are good and loyal. They will serve you selflessly,' the king said.

'You are all very kind, but I have vowed to shun all attachments. I beg you to put the thought aside. My only desire is to serve the poor, the meek, and the holy.'

'But you can do that as a prince,' Ila said.

Mayarani put her hand on Neelkanth's chin. 'Son, you are young at present but be sure that you will become restless without a woman when you grow up,' she said, unwilling to give up on her wish without a fight.

Neelkanth stared at the Shaligram sitting on top of the bed of flowers and inhaled deeply. 'Mother, my only wish is to sit at the feet of God and enjoy his bliss.'

'The forest is wild. There are lions and tigers. Many have perished, eaten alive by them. Give up this futile desire and enjoy the life of a king.'

'Mother, I have lived with them for more than a year. Never have I felt fear in their presence nor suffered loneliness for being alone. God is in my heart. Every breath is filled with his love. Every sound is filled with his name. He is the ultimate king of this entire universe. How can I then give him up for the rein of this kingdom! I would not do so even for the kingdom of the world. Rather than falling from the path of my sacrifice, I shall turn thousands towards that same path,' said Neelkanth with the determination not seen by the royal family.

The king stood up. 'You have a heart of an emperor, my child. Worthier than the king who adorns this crown. Sleep well,' he said with disappointment and left with his family.

Neelkanth watched them leave, closed his eyes, and sat in meditation. He opened his eyes when the palace fell silent, collected his things, and quietly slipped out of the palace.

He walked with haste for many hours and rested near a river as the sun crept over the horizon. After washing, he sat down in meditation. He only opened his eyes when the sound of galloping horses drew near. Neelkanth saw that it was the king's minister.

The minister knelt and bowed. 'Child yogi, the king and his family are in tears. They are inconsolable from missing you. They have lost all interest in life. Your sudden departure has left them without a reason to live. Young though you are, you know the way of a kingdom. Without the protection of the king, the kingdom will fall into decline, and the people will suffer. The king is righteous, just and generous. The people need his protection, so please return, if only for a while, to console them. They will die otherwise.'

Neelkanth looked down. The royal family had looked after him like a son. His heart felt the pain of their sorrow and his eyes misted with tears. He got up without uttering a word and followed the minister. The minister sent a rider ahead.

The royal family came rushing out of the palace gates when Neelkanth entered. They fell at his feet. Sushila and Ila took his hands. They led him to the throne, thinking that Neelkanth had returned to accept their father's offer.

Neelkanth reluctantly sat down on it. 'Do not cry. You have my assurance that your daughters will find husbands worthy of the crown you wear. Do not worry. Be happy in the memories we have shared. You have looked after me like you would your son. The princesses are good girls, devoted. They have served me like sisters do a brother. Allow me to continue on my journey to fulfill the task for which I have come. Take joy in the knowledge that this will not be our last meeting. We will meet again when I reach Saurashtra in a few years but allow me to leave with your blessings for now.' Neelkanth came down the throne and touched the feet of the king and his sister like they were his parents.

Mayarani's trembling hands reached for Neelkanth's head in blessings.

Neelkanth saw the tears. 'Think of me, mother, whenever you feel sad. Not only will you see me, but you will know exactly where I am in my journey.'

Mahadut joined hands with his daughters and sister. Tears streamed down their cheeks as they surrounded

Neelkanth in an embrace. 'Go, my son. Go with our blessings,' the king said.

Sushila and Ila walked with Neelkanth to the palace gates, followed by the king and his sister. Cheering crowds on either side of the dirt road applauded as they led Neelkanth out of the town.

7

Divine Consciousness

Neelkanth entered a dense forest after leaving Bhutolpur. Lions and elephants lowered their heads as he passed. Monkeys gathered on trees and followed him, leaping between branches until he exited the woods onto a field. Neelkanth's eyes fell on an elderly yogi sitting in meditation under a banyan tree in the grove in the distance. He keenly studied his silver hair and the long beard and felt a strong desire to visit him.

The yogi opened his eyes when Neelkanth approached him. Never had he been attracted to anyone or anything while in meditation. There was something about the child yogi approaching him, the serenity in his fixed gaze, the sacrifices in the emaciated slender frame, the lack of possessions, and the unhurried steps – he felt a peace he had never felt before. Was he the one he had been waiting for all these years? Was he his beloved Sri Krishna in disguise? The elderly yogi felt compelled to stand up and walk towards Neelkanth.

Their hands touched as they stood staring at each other, like familiar souls meeting after a long time. 'I am

Gopal Yogi. Welcome to my humble ashram. My child, never before have I felt drawn toward anyone. Are you who I think you to be or am I dreaming?'

Neelkanth smiled. 'I am Neelkanth and I have been on a pilgrimage in the Himalayas. I have met many people along the way, but I have not met anyone like you.'

'Child, I feel as if Sri Krishna himself has come in the form of a child to bless me for my long years of austerities.'

Neelkanth squeezed the yogi's hands without saying anything.

'I have mastered the highest form of yoga,' the yogi said as he led Neelkanth inside his mud and straw hut. There, he poured some water into a wooden bowl and served Neelkanth with some fruit. Neelkanth unfolded the Shaligram from around his neck and offered the water and fruit before taking some himself.

'Indeed, I am blessed,' the yogi said, looking at his devotion.

Neelkanth pressed his palms together. 'I have traveled widely. I believe I know how to meditate, but I am still not well practiced in the skilled art of yoga. I have come here with a wish to learn more. Will you please accept me as your pupil and teach me the highest form of yoga? I will do as you say.'

'Child, my heart is not easily swayed. Never before has it felt the desire to accept a student as I do today. It would not be so unless you were worthy of learning Raja Yoga, the most difficult form of yoga. It will be a joy to teach you all that I know. Yet, I must warn you that Raja Yoga is not learned in mere months or years. It requires a lifetime of sacrifices, commitment, regular practice, and constant vigilance before one can realize the final stage of Samadhi, the perfect state of super consciousness and pure existence. Are you prepared for that?'

'I would not have come otherwise,' said Neelkanth, without hesitation.

Gopal Yogi placed both his hands on Neelkanth's head in acceptance.

Neelkanth woke up early in the morning and sat in meditation near the stream running through the grove. Gopal Yogi summoned him under the shade of a banyan tree and presented a pile of loose paper bound with a string. 'I want you to recite and memorize all these verses,' he said.

Neelkanth picked up the pile, stained with years of use, with verses written in Sanskrit. 'I am fluent in Sanskrit,' he said and read the first line on the first page, 'The Land of Dharma.'

'No truer words were ever spoken. Mother India has protected dharma throughout the ages of man,' said the yogi. 'These words will form the foundation of your knowledge.'

Neelkanth bowed without saying any more. He had memorized the words of the Bhagavat Geeta as a child. His father had made sure of that. 'Study it well and understand the deeper meaning of each verse,' he had told him, 'because it will form the foundation of all your knowledge.' Neelkanth had kept them fresh by constantly reciting them as a child whenever he was alone; he had taught them to his friends because his father had told him that his understanding would truly be tested when he explained the meaning of each verse to others. In the four years he had been traveling through the Himalayas, he had recited the entire eighteen chapters of the Bhagavat Geeta more times than he could remember, with a challenge to himself that he would only go on to the next verse once he had understood the meaning of the first. He found divinity in words, a higher intellect, not of this world. He found an appreciation of life beyond wisdom, and he found meaning to his life; he found humility, courage, hope, and resilience. They gave him the will to keep going during his most difficult days in the Himalayas, to find a life beyond mere living, beyond the daily grind of surviving, beyond materialism, beyond even the human body. A life that few searched out because few understood it. Once that life is achieved, there is nothing more to do.

He did not want to give Gopal Yogi the impression that he knew it all, so, for a whole month, he patiently recited the verses loudly while washing, he recited them while cleaning the hut, while sweeping the courtyard, and while cooking their meals. Gopal Yogi observed and listened to him with the pride of a teacher who had discovered his greatest student. He encouraged him, sometimes corrected his pronunciation, sometimes stopped him and explained the meaning, and, at other times, asked him the meaning. And by so doing, Gopal Yogi took joy in Neelkanth's quick intelligence, glad, that at long last, he had found a student worthy of the knowledge he had acquired.

On the morning of the last day of the month, Gopal Yogi summoned Neelkanth to join him under the banyan tree. 'I have observed you with immense joy,' he said. 'However, before you can proceed to the next stage, you must pass the test I am about to give you.'

Neelkanth bowed without saying a word. It was the way of the wise Neelkanth was not surprised by, because even his father had given him regular tests before allowing him to progress to the next stage of his education.

'Recite verses 29th and 30th of the first chapter,' the yogi said.

Neelkanth closed his eyes and placed himself as an observer on the great battlefield of Kurukshetra. He thought of Sri Krishna, he thought of Arjuna, he thought of their great chariot parked between the opposing armies. Neelkanth witnessed Arjuna slump to his knees in dejection and his voice opened, 'My limbs fail me and my throat is dry. My body trembles and my hair stands on end. My bow slips from my hand and my skin burns. I cannot keep quiet, for my mind is in turmoil.'

'The 4th and 5th verses of the second chapter.'

'My Lord! How can I, when the battle rages, send an arrow through Beeshma and Drona, who should receive my reverence? I would rather be happy with a beggar's crust than kill these teachers of mine, these precious noble souls! To slay these masters who are my benefactors would be to stain the sweetness of life's pleasures.'

'Verses 37, 38, and 39 of Chapter 3.'

Neelkanth closed his eyes. 'As fire is shrouded in smoke, a mirror by dust, and a child by the womb, so is the universe enveloped in desire. It is the wise person's constant enemy; it tarnishes the face of wisdom. It is insatiable as a flame of fire. It works through the senses, the mind, and the reason; and with their help, it destroys wisdom and compounds the soul.'

'Verse 41.'

'It is said that the senses are powerful. But beyond the senses is the mind, beyond the mind is the intellect, and beyond and greater than intellect is He.'

'Perfect,' the yogi smiled. 'Verse 3 of Chapter 7.'

'Among thousands of men, scarcely one strives for perfection, and even amongst those who gain occult powers, perchance but one knows Me in truth.'

'Verses 20, 21, and 22 of Chapter 10.'

'O Arjuna! I am the Self, seated in the hearts of all beings; I am the beginning and the end of life, and I am the end of them all. Of all creative powers, I am the Creator of luminaries, the sun, the whirlwind among the wind, and the moon among the planets. Of the Vedas, I am the hymn; I am the electric force in the powers of nature; of the senses, I am the mind; and I am the intelligence in all that lives.'

Gopal Yogi tested Neelkanth for about an hour, asking him to recite the verses without prompting, without a hint of what it was about. Each time, Neelkanth closed his eyes, looked within his heart, and recited them without a moment's hesitation.

He gazed at Neelkanth with joy after Neelkanth recited the final verse. 'Faultless,' he simply said. 'Are you sure you are not Sri Krishna in disguise? How else would you know His every word?'

Neelkanth bowed gently, humbly. 'A student is only as good as his master. Thank you for your patience and kindness.'

'Patanjali has divided the path of Raja Yoga into eight limbs,' Gopal Yogi said.

'Limbs, Master?' Neelkanth asked.

'Yes, they are like the limbs of the human body, the two arms, the two legs, the two eyes, and the two ears. You will see why when we complete the course. You have already mastered a few, judging from what I have seen in our short time together. The first limb is Yama. It is about good conduct and restraint in external matters. You have already mastered all of them, so I will not spend any more time dwelling on it...'

Every morning and evening, Neelkanth sat in front of Gopal Yogi for his lessons. He meticulously went through the seven remaining limbs, Niyama, Asana, Pranayama, Pratyahara, Dharna, Dhyana, and Samadhi, describing their characteristics in immense detail.'

Neelkanth soaked the knowledge like a dry bean soaked in water.

After months of lessons and practice, Neelkanth bowed in front of the yogi. 'Master, I can now see the intense glow in my heart. But what is the source of that glow? Please teach me.'

Gopal Yogi smiled. 'These are difficult skills that take many lifetimes to master. Look closely, my child. Close your eyes and look. Delve into the depth of that glow and find its source. Tell me what you see.'

Neelkanth closed his eyes and looked into the depth of his being, his soul – pure, divine, and luminous. He penetrated its core. As he did, a glow enveloped his entire body, and he rose from the ground and floated in the air.

Then he saw it. An image of himself in the core of his luminous soul, gloriously adorned like an emperor on a throne. The face was the same, but he did not believe what he saw as he absorbed the calm serenity of the image for a long time.

Gopal Yogi stared at him, lost in the aura of his pupil. His palms came together and he bowed as the realization sunk in that this was a pupil from a different world, a different realm, divine. How else could he accomplish in a year what would normally take many lifetimes? 'Please be as you were,' he said.

Neelkanth's body gently floated down to the ground. He opened his eyes and calmly bowed his head at the feet of Gopal Yogi. 'Thank you,' he said.

Gopal Yogi stared at Neelkanth for a long time without saying a word, unable to believe that Neelkanth had mastered the highest form of Yoga in less than a year. 'Child,' he said, 'these skills are not mastered in months nor years but take many lifetimes. Yet you have mastered them in no time at all. Tell me truly, who are you?'

Neelkanth met the eyes of Gopal Yogi without saying anything.

'You are clearly not human but divine. I feel as if my beloved Sri Krishna has come to bless me for the years of penance,' Gopal Yogi said again.

Neelkanth smiled. 'Do not belittle the teacher,' he said. 'A pupil must also be worthy of the teacher who teaches him. I want to learn everything you know.'

They sat down again the next morning. 'I will now teach you the science of action, although, having lived with you for nine months, it is clear that you are already well versed in its knowledge.'

Neelkanth sat up. 'Tell me all you know, but before you do, tell me about the qualities of nature.'

Gopal Yogi glanced at Neelkanth with a sparkle in his eyes. 'You ask an important question because before we can understand our nature, we must understand the qualities of nature that surrounds us. Child, look around you and tell me what you see.'

Neelkanth stood up. 'I see the hills. I see the woods. I see streams of pristine water running through them. I see the soft blades of grass. I see fruit trees, a world of plenty. Everything one would ever want is found in nature.'

Gopal Yogi raised his hands. 'Isn't it just the most beautiful thing you ever saw?'

'Oh, it is, it is, master.'

'It sustains us all; therefore, it is the source of all. It provides everything we will ever need, yet it is not dependent on us. It is well-ordered; therefore, we find peace in her. It is dynamic, but it still keeps its order and does not fall into chaos.'

Neelkanth closed his eyes and listened to the song of the birds, the ripple of the flowing water, and the occasional roar. 'It gives us the air to breathe. It gives us the sweet water to drink, to wash, and to grow crops and fruits. It gives us the wood to build shelter and so much more, yet it does not ask for anything in return.'

'Child, nature is like a mother who gives without asking for anything in return. Ruin finds those who only take without giving, without sacrificing anything. Worship the powers of nature, treat them with respect, and nurture them. If you cut a tree for wood, make sure you plant two more to replace them. If you take water for the crops, make sure you give some from the harvests to feed those with little. If a miner takes gold from the mines, let him use some to serve the vulnerable. Otherwise, a day will surely come when there will be no trees to cut, nor crops to harvest, and only death and ruin will lie everywhere.'

'To give is to sacrifice,' Neelkanth said.

'No, to give without expecting anything in return is to sacrifice. The important thing to learn is to help the revolving wheel of life. Do your duty always, but do so without care for the result or reward, and do not let your ego think that you are the doer. Does not nature revolve happily in the cycle of birth, death, decay, and rebirth; do not the seasons revolve without interference year after year; does the moon not revolve every month; does the sun not rise daily in the east and set in the west; indeed, does not the water cycle give us sweet water.'

Neelkanth bowed. He agreed with the sentiment Gopal Yogi expressed because he had proved it with little since he left Ayodhya. 'Tell me about the paths to freedom and liberation.'

The yogi closed his eyes and thought for a long time. Neelkanth waited patiently, intrigued by his ability to concentrate for so long. 'In this world, there are two paths to freedom and liberation,' said the yogi even before he had opened his eyes. 'There is the path of wisdom for those who love to meditate and the path of action for those who are prepared to work. It seems to me you have already mastered the art of meditation. Yet, know that, amongst thousands, there is just one who will choose the path of wisdom because few can sit for long hours and meditate. Indeed, few have the discipline to sacrifice. You are that one.'

'Master, do we not use both paths? No one can refrain from action, for were we to do so, even the sustenance of this body would not be possible; nor can we stop ourselves from thinking because even while refusing to think, thousands of thoughts surface in our mind.'

'Therein lays the dilemma. Which path to take to attain freedom and find liberation from the cycle of birth and death?'

'Do they not complement each other? Do they not depend on our nature, the time, the place, and the circumstances?'

'How many of us can judge our natures? How many of us find time to examine our hearts and discover our natures in our daily rush to live and survive? We are all servants of this human body. We live to serve its every need, for were we to stop acting, even the maintenance of this body would not be possible. The body compels us to act whether we will or not. Those who control the senses and the mind control the world. The science of yoga you have mastered is one such path to gain control over the senses because by sitting still in meditation, you are learning to keep the mind from straying.'

Over the next few months, Gopal Yogi taught Neelkanth the science of spiritual knowledge, the science of universal self, residing in the cave of the heart.

Neelkanth soaked it up like parched ground absorbing water after a long drought.

'I have taught you all I know,' Gopal Yogi said one evening. 'I feel as if I have fulfilled the purpose for which I was born. Isn't it every master's wish to pass on all that he knows to a worthy pupil?'

'I am honored to have had such a wonderful teacher as you who practices what he teaches. Thank you.' Neelkanth knelt and placed his head at the feet of the yogi. Gopal Yogi placed both his hands on his head and blessed him. 'I feel so at peace for having passed on the knowledge.'

A divine radiance embraced Neelkanth's body. The yogi saw Ram in his princely robes with bow and arrow; he saw Narasimha, the half-man, half-lion; he saw Vishnu, he saw Shiva, Vaman, the dwarf avatar; he saw the earth, the mountains, and the rivers; he saw the sun, the stars, and the universe, he saw his beloved Sri Krishna with his conch and the disc, serene, as he stepped forward and embraced him. 'Why did you not tell me?' Gopal Yogi trembled as he knelt and touched Neelkanth's feet.

Neelkanth raised him from the ground. 'You must rest now,' he said simply. 'It is late.'

'I feel so tired,' the yogi said and laid down. Neelkanth massaged his feet. He held his hand when the yogi's breathing became shallow and he slowly faded away. Tears streamed down Neelkanth's eyes as he walked out of the hut to collect wood to cremate the body.

As orange flames engulfed the body, a white ball of light rose from the body and hovered in front of him before descending to his feet. Neelkanth watched it until it disappeared behind some clouds. 'To my home,' he whispered.

After that, Neelkanth could feel the slightest change in the vibrations around him when he left the ashram. The mastery of Raja Yoga had given him a consciousness beyond nature, an external awareness of the energies that shaped and molded its rhythm. The external energies joined with an internal consciousness that surpassed even nature and emanated a divine glow from the heart like none other. He had traced its origin to his soul residing within his heart.

Walking through the woods, he sensed that the trees were trapped souls. He could feel their pain and the relief of liberation when he touched them. The flowers and the shrubs, the insects and the flies, the lions, the tigers, the deer, the antelope, and the elephants were all part of the cycle of 8.4 million births, a revolving wheel in the cycle of birth, death, decay, and rebirth, which every soul endured before being granted the most precious birth of them all, a human being. 'Do not waste this one chance,' Gopal Yogi had repeatedly drummed the message into his mind until it became a chant that echoed in his heart even in sleep.

Feeling completely at peace, he came down a steep forest of pine to reach the white waters of the Ganga. There, he bathed and meditated before visiting a Shiva temple in the village of Bokra where he rested for three days with the permission of the priest who, like the priests of many other temples Neelkanth had visited in the region, saw the aura of a child Shiva in him and felt compelled to serve him.

On the way to Nepal, Neelkanth met a band of monks. Impressed by his austerity, their leader walked with him. They spoke about their travels in the Himalayas, their deep craving for peace and solitude, and their liberation from the cycle of birth and death.

They become so engrossed in their discussions that they reached the edge of Kathmandu before they realized.

'This is where we stop,' the leader said. 'We don't want to end up in the prison of the king. Rana Bahadur has been suffering from a chronic disease for years and has been trying to find a cure from holy men on pilgrimage. He imprisons and tortures them if they are unable to provide a cure. He has imprisoned thousands.'

Neelkanth saw the fear in the leader's eyes. He looked up at the palace on the top of a hill and saw his chance to free the pilgrims. 'The godly should never be afraid. Follow me,' he said bravely.

Though so much older than Neelkanth, the leader had developed a deep affection for him after their long walk together. There was something about the courage of Neelkanth that intrigued him because he had never met anyone who was so sure about everything, so in tune with nature and the thoughts of men, especially someone so young. He sensed a motive, a purpose to their visit to Kathmandu. He nodded to his disciples to follow Neelkanth to the gates of the palace. They were immediately surrounded by the king's guards.

'Told you,' the leader said, feeling vindicated.

Neelkanth smiled calmly. 'There is nothing to fear for the pure of heart.'

'Our orders are to take all visitors to the king,' a guard said.

The king's minister came forward as they entered the palace courtyard. 'Who is your leader? The king wishes to meet you,' he said.

The leader of the monks took a step back while Neelkanth boldly stepped forward. 'These monks are innocent,' he said, looking at the minister in the eye. 'They are men of God and are merely passing through. Take me to the king.'

The minister looked down. 'You are only a child. How can you be the leader?'

'God does not look at the age of a person but the purity of his heart. The fact that I am a child does not make me unworthy to lead.'

'We are in the city because of this child,' the leader stepped forward.

'So be it,' the minister said and led Neelkanth to the palace.

The king stood up when he saw Neelkanth approach him. He had met thousands of yogis during his reign, but none like the child who walked toward him. He stood up when he did not sense any fear in Neelkanth.

'You are aware of my illness,' the king said. 'And the consequences that will follow should you fail to find a cure.'

'I have heard,' said Neelkanth, bravely staring at the king in the eye. 'What illnesses we suffer are the result of our vices. Offer prayers to God, give up your vices, and the cure will be found.'

119

'If it is that simple, why hasn't anyone offered the solution before?' the king asked.

'For fear of invoking your anger. You have imprisoned thousands through no fault of their own. Release them all, ask for forgiveness, and the cure will be yours.'

The king stared at Neelkanth intently, not knowing what to make of his confidence. 'Do not make promises you cannot fulfill,' he said, laughing.

'God is ever forgiving. He will surely look upon you with compassion if you release the innocent.'

'Many monks have tried to trick me before. How can I be sure that you too will not do the same?'

Neelkanth took a deep breath. 'How can you invoke the compassion of God by imprisoning his soldiers? Are you not inviting – adding to your misfortune? These monks have done nothing wrong. They are seekers of God, so release them.'

The king stared at Neelkanth for a long time. He searched his heart and felt an inner peace he had not experienced before. 'Do what you must,' he said.

'Please bring me some water,' asked Neelkanth.

The king nodded his head to his attendant, who rushed out and brought a jug of water. Neelkanth poured some water into a glass, closed his eyes, and offered it to his beloved Sri Krishna. 'Take this water. It will cure all your illnesses.'

An ominous silence filled the hall as the king drank the water. The courtiers had witnessed the king's fury after each failure. They anticipated the same again. Neelkanth sensed their anxiety but kept his gaze on the king.

The king jumped with joy. 'The pain is no more, no more!' He danced wildly as everyone started to clap and cheer.

Neelkanth smiled when the king settled down on his throne. 'Now, you must fulfill my wish. A good deed cannot go unrewarded.'

'Release all the monks,' the king ordered at the top of his voice.

Neelkanth bowed and turned, having accomplished what he had come to do. His eyes stared at the exit door. The courtiers stared at him in awe, wonder, and reverence, for the child yogi had cured what many older yogis had failed to cure. The king clapped when Neelkanth took the first step. Soon the entire hall echoed with cheer and applause. People bowed, bent low, and touched the marble floor upon which Neelkanth stepped and walked out of the hall. A satisfied smile grew on his face for having freed the monks. The guards outside stepped forward to stop him but stepped back when the minister nodded to allow Neelkanth through. Neelkanth sensed the call of the godly as he stared at the mountains and walked out of the town.

8

Fake Monks

Neelkanth visited several mountain monasteries along the way before returning to Nepal. There, in a small village of Sirpur, he cautiously entered a garden, unaware whether he was allowed or not. It was late evening, so it seemed the only thing to do. He found an isolated spot under a tree and sat down in meditation but soon sensed the presence of someone near. His eyes fell on a royal couple sitting on the ground. Neelkanth bowed.

'Welcome to Sirpur,' the king said. He marked Neelkanth's forehead with the red vermillion spot and placed a garland around his head to welcome him.

'Child,' the queen said, 'looking at your emaciated body, it is clear that you have performed severe penance. Please visit the palace and share a meal with us.'

Neelkanth bowed. 'Mother, an ascetic belongs under the roof of the sky,' he said, wary of accepting the offer after his experience in Bhutolpur. 'It is late now, but I will take some food tomorrow if you bring some.'

'This is Gopal,' the king introduced a man standing behind him. 'He will look after you.' The royal couple bowed and left, respectable of Neelkanth's wish. They were a devoted couple who held holy men in immense reverence and never liked to upset them.

That night, it rained all night. Neelkanth lost consciousness and fell into a trance. As the waters rose, mud began to swirl around him and, by morning, covered his entire body.

When Gopal returned to check on Neelkanth in the morning, he did not see him anywhere. He panicked and fell to the ground, worried about how the king would react once he discovered that Neelkanth was missing. Lightning flashed and the sky crackled. The clouds opened with a heavy downpour. The water washed the mud from Neelkanth's body. Gopal raised his head and saw the top of Neelkanth's head and jumped to his feet. He sent some guards to fetch the king, who came running. The king asked the guards to take Neelkanth to the palace. There he washed him with warm water, rubbed his body with a warm towel, and massaged it with oil.

Neelkanth opened his eyes and looked around. 'How? When did I get here?' He sat up. 'Have you checked on the monks in the garden? I have lived in the Himalayas for years. So, please do not worry about me.'

'Child, you should not worry about the others,' the king said. 'Your body has become weak due to your austerities. A child of your age should be full of life and play. Please stay in the palace until you are fit and well.'

Neelkanth pressed his palms together. 'Thank you for your kindness but I prefer to stay in the open. The sound of birds and nature in full bloom is so much more pleasing to the ears and eyes. There is a peace about the natural world that is so soothing. Allow me to return to the garden.' Neelkanth got up and walked back to the garden. Gopal and the king followed him. Neelkanth sat down under the same tree.

After the king left, Neelkanth told Gopal about the many beautiful gardens he had visited on his pilgrimage. He spoke about the gardeners who had looked after him. The charity of their owners who had made them available to the visiting ascetics and served them selflessly. He told Gopal about how some ascetics took advantage of this generosity. Gopal served Neelkanth like a servant, cooking all sorts of delicious foods daily. The king made it a point to visit Neelkanth every morning to listen to his tales of the Himalayas and stayed until lunch to ensure that Neelkanth ate. Neelkanth ate a little and asked the rest to be distributed to the other monks.

'You will fade away if you continue to eat so little,' the king said one day. 'Then where will I be?'

'You will be fine. God will always look after you, for you have a generous heart.' Neelkanth's eyes fell on a monk running towards them. 'Gopal has fainted,' the monk said.

The king jumped to his feet and followed the monk to the house of the monks, where Gopal lay on the floor, surrounded by all the other monks, trying to revive him.

'He cannot be revived,' one monk said. 'Perhaps you can tell this child with whom you have become so besotted to revive him.'

Neelkanth saw the lentil seeds scattered on the floor and knew they had cast an evil spell on Gopal. He knelt and whispered the name of his beloved Sri Krishna in Gopal's ear. Gopal immediately opened his eyes, saw Neelkanth before him, and instantly sat up. 'What happened? I must have fainted.'

Neelkanth stood up and offered his hand. Gopal pulled himself up.

'You must go to your room and rest,' the king told Gopal.

Gopal glanced at Neelkanth as if to seek his permission.

'I will be fine,' Neelkanth said. 'Go and rest.'

Some monks came forward and bowed at Neelkanth's feet. Neelkanth followed Gopal with his eyes until he felt sure he was safe. As he turned to the king, he saw a line of monks fall to the ground like dominoes.

'What's happening?' the king asked in concern. 'Is there some illness spreading through the garden?'

'No. No illness, just some mischievous people trying to assert their powers.' He stared at the elderly monks standing in front of them. Neelkanth glanced at the unconscious monks and they instantly sat up.

The king looked at Neelkanth. 'How? Why?'

'There are people amongst us who think they are greater than God. Little do they know that the spells they utter to assert their power are worthless without the grace of God.'

The king glared at the monks. 'Answer me. Is this your doing?'

The monks stared at the king in defiance. 'You have become too attached to this child, forgetting that we have lived a long and devoted life in the service of God.'

The king turned to his guards. 'Surround these infidels. Not only are they a disgrace to themselves, but they also dishonor the generosity of the kingdom. Escort them to the borders of our kingdom. If you ever step into the borders of this kingdom, I shall place you all in prison. Go now and never return.'

As the monks were escorted out, the king turned to Neelkanth. 'You have saved me.'

'You have a pure heart. It does not discriminate. It is a quality that has earned you the grace of God. You must protect your subjects. If you are to truly protect them, then you must learn the art of good judgment of people. Who to punish and who to honor? Learn the lesson that all you see is not what it seems.'

The king knelt before Neelkanth. 'Please stay here for as long as you wish. I shall serve you with honor and kindness always.'

Neelkanth placed his hand on the head of the king. 'I shall stay in the garden.'

'Gopal will serve you,' the king said.

Neelkanth glanced at Gopal standing behind them and smiled. 'My heart is pulled towards the meek and humble. Come, Gopalji,' he said.

A man rushed to Neelkanth just as they were about to leave. 'Help me, child yogi. I have been greedy. My greed has turned a complexion that was once so fair into this wretched darkness. It has eroded all trust and respect. Please help me to return to my former self.'

Neelkanth examined the dark complexion of the face. 'God gives plenty, but he does it so that we can serve those in need. Wealth is useless unless it is used to serve the poor, the meek, and the holy.'

'Please help me by reversing the curse,' the man cried.

'Give up your greed and learn to serve, then all you had will return in abundance.' Neelkanth placed his hand on the man's head. 'You are a priest, and as such, you must never forget your duty to the good people of our land. Serve them all like you serve God and your former glory will return.'

'I will use everything I have to serve,' the priest said.

The king came forward when the priest left. 'Stay in the palace. You will be the king's councilor. Your kindness will certainly serve my subjects well. They strive hard and pay their taxes, but I lack the wisdom to guide them.'

'I am a servant of God,' Neelkanth said. 'Grand palaces and houses do not suit such a person. The garden will be fine.' Neelkanth glanced at Gopal, who followed him without saying a word. Gopal served Neelkanth with devotion, ever at his call until the New Year celebrations.

'There is much that I still need to do,' he said to the king.

'How will I find someone like you to guide me,' the king said.

'I will always be here. Remember me always. I shall never be far away.'

The king took Neelkanth's hand and led him to an elephant decorated with fine silk, garlands, and a golden stage. The elephant blew a trumpet when she saw Neelkanth. Neelkanth patted it with his hand. 'You are the king, so you must take the seat on the elephant. I will walk with the elephant,' he said.

The king folded his hands. 'I am just a king of this small city, but you are a yogi of this entire world in the guise of a child. My subjects are waiting outside the gates, eager to see you ride on an elephant. Do not disappoint them.'

Neelkanth remembered his ride on an elephant behind Lord Badrinath. 'I have only ever ridden on an elephant once before because I have vowed to travel on foot. Please do not make me break my vow again.'

'Child yogi, if you do not sit on the elephant, I shall never again sit on it either,' the king said. He dipped his finger in a vermillion cup and marked Neelkanth's forehead with a red spot.

The queen garlanded him and served him some sweets. 'It is customary to take some sweets before a journey,' she said. Neelkanth took some and asked the rest to be distributed.

The king helped Neelkanth to the stage on the elephant while he stood behind with a fan in his hand. Neelkanth asked him to sit beside him. It surprised him that the king, so used to being fanned by a servant, wanted to fan him like a servant. He realized it was among the many reasons why he felt compelled to visit the kingdom. As the elephant approached the palace gates, crowds cheered and clapped.

'You have won the hearts of my subjects,' the king said from behind.

Neelkanth stood up and waved. As they made their way through the street, people threw flowers at the feet of the elephant. They looked up in amazement when balls of light appeared in the sky and hovered above the city. They gasped at the sight of the gods sprinkling flower petals from their chariots in the sky. The king looked up and saw them too. 'You are not of this world,' he said.

'I am merely the servant of the poor, the meek, and the holy,' Neelkanth said. 'Serve your subjects well.' Neelkanth stepped down at the entrance to the city, turned to the crowds for one last time, and bowed before making his way down the road. He did not look back.

Neelkanth arrived in Kamakshi after a long track through the woods. Curious villagers and ascetics gathered around him as he entered the garden. They were struck by his youth and sacrifice. They asked all the usual questions to learn more about him. Neelkanth dodged the questions in his usual manner and instead spoke about his pilgrimage through the Himalayas and his eagerness to serve the poor, the meek, and the holy.

'You have come to the right place,' an ascetic said. 'This is a sacred village where pilgrims come to seek love and forgiveness, yet all they find is fear and greed.'

'There is a wicked priest, Pibek, who uses spells to coerce, subdue, and kill the villagers. He claims the grace of Goddess Shakti. He is ruthless when drunk and kills at will.'

'He takes all we make and leaves us with little to feed our children.'

Neelkanth listened intently and realized the purpose of his visit there. He glanced at everyone, saw their thin bodies, and took pity on them. 'Don't worry,' he said with the calmness that belied his youth. 'Let us see what happens. After all, isn't Kamakshi a place of love? Is God not all love? Is there anyone more powerful than God?'

The villagers gathered around Neelkanth, feeling encouraged. Neelkanth saw a group of half-naked dancing men and women approaching. Behind them walked a man, tall and dark, a garland of skulls in a golden necklace, wide nostrils pierced with a golden ring, long dangling earrings protruding from an elongated ear.

'Pibek.' Frightened villagers gathered behind Neelkanth.

'I see what you mean,' said Neelkanth, keenly studying Pibek. The grotesque paraphernalia of ornaments was intended to instill awe and fear in the observers. His body was painted with ash, his eyes were red with anger, his forehead was marked with red vermillion, and his long dark hair was held in place by a red hair tie.

'Don't be afraid. Stay behind me and let us see what he does.' Neelkanth bowed when Pibek stood in front of him.

Pibek struck his trident on the ground. 'Child, break your sacred Brahmin's thread, cast aside your tulsi beads, and become my disciple.'

The ascetics stepped back. 'Don't look at him,' Neelkanth told them.

Pibek closed his eyes, chanted a spell, and threw some lentils on a banyan tree. The tree instantly dried.

The ascetics placed their hands on the necklace of tulsi beads.

'Don't break your offering to God,' Neelkanth said. 'There is no one greater than God. Surrender only if something should happen to me.' He fixed his gaze on Pibek. 'Why hurt those who cannot defend themselves?

Attack me and if you should defeat me, they will all become your disciples.'

'What is a child against the might of Pibek!' Pibek shouted, laughing wildly.

'You may do whatever you want. I am not going anywhere from here.' Neelkanth closed his eyes in meditation.

Pibek uttered a spell and threw some lentils on Neelkanth. The lentils fell to the ground and burst into smoke. Two ghosts armed with tridents emerged from the cloud. Pibek told them to attack Neelkanth, but the ghosts turned on him and started beating him with their tridents. Pibek fell to the ground, bleeding.

'Just you wait!' Pibek bellowed.

'I am not going anywhere. You do what you want,' Neelkanth challenged him.

Neelkanth's calm demeanor incensed Pibek even more. 'I will not be called Pibek if I do not see your death by the end of the day.' He rose with the aid of his disciples. 'Just you wait.' He chanted a spell. Hanuman flew down from the sky and landed on the ground with a thud. The ground shook so much that all who had gathered to watch fell to the ground.

Neelkanth smiled, pleased to see Hanuman. Hanuman bowed. 'Why have you summoned me, my Lord?'

'You will remember my words when we last met that you should only come when I think of you. I have not thought of you today, and yet, you came.' He pointed at Pibek standing behind him.

Hanuman turned. 'You have summoned me?' Hanuman glared at Pibek.

'I need your help to kill this arrogant boy.'

Hanuman thumped his feet on the ground and grew in size until he towered over everyone. People stepped back.

'Now your time has come,' Pibek said to Neelkanth.

Neelkanth laughed. 'Call whoever you wish.'

Hanuman looked down at Pibek. 'Your time has indeed come.' His voice thundered over the village. He reached for Pibek, picked him up with one hand, and threw him to the ground. 'How dare you insult Neelkanth?' Hanuman glared down at Pibek's bloodied face and reached for him.

Pibek's disciples rushed to Neelkanth and bowed. 'Please show mercy. Pibek is drunk and has lost his senses. He does not know what he is saying.'

Neelkanth glanced at Hanuman and nodded. Hanuman put Pibek down. Pibek crawled to Neelkanth. 'Have mercy on me. I am a fool who has been blinded by the dark powers. I have killed, looted, and destroyed all who have stood against me.'

Ever forgiving, Neelkanth gazed at Pibek with kindness and placed his hand on his head. 'The powers you possess are through the grace of God. Rather than using them to help people, you have used them to frighten, loot, and kill them. It is not the way of the good or the godly. Give up your reckless actions and serve the people you have looted, bow to the families whose elders you have killed, and beg for their forgiveness. Only then will you regain your true purpose.'

'I will redeem myself and serve this village till death,' Pibek said.

Neelkanth blessed Pibek and forgave him. Everyone started to applaud. It was not in Neelkanth's nature to hold a grudge against anyone who asked for forgiveness, no matter how bad. Having witnessed how Neelkanth subdued Pibek, people realized the power of the teenage yogi. They lined in front of him and came to seek his blessings.

Over the next month, they treated Neelkanth like God, worshiped him, listened to him, and hung onto his every word, even though he told them he was merely a servant of the poor, the meek, and the holy. He was happy to stay in the village to ensure that Pibek did not revert to his old ways. Pibek kept his promise. With his purpose fulfilled, one night, when all was quiet, Neelkanth quietly left the village, happy that the people of the village would no longer suffer the tyranny of Pibek.

9

Liberation

Neelkanth purposefully followed the dirt road to the mountains in the east. It was a warm night and chirps of crickets filled the air. Faint traces of light pierced through the clouds at the horizon in a warm rosy glow. Approaching the top of a hill, his eyes fell on a chain of ridges in the distance, and he stared at it for a while as he thought about fulfilling the wishes of millennia and more. There was joy in his heart as the arc of the sun appeared on the horizon – a joy he had not felt since leaving home. His voice broke into a song as he climbed down the hill.

A dense forest faced him in the distance like an impenetrable wall. Neelkanth approached it like a seasoned traveler, having confronted many such obstacles. But he also found that while his resolve was ever firm, others had different ideas. A guard stopped him at the end of the dirt road.

'Child, there are a lot of wild animals in the woods,' the guard said. 'Many have entered and not returned. No one is allowed to enter by order of the king.' The guard pointed to the dirt road leading to the village as if to tell him to go into the village. 'Only the woodcutters are allowed, and that only in the vicinity.'

'I am not afraid,' said Neelkanth.

The guard put his palms together. 'Child, you are not much older than my children. If I allow you to enter and you die, it is I who will feel the grief of a father who has lost a son, not forgetting the punishment of the king for being disobedient. Please don't insist on entering.'

It was not in Neelkanth's nature to put anyone into difficulty. He sat down in the shade of the trees and took a short sip of the water from the gourd. He saw his chance when a herd of cows approached the guard. While the guard was counting the number of cows, Neelkanth crouched and sneaked into the forest with them.

The cries of wild animals echoed around him as he fought through the vegetation, shaded by the branches of tropical trees. He stopped by a river of crystal clear water and sat down on the shallow edge to wash the tiredness out of his limbs before moving on. It was evening when he reached the base of the mountains and decided to rest for the night.

He started the climb early in the morning. The vegetation was still dense and made the climb more arduous than he had anticipated, but the pull of those waiting above compelled him to push on. As the sun crept up above the chain of ridges, echoes of sacred hymns hummed over the mountains and the scent of burning rosewood reached his nostrils. Neelkanth stopped, inhaled deeply, and ran his eyes through the mountains before sitting down in meditation on a raised stone.

He opened his eyes when he felt the presence of someone near. They fell on a prince and a line of yogis stretching far, standing in front of him with pressed palms.

'Who are you and why are you all here? What are the flames ponds and why do you sit in front of them?' asked Neelkanth.

'Child, I am the mountain brought alive by your presence,' the prince said. 'These are yogis who have been performing penance on the mountains for millennia in the hope of seeing God. Each sits in front of a deep pond that is filled with water during the day but erupts into a flame at night. That is when these yogis also appear. Only those who have attained yogic powers can see them. You are a yogi and therefore see them. There are 900,000 such yogis in these mountains.'

Neelkanth looked at the long line of yogis, their bodies emaciated by years of penance and sacrifice. I am one, they are many. How will I meet so many yogis? Neelkanth thought. There are so many other places I have to visit. His eyes filled with kindness, and using the powers of yoga he had acquired from Gopal Yogi, Neelkanth replicated into 900,000 figures. Each stood in front of one yogi and fell into an embrace. 'It is the least I can do for your sacrifice and prayers of a thousand years,' he said to each of them.

The eyes of the yogis filled with tears and their voices choked with emotions, grateful for a chance to embrace Neelkanth. Compelled by their long penance, sacrifice, and devotion, Neelkanth stayed with them for three days to give them the joy of sharing his experiences. On the third day, he asked for their leave. 'There are so many holy places I still have to visit. You have all shown your desire to be with me. Remember the vision of this child. Go now, to where you all belong.'

The yogis transformed into balls of glowing light, which rose high and disappeared in a flash. Neelkanth knelt and bowed his head to the ground in reverence of their long penance. He climbed down the mountains and followed a path through the forest cleared by a herd of elephants. He passed through Balakund, where the waters of the spa eternally ignited with flames. He sanctified the birthplace of Chaitanya Mahaprabhu in Navdweep before reaching Gangasagar, the confluence of Ganga and the sea. There, he bathed in the sea before taking a ferry to reach the beautiful, secluded grove of Kapil Muni.

As Neelkanth entered, his eyes fell on a monk in orange robes coming toward him. They both rushed forward with open arms and fell into an embrace.

'Oh, I have waited so long for you to appear,' the monk said.

Neelkanth bowed. 'I have heard that your ashram is an ideal place for meditation.' He studied the emaciated figure of the monk.

'I am Kapil,' the monk said. 'This ashram has given me many years of peace, solitude, and silence. It would be an honor to serve you for however many days you wish to stay.'

'Please find me a good spot to meditate,' asked Neelkanth.

Kapil Muni took Neelkanth to a solitary tree near the river. Neelkanth stared at the clear water shimmering in the afternoon light, then sat down, and closed his eyes. He listened intently to the sounds of nature but heard nothing except the soothing, gentle ripples of flowing water. 'This is ideal,' he said. He placed his gourd down on the side, took off the Shaligram from around his neck, and stepped into the river.

He sat down in mediation afterward and allowed his thoughts to take him where they may. He thought about his parents, he thought about his brothers, he thought about Suhasini, and he thought about his friend Veni. Yet, none of them pulled him back. He wondered whether he was finally free of them, free from the knot of regret that now and then resurfaced to fill him with guilt. He thought about his travels through the Himalayas and the meeting with Rishis Nar and Narayan in Badrivan. He thought about the other rishis who enjoyed their company, and for a moment, he wondered why he couldn't enjoy the same joy after the sacrifices he had made. But instantly put that regret out of his mind when he remembered the encouraging words of Rishi Narayan about a greater purpose he had come to fulfill.

He thought about Gopal Yogi, the year-long peace he had enjoyed in his ashram, mastering the highest form of yoga, but there was no regret there, too, because Gopal Yogi, in death, had gone to a place where all good souls return. He thought about the many kings and their queens and the mothers whose maternal love always pulled his heart to respond. He thought about princesses Ila and Sushila, and he instantly knew they were fine, married to the men of their choice. He thought about Mohandas,

Gopal, and the many gardeners who had allowed him to enjoy their gardens. None of them pulled him anymore. He thought about Shiva, Parvati, Mother Ganga, and the meeting with Laxman. They pulled on his heart like no one else, but he knew they were not of this world, so he did not mind. Then he thought about the widow he had rescued from the funeral pyre of her husband, and the poor Dalit villager, the many pilgrims in search of God, and he knew exactly why he had left home, what he must do, where he must go. Relief emptied his mind and left a peace like none other. He forgot all sense of time, place, hunger, being and not being, and existence.

He opened his eyes six days later, aware that the people of India had lost their purpose. The fake monks had blinded their eyes through deception, greed, and superstition. The violence of conquering rulers had stained her soil with blood. It was time to re-establish the true essence of the Vedas, the infinite power of *Ahimsa* in word, thought, and deed, clean living, and the glory of God. He stood up with renewed determination. 'I shall use *Ahimsa* as my guiding principle upon which all my teachings will be based,' he said loudly. He had not felt so at peace with himself since he left home. He bowed to Muni Kapil for providing him with such a peaceful ashram for reflection before leaving.

Walking along a well-trodden dirt road, Neelkanth came across a small village in the evening. His pace picked up as the long shadow of his emaciated body fell on his left and the sound of children playing in the distance reached his ears. The children surrounded him when he approached them, intrigued by a child visitor in the garb of a yogi. 'Come play with us,' one boy said, offering a wooden bat.

Another boy stepped forward. 'We will throw the ball and you have to hit it as far as you can.'

Neelkanth wiped his brow. He remembered playing something similar in Ayodhya. 'Keep your eye on the ball,' a boy shouted.

As the ball bounced in front of him, Neelkanth gently nudged it to another boy. 'Strike it hard,' the boy shouted.

Neelkanth focused his eyes as the boy bowled and struck it with all his strength and saw it fly to the boundary of the ground. 'A six!' the boys cheered as they came running towards him.

Neelkanth gave the bat to a boy. 'I am looking for the temple.'

'It is at the other end of the village.' They all pointed in the direction of the dirt road.

'I will show you,' one boy said. He took the gourd from Neelkanth. 'I am Jairam. I visit the temple every day to listen to the story of Ram.'

Neelkanth glanced at him from the side of his eyes, pleased to hear that the same story of Ram that had excited him as a child still excited other children, forgetting that he was still no older than fifteen.

They climbed the stone steps of the temple. Neelkanth fell to the ground in prostration as soon as his eyes fell on the statues of Ram, Laxman, and Sita.

Jairam glanced and quickly followed. He had the same reverence for Ram as Neelkanth but had never seen anyone prostrate like him. 'Jairam,' the priest stood above them. 'Who have you brought to visit our humble temple?'

Jairam didn't know what to say. Neelkanth helped by introducing himself.

'Child, I have met many traveling yogis in my life but never met a child yogi like you. We are a poor village, living on what the land provides. But we are happy. The folks are very devoted and come to the temple every day.'

Neelkanth stared at the priest for a while without saying anything as he realized why he had felt compelled to come. The priest invited Neelkanth for a meal but showed him a stream of crystal clear water on the side of the temple when Neelkanth expressed a wish to wash first. 'You will not find purer water to bathe anywhere near,' he said.

Neelkanth thanked the priest. He saw that Jairam had gone and sat down in meditation until the priest summoned him for dinner. He served him all the food that had been offered to the deities for dinner. 'You must eat to grow,' he said every time Neelkanth said that he was full.

'But I have lived on air for days,' said Neelkanth.

'All the more reason to eat more. You will need the strength for your pilgrimage.'

Served as it was with love, Neelkanth ate until he had eaten everything. Love was what Neelkanth sought in the hearts of the people he met, and the message of love was what he preached whenever he had a chance.

After the prayers in the morning, the priest sat down in front of a few children from the village to recite the story of Ramayan. Neelkanth sat down behind them, listening intently. He was glad that it aroused the same love in other children and particularly liked how the children questioned the priest when they did not understand something. It was what his father had taught him. 'Only when you question do you master the true essence of our scriptures,' he had told him many times. Neelkanth enjoyed the exchanges between the priest and the children so much that his stay in the village extended to more days than he had planned.

'Sita is an ideal wife,' a girl said one day. 'What are the qualities of the ideal wife?'

The priest looked at the girl thoughtfully. 'An ideal wife should obey and serve her husband like she serves God.'

'If the wife must serve her husband like God, it must also follow that the husband must serve his wife like a Goddess,' the girl challenged.

The priest stared at the girls but was unable to respond. Neelkanth looked at the priest and pressed his palms together as if to ask him if he could answer. The priest nodded.

'The husband must also honor his wife like a Goddess. All husbands should have the following five qualities. Courage, strength, love, consideration, and kindness. Ram was an ideal husband and had all these qualities. Otherwise, King Janak would not have allowed Sita to marry him.'

Intrigued by the response from Neelkanth, the girls turned to him. 'So why did Ram abandon Sita after returning to Ayodhya after the exile? Where was his love for Sita then?'

Neelkanth glanced at the ground thoughtfully. 'You ask an important question,' Neelkanth praised the girls. 'Ram had all the qualities. His love for Sita was unquestionable. There are many versions of the Ramayan, yet the best version is the original version written by Sage Valmiki, who writes that they ruled the Kausalya Kingdom together for many years. Sita was not banished because of the suspicions of his subjects but supported by Ram, who never doubted her purity. Others have added their endings to generate renewed interest, but it is Valmiki's Ramayan that tells the story as it truly was.'

'Sage Valmiki was originally a thief,' the girls said together.

'Indeed he was. But we can all change for the better, is that not so? Is life not about making progress from one day to next, from one year to another?'

'Yes,' cried the children together.

'Are we not born to improve?'

'Yes!'

'Is there any man who is perfect except Ram?'

'No!'

'Is there any woman who is perfect except Sita?'

'No!'

The priest laughed at the way the children hung onto Neelkanth's every word. 'We must all strive to improve, be better, and forgive each other for our flaws. If we can do so throughout our lives, then we will have fulfilled our duties as husbands, wives, sons, and daughters.'

The children started clapping. Neelkanth waited for them to stop. 'I have listened to the Ramayan for more times than I can remember, but never have I enjoyed myself so much as I have today,' he said. 'I hope you will all be the ideal husbands the girls will want to marry, and the girls will be the ideal wives the boys will want to marry.'

'Oh, please tell us about the qualities of an ideal wife,' the girls asked.

Neelkanth stared at them, but he was not looking at them at all. He thought about his mother for a long time and bowed. 'Faithful, selfless like a mother, loving, resilient in the face of adversity, and diplomatic.'

The girls smiled. 'We will try to be as you say.'

The priest glanced at Neelkanth and smiled. 'Thank you. That's enough for today,' he said.

The children bowed to the priest and then turned to Neelkanth without hesitation, knelt, and bowed their heads at his feet even though he was not much older than them.

'May you all grow up to be the best that a wife can be and the best that a husband should be,' blessed Neelkanth.

The priest brought some fruits, nuts, and warm milk for Neelkanth. 'You are an ancient soul in the guise of a child,' he said.

Neelkanth spoke about his long pilgrimage through the Himalayas while they ate, particularly about his year with Gopal Yogi.

A man appeared at the entrance of the temple. He was breathing heavily. 'What's the matter?' the priest asked, jumping to his feet. He served the man a glass of water.

'My daughters…' he gasped.

'Yes, they were here. What has happened to them?'

The man knelt before Neelkanth. 'My daughters said there was a boy in the temple who was wise beyond his tender years and pressed me to ask him to come and visit our home. Are you Neelkanth?'

Neelkanth bowed.

'They are both curious girls, keen to learn, and very intelligent,' the man said.

'They asked some probing questions that I could not answer. Thankfully, Neelkanth was present and was able to answer them to their satisfaction,' the priest said.

'It is God's grace,' said Neelkanth.

'Will you do us the honor and visit our home?' the man asked.

Neelkanth glanced at the priest as if to seek his permission.

'The family has created a beautiful Krishna temple you must see,' the priest said.

'All the more reason to visit,' said Neelkanth. He got up and followed the man out of the temple through the dirt road bordered by wildflowers. Jairam came running towards them when they entered a rose garden in full bloom, exhibiting a spectral of exciting colors. Neelkanth inhaled their sweet scent. Jairam took Neelkanth's hand and led him to his two sisters and mother, standing on the veranda. Neelkanth bowed as the girls' placed a garland of red and white roses around his head. Jairam led Neelkanth to a room where a white marble statue of Krishna and Radha stood, beautifully adorned in rich silk clothes. Neelkanth's heart warmed to the family. As he knelt to prostrate, Jairam held his hand. 'Please wait,' he said and laid a long orange duvet on the floor.

Neelkanth placed his hand on Jairam and prostrated. He lay on the floor for some time in prayer for the good of the family. When he got up, Jairam folded the duvet and placed it on the ground for Neelkanth to sit. The family sat around him. 'Who are you?' the father asked.

'I am the servant of the poor, the meek, and the holy,' said Neelkanth. He briefly told them about his travels from Ayodhya, tactfully dismissing any questions about his family, except to say that he had left home after his parents passed away because he wanted to impress upon the children his reverence for his parents.

Jairam's mother stared at Neelkanth's emaciated body and teared up. The girls took her hands to comfort her.

'Let us hold hands and form a circle,' said Neelkanth, gazing at the mother. 'You will find what you have wished for.'

'What have we wished for, Papa?' Jairam asked.

'I have wished that God should visit our home in person,' the father said without hesitation. The room filled with a sudden flash which blinded everyone and later merged into the body of Neelkanth. Neelkanth smiled. 'God is here, in person, as you had wished. Recognize Him and you will never need to be reborn again.'

Jairam got up, knelt, and bowed his head at Neelkanth's feet. 'Please stay with us for a few days,' he said.

'Oh, please stay,' the girls said together.

'Good food and rest will help you to regain your strength,' the mother said.

Neelkanth sensed the love of the family, their togetherness.

'Ma makes delicious food,' the girls said together. 'We will help her.'

Neelkanth smiled. 'Only if you tell me your names,' said Neelkanth.

The girls glanced at each other. 'I am Lakshmi.'

'I am Sita.'

'I should have guessed,' said Neelkanth, grinning.

'We will bring fruits and flowers for your morning prayers,' Jairam said.

'Please stay and allow us to serve you,' the father said.

Neelkanth looked down. 'How can I not stay when all you have offered me is love? Love is what I crave and love is what I look for in the heart,' he said, wiping a tear.

When Neelkanth woke up early in the morning, the house was infused with the aroma of spices and incense. Jairam sat down beside Neelkanth with a plateful of freshly cut fruits.

'You must have woken up early to get this ready,' said Neelkanth, staring at the red mark on his forehead.

'Papa has instilled this habit in all of us,' Jairam said. Lakshmi and Sita came with a plate of freshly picked roses. Neelkanth placed the Shaligram on an orange handkerchief and arranged the roses around it. He sat in meditation for a long time, turning the rosary while the girls sang and Jairam accompanied them with the drums.

Neelkanth felt overwhelmed with love for the family when the mother cooked them hot idli sambar, uttapams, and parathas for breakfast. Having controlled his diet since leaving home, he ate little, despite the father's insistence that he should eat more to regain his strength. 'My body can only take a little at a time,' said Neelkanth.

After breakfast, Neelkanth asked Jairam about the freshly cut lotus flowers. Jairam told him about the wonderful lake outside the village. 'I go there with my friend Krishna Tamboli to collect the flowers every day for the puja.'

'I would like to visit the lake,' said Neelkanth.

Jairam's eyes lit up. 'Of course, I will take you. We can sail in a raft. You will like it there. It is so nice. We will go there in the evening. It is cooler then.'

The rays of the sun flashed over the tips of the trees in the forest on the opposite bank when they reached the lake, casting a long shadow of the trees on the lake. Tamboli had kept the raft ready. Jairam took Neelkanth's hand as he stepped inside the boat. Neelkanth sat down on a plank opposite Jairam as he took the oar while Tamboli unfurled the sails.

'The forest on the opposite bank is full of wild animals,' Tamboli said. 'It groans with the call of the wild animals at night. I go to sleep every night listening to them.'

'Do they not frighten you, Krishna?'

'No. What is there to fear? I have heard them for as long as I can remember. They never cross the lake to come to this side or anywhere near the village.'

'They are wild animals and prefer the wild of the forest,' said Neelkanth. He got up and sat down next to Jairam. 'Let me steer the raft.' He took the oar from Jairam.

'Have you done it before?' Jairam asked.

'Ayodhya is on the banks of the great Saryu,' said Neelkanth.

A cool breeze blew as they sailed to the middle of the lake. Neelkanth raised his hand to feel the direction of the wind and adjusted the oar slightly to catch the wind. The raft picked up speed in the direction of the opposite bank.

Tamboli crawled to Neelkanth. 'You're sailing towards the forest!' he said.

'No one from the village ever goes there!' Jairam shouted. 'The wild animals will kill us.'

Neelkanth didn't say anything and stared at the line of tall, dark trees as they approached the shore. As soon as the raft scraped the sandy bank, Neelkanth jumped out.

'No, Neelkanth!' Jairam shouted. 'The lions will kill you.'

'It isn't safe!' Tamboli shouted. 'The animals come to the lake to drink water in the evening.'

Neelkanth ignored them and carried on. The boys rushed behind him. Neelkanth entered the forest and kept on walking. Fearful of his life, the boys followed him. Loud screams echoed through the forest.

'They can sense our presence,' Tamboli said.

'Smell us, you mean. We will soon be meat,' Jairam said, pulling Neelkanth's arm.

Neelkanth glanced at Jairam. 'Don't worry. I have been traveling and living with wild animals for years.'

The leaves rustled as a sudden gust caught the trees. The birds flew as two screeching monkeys leaped up the higher branches. The boys watched them. 'They can sense the wild animals approaching,' said Neelkanth.

A black bear suddenly came charging at them. Neelkanth pushed the boys out of the way. They found the nearest tree and started climbing.

'Neelkanth!' Tamboli cried.

Neelkanth stared at the bear and held his position. The bear rose on its hind legs as it approached and gave a ferocious growl before coming down with a thump in front of Neelkanth.

'Run, Neelkanth, run!' Jairam shouted.

Neelkanth placed his hand on the bear's head and stroked him. The bear raised his head. Neelkanth saw the tears in his eyes. 'All will be well,' he calmed the bear.

The bear bowed his head and scuttled off in the direction he came from. Neelkanth stared at the bear until it disappeared behind the bushes. The boys came down from the tree.

'How did you do that?' Jairam asked, still trembling.

'Let's go.' Neelkanth started walking back to the raft without replying.

He took the oar as they set sail and guided it to the middle of the lake. The boys sat opposite him on the plank.

'How did a wild bear become so tame?' Tamboli asked. 'Why did it bow at your feet?'

'The bear was Jambuvan,' said Neelkanth. 'He had served Sri Krishna but always doubted him when he was on Earth and was, therefore, born as a bear. I have quashed his doubts. Soon, he will die and be born again.'

'How do you know all this?' Tamboli asked.

'Neelkanth is a great yogi,' Jairam said.

A flash of white light sprung from Neelkanth's body and blinded the boys. Neelkanth guided the raft to the bank while the boys recovered. They took Neelkanth's hands and walked with him to the house. Jairam told the story to his family after Neelkanth went to sleep. The story spread to the villages nearby during the night, and a large curious crowd gathered outside their house in the morning.

Neelkanth came out after his morning prayers and sat down on a seat Jairam had erected under the shade of a tree. He bowed as he ran his eyes through the crowd and put them all in a trance with his yogic powers. He walked around them and placed his hand on their heads in blessing before returning to his seat. They all came out of the trance when Neelkanth snapped his fingers.

'You are none other than Shri Krishna, returned to redeem us all,' the father said, bowing his head.

'I am the servant of the poor, the meek, and the holy,' said Neelkanth. Everyone came forward to pay their respects. Looking at the crowd, Neelkanth knew he had done what he had come here to do.

He woke up early the next morning. Dawn had not yet broken, but he could hear the growls of the lions and tigers in the distance. As he stepped out of the house, he felt an emptiness he had not felt before. They were a good family, devoted to each other and God. He sighed deeply and started walking south, unsure why he felt the way he did.

10

Jagannath Puri

The journey south through the deserted groves was contemplative with the devotional poems of Mira and Tulsidas. His gaze fixed ahead, there was an unusual urgency in his pace.

'Jagannath Puri,' he said loudly as if the pull of the ancient city had compelled him to race ahead, walking for days during the cool early mornings before resting in the afternoons.

He had not looked back until he heard a familiar cry of his name. Jairam came running towards him, panting, gasping for breath. He fell at his feet in tears.

'I...I have searched for you everywhere, Neelkanthji.' Jairam knelt in front of him, his palms together in reverence. 'Please return home.'

Neelkanth raised him from the ground. 'Jairam. You, here? But why?' There was concern in his voice. 'Are you lost? Are your parents and sisters well?'

'Lost? Oh, no,' Jairam said, still crying. 'I have found what I have searched for twenty days and twenty nights.'

'Why, Jairam? Is your family not well?'

'They have all lost the will to live. My mother pines for you. My sisters cry all day long. My father has even searched the forest, only to return bereft and broken after not finding you. Please return to the village. Make my family whole again and restore their will to live. Oh, please, forgive our faults, Neelkanthji, and return. They will die without seeing you again.'

Neelkanth gave Jairam the gourd. 'Drink some water and calm down. Then tell me everything.'

Jairam raised his trembling hands and tried to drink the water. Neelkanth held his hands to steady them. Jairam drank some water. Neelkanth then led him to the shade of a tree.

'Oh, please come back to our home, Neelkanthji,' Jairam said again. Neelkanth sat him down. Jairam inhaled deeply. 'My parents have stopped eating. All they do is cry for you. Villagers gather outside our house. They cry and speak about you. My dearest friend, Tamboli, wanders all day long, crying, calling your name. All he wants to do is enter the forest. He is sure you have entered it again to save more animals. Only his parents prevent him from acting so recklessly. How can I allow you to go with so much sorrow? The village will die without you. You have become its life, its breath and its joy.'

Neelkanth wiped Jairam's tears with his fingers. 'Jairam, we are near Jagannath Puri. It would be such a shame if we returned without visiting the temple.'

'Do we have time? It has been twenty days since I left the village. Will they even be alive if they haven't eaten all this time?'

Neelkanth closed his eyes and observed them with his yogic powers. 'They are all alive and eating,' he said. He did not tell him that they were still eagerly awaiting their return.

'How do you know these things?'

'Don't you trust me, Jairam?' Neelkanth looked into his eyes.

'I am sorry. I don't know what I am saying, mad with grief as I am.'

'The vision of Lord Jagannath will lift your spirit.' Neelkanth stood up and held out his hand. Jairam took it.

They walked together, hand-in-hand, like best friends, and reached the shore after passing through the woods. Jairam approached a man waiting near a raft. 'We wish to go to Jagannath Puri. Will you be able to take us there?'

Neelkanth smiled at the man with kindness. The man gazed at his emaciated body, the old loincloth, and the bun of dark hair on the top of his head. He saw the young Shiva in Neelkanth and instantly stepped forward, his palms pressed together. 'I have been ferrying pilgrims to Bhubaneshwar for many years, but I feel as if Lord Shiva himself has come in person to bless me for the years of service to pilgrims.' He took Neelkanth's hand and led him into his raft. He dusted a cushion for him. 'You are not a mere child,' he said as he picked up a green coconut and sliced its head before serving it to Neelkanth. Neelkanth drank a little of the coconut water and gave the rest to Jairam, who accepted it with glee, happy to quench his thirst with his favorite drink.

'Ummm,' he cried after his first sip as he held the water in his mouth to absorb the flavors. 'You see we are not the only ones whose hearts you touch. I bet you have left many broken hearts scattered across all of North India.'

Neelkanth grinned. 'Jairam, I did not leave home only to get attached to other people. Though I care for them deeply, I must continue to travel to lift the people from this malaise. Our country has been ravaged for centuries by invaders. They have stained the heart of India. The true meaning of our ancient traditions and values has been shattered by violence and greed. I want to restore the ancient value of *Ahimsa* that has guided this holy land. I want to serve the poor, the meek, and the holy who have been suffering for far too long.'

'All that is good, but I hope you realize how you touch the hearts of the people you meet,' Jairam repeated.

'People are searching for peace everywhere I have visited. They feel lost and cheated by the fake monks who have exploited them for centuries. Jairam, the true essence of the Lord's words has been lost.'

They arrived at the banks of Indradumyna Lake in the early morning, where traders from all over the region had gathered to make their way to the town of Jagannath Puri, a few miles away.

Neelkanth thanked the man. Jairam took his hand. Neelkanth gave him a side-long glance before running his discerning eyes through the crowd. 'Traders gain on the goodwill of the pilgrims. Little do they know that those who prey on the meek find little joy with their ill-gotten gains.'

He found an isolated spot on the bank, bathed, and performed his prayers. Jairam collected some wildflowers.

Then, he cut some fruits and offered them to Neelkanth. After the prayers, they joined the many pilgrims on the dirt road to Puri.

As the great dome of Jagannath came in sight, Neelkanth picked up his pace. Jairam held his hand, afraid of losing him amongst the large crowds converging on the temple. Jairam was not surprised as they easily gave way when they glanced at Neelkanth. Many bowed as they approached the stairs of the temple.

'I hope you realize the devotion you awaken in people when they see you,' Jairam said.

Neelkanth squeezed Jairam's hand to reassure him as he pulled him along with him until they stood in front of Lord Jagannath.

Neelkanth prostrated while Jairam stood, holding the gourd, his eyes filling with tears of love for Neelkanth as he observed his deep devotion, humility, and an inner craving for the Lord he had not witnessed in anyone. There was a gentleness about everything Neelkanth did that Jairam liked because they were the qualities his parents had nurtured in him and his two sisters. Though surrounded by throngs of pilgrims, he felt at peace. 'Bow to Lord Jagannath and ask for anything but for my return,' Neelkanth said when he got up. 'He will grant your every wish and more.'

Jairam bowed and prostrated. The priest came forward and took Neelkanth's hand. Neelkanth waited for Jairam. The priest took them to the inner sanctum. 'Only the lucky few have a chance to be here,' he said. 'Stay here for as long as you like. I shall serve you with the Lord's offering.'

Jairam grinned, not surprised about anything that happened to them.

'Lord Jagannath will reward you for your kindness,' Neelkanth blessed the priest. 'The devotion of the pilgrims is heart-warming. Serve them well.'

'See what I mean,' Jairam said with a broad grin.

'The Lord looks after the pure of heart,' Neelkanth said, dismissing any thought in Jairam's mind that he was special. 'But we cannot stay here, of course.'

'Why?' Jairam frowned, disappointed, unwilling to give up the sanctuary of the temple so easily.

'It is too crowded. I prefer the seclusion of the shore.'

Jairam followed Neelkanth to the shore without protest. Neelkanth selected a secluded banyan tree not far away from the temple. They visited the temple every morning and sat in meditation before the famous Garud pillar in the temple. There, they listened to the discourses on Shrimad Bhagwat. The priest served them the food offered to Lord Jagannath. Neelkanth took a little and left the rest for Jairam, whose appetite seemed to be growing by the day. Neelkanth assumed he was going through a growth spurt.

When they returned to the shore, Neelkanth taught Jairam the simple basic positions of yoga. His lessons attracted many pilgrims, pulled by his austere nature. Soon, the news reached the King of Puri, who arrived at the temple one morning to meet Neelkanth sitting in meditation. Neelkanth opened his eyes and bowed.

'What is your name? Who is your father and who is your mother?' Why have you deserted your home at such a tender age?' the king asked.

Neelkanth looked at the eyes of the king and saw the purity of his soul. 'I am Neelkanth. The Lord is my father and my mother. I have been traveling across the north of India for four years, in search of the godly, to quash the superstition that has stained our *dharma*, which was once so pure.'

The king sat down on the floor, intrigued by Neelkanth's response. 'Child, it is hardly surprising that the original meaning of our scriptures has been lost because invaders have ruled us for more centuries than my ancestors can care to remember. First, the Mughal Empire and now the British. It is only through the grace of Lord Jagannath that our kingdom has remained untouched.'

'I promise you, Mother India will once again reclaim its inheritance,' said Neelkanth.

'Victory to Lord Jagannath!' The king raised his arms above his head and cried out in joy. 'Child, please accept me as your disciple. Come and stay in the palace while you are in Puri and give your discourses to the pilgrims. Your wisdom is rare to witness. It fills my heart with joy. Let the pilgrims witness the powers of a true yogi.'

Neelkanth raised his hand and placed it on the head of the king. 'It would not befit a yogi to live in luxury. The sky is my roof, the sun my strength, Mother Earth supports me with all the generous gifts it showers upon us without asking for anything in return.'

'If you will not stay in the palace, will you at least sit beside Lord Jagannath during the Rath Yatra?'

'It is the reason I have come. I shall gladly sit on the chariot if we can purify the soil that has been stained by fake monks who prey on the innocent pilgrims.'

'The boy speaks the truth,' the priest said from behind. 'There is a band of monks who have for years preyed on the goodwill of pilgrims.'

'Where are they?' The king jumped to his feet. 'I shall send my army at once to quash them.'

Neelkanth asked the king to sit down. 'Not yet. Concentrate your mind on the preparation for the Rath Yatra.' He got up.

'Please visit the palace to bless our house?' the king asked again.

'There is no home like the home that the Lord provides.' Neelkanth glanced at Jairam. Jairam got up. The crowd that had gathered around them bowed and gave way as they left.

'Why did you not accept the offer to stay in the palace?' Jairam asked when they entered a dirt road. 'It would have been nice to live in a palace for a change.'

Neelkanth laughed. 'Jairam, do I sense some frustration with living under the protection of Mother Earth?'

'I have never had the privilege of visiting a palace, have you?'

Neelkanth thought about his adventures in the Himalayas. 'It is nothing special. Just nature's many gifts reshaped.'

'Ahha, you have tasted the good life!'

'Jairam, you haven't yet seen the beauty of God's eternal divine home. There is nothing in creation that is comparable.'

'And I presume you will tell me you have,' Jairam glanced at him.

'One day, Jairam, one day,' said Neelkanth grinning, without adding any more.

They approached the banyan tree. There were some seagulls diving in and out of the sea. They watched them for a while before entering the water. Neelkanth dipped his hands in the water and splashed some water at Jairam. Jairam laughed and threw some water back, beginning a water fight, which continued until Neelkanth disappeared underwater and reappeared behind Jairam and playfully pulled him down.

They returned to the banyan tree after an afternoon of fun and frolic in the waters. It reminded Neelkanth of his time with his friends in Ayodhya, of carefree swimming, fun, and games in the Saryu. And for a brief moment, just for a few seconds, he wondered what they were all doing.

Jairam looked at his gaze in the distance. 'I bet that afternoon reminded you of your childhood,' he said, forgetting that they were both still children.

A few days later, Neelkanth sat in front of Lord Jagannath on a huge chariot with Jairam behind him like Laxman to Ram. There was a broad permanent grin on Jairam's face as he watched the king pull the chariot with the rest of his subjects. The sound of trumpets, drums, and cymbals resonated around them in a mist of colored powder showered over the chariot by the onlookers. Neelkanth had never seen a festival like it, while Jairam remembered his many visits with his family, never expecting that one day he would have the chance to ride on the chariot with Lord Jagannath himself.

Neelkanth kept a steady gaze ahead, enjoying the warmth of the public. Jairam watched the crowds when his eyes fell on a band of naked monks he had seen near the lake. Their red eyes were fixed on Neelkanth. He gazed at Neelkanth in fear and wanted to tell him but held back because he appeared so serene amid the joyous jangle of the crowds. Perhaps, on the way back to their banyan tree ashram, he decided.

It was evening by the time they returned to the banyan tree. A cool wind blew from the lake. Jairam tried to wrap a shawl around Neelkanth. Neelkanth immediately raised his hand to stop him. 'A yogi should bear all. I have traversed the snowy peaks of the Himalayas barefoot with just this loincloth, so what is a cool breeze.'

Jairam sat down beside him. 'I enjoyed the day,' he said.

'Yes, it was very kind of the king to allow us to ride on the chariot.'

'Such are the joys of serving you. Who would have thought little old me would get a chance to ride the chariot of Lord Jagannath himself?'

'The fruits of your selfless service. You are greater than you think.'

Jairam stared at Neelkanth, expecting him to tell him more, but Neelkanth closed his eyes to meditate. Jairam saw the band of monks coming in their direction. He instantly sensed trouble. Their evil glares during the Yatra imprinted on his mind like a poignant memory of childhood.

'I know,' Neelkanth said even before Jairam could say anything. 'Sit down here and let them come.' Jairam did as asked. He had learned to trust the judgment of Neelkanth.

A monk nudged both of them. 'We want to cook our evening meal. Get up and gather some spinach leaves.'

Neelkanth remained in meditation. Jairam glanced at him and closed his eyes, hoping that ignoring them would drive them away. The monk shook Jairam. Another kicked Neelkanth. Jairam got up and hid behind Neelkanth. Neelkanth calmly opened his eyes.

'Go and pick some spinach leaves,' the monk shouted.

Neelkanth looked up and stared at the monk's bloodshot eyes, his long dark beard, hair tied in a bun on the top of his head, silver earrings hanging from his ears, a garland of dry acorns around his neck, and a sword around his waist – it was a paraphernalia of contradictions. 'There is life in the leaves. I will not pick them,' said Neelkanth.

The monk pulled out his sword and tried to strike Neelkanth.

Another monk placed his sword in the path and stopped him. 'He is with us,' he said.

Neelkanth stood up. 'There is no need to argue. It does not befit a monk to show such anger.'

'Who are you to tell us how to behave!' The monk raised his sword. Monks from all sides came running and started to push each other. Neelkanth stepped to the side as Jairam screamed when the monks started to fight amongst them. Trumpets blared and drums beat loudly to summon the different factions, frightening the birds nestling in the trees.

Jairam saw his chance and ran in the direction of the palace. Neelkanth closed his eyes and sat in meditation. The sound of metal blades and piercing cries echoed around him as swords cut through flesh, maimed, and killed.

A cavalry came riding on the dirt road and attacked the monks. A fierce battle ensued between the soldiers and the monks. The king came to Neelkanth after many of the monks fled. He knelt before Neelkanth and touched his feet. Only then did Neelkanth open his eyes.

'It is dangerous here,' the king said. 'If you will not stay in the palace, at least stay in the garden. You will be safe there.'

Neelkanth looked at the bodies around him. 'Death comes to us all. Whether in youth or old age. It is an inevitable part of life.'

'These monks are a stain on the holy soil of Puri,' the king said.

'You are a king with the power to protect the pilgrims from them.' Neelkanth glanced at Jairam, who took the hint and got up.

They followed the shore south to Manaspur and entered a garden in the evening on the outskirts of the town. The gardener greeted them as soon as they stepped through the gates. 'This garden has been created by the king for ascetics, especially like you,' he said and led Neelkanth to a tree. 'You will find it's cool and quiet here.' The gardener stared at Neelkanth's emaciated body, and his eyes misted. 'Child, will you have some food?'

'I am famished,' Jairam whispered in Neelkanth's ear. 'We haven't eaten all day.'

'We will have some fruits,' Neelkanth said. He asked Jairam to sit down when the gardener left. 'It appears you are finding the life of a wandering ascetic difficult.'

Jairam realized he had overstepped his mark. 'I am a son of a father who has given me everything that I have wished for and more. It is difficult. The naked monks have crushed my will to go on.'

Neelkanth listened but did not say anything. He saw the gardener approaching with a plateful of cut fruits and milk. Jairam reached for the plate as soon as the gardener placed the plate in front of them. 'Jairam,' Neelkanth simply said to stop Jairam. He untied the Shaligram from around his neck and placed it on a stone.

Having observed Neelkanth's devotion to the Shaligram over many days, Jairam knew the reverence he held for the stone. His father had explained to him once when he had asked him about worshipping stone statues and pictures. 'God is all-pervading,' he had told him. 'He is everywhere. Even a dry leaf cannot be moved without his will.'

Jairam picked up the plate and offered it to the Shaligram with the same reverence he had seen Neelkanth display.

'Now you can eat,' said Neelkanth, smiling. While Jairam reached for the bowls of guava fruits, Neelkanth picked up the small brass jar of milk and drank a little before offering the rest to Jairam. 'The act of offering everything to God first is a mark of our devotion,' said Neelkanth.

'You are my living God,' Jairam said.

It was the last thing Neelkanth had expected Jairam to say.

'I am a servant of the poor, the meek and the holy,' Neelkanth reminded him as he placed his hand on Jairam and blessed him. While they ate, Neelkanth spoke about his year with Gopal Yogi. 'You are the only other person

I have spent so much time with since and yet,' he gazed at Jairam with love, 'I sense that your heart is not here.'

Jairam looked down and thought about his parents, eagerly waiting for his return. 'My parents are pining for our return. Is it not the duty of a son to serve them and make them happy? I know your heart is set on traveling south.'

'Let us rest for now, Jairam. Tomorrow is another day. Let us see what it brings.'

Jairam got up early in the morning, bathed, and went to collect some fruits and flowers. When he returned, the gardener was sitting with Neelkanth in prayer. Jairam saw the fruits and flowers, the garland of pink roses around Neelkanth's neck, and more spread around the Shaligram. He sat down without disturbing anyone.

Neelkanth opened his eyes and reached for the flowers Jairam had brought and placed them around the Shaligram. 'The Lord God will not be pleased if he does not receive the flowers of his choicest devotee,' he said, grinning. 'Today, we will serve a hot idli sambhar with yogurt.' He brought out a clay pot and placed it in front of Jairam. 'It has already been offered. Eat well because the king is visiting as he does every morning.' Their eyes fell on an entourage on the path leading from the gates.

Jairam stopped. 'I shall enjoy the breakfast after he is gone. It is rude to eat in front of a dignitary?'

'King Satradharma of Manaspur,' the gardener announced as the king stood in front of Neelkanth and bowed. The king sat down on a rug his attendant placed on the ground.

Neelkanth put his palms together and bowed.

'I hope you have been well looked after?' the king asked.

'The garden is an oasis of peace. A good resting place for pilgrims,' said Neelkanth.

The other ascetics gathered around them.

'You are a generous king and the Lord will certainly grant you liberation.'

'It was my father's wish that no pilgrim should pass through Manaspur hungry.'

'You have done well to uphold his wish.'

'Is it not a son's duty to honor the wishes of his parents?'

'Indeed. Yet, many take advantage of your generosity,' said Neelkanth, running his eyes through the growing crowd of monks gathering around them. He saw some glowering at him, their eyes filled with envy.

'At least they will not leave hungry,' the king said. 'Yet, in all the years I have ruled this land, never have I seen a yogi so young and so at peace.'

'It is the peace attained from realizing the true glory of God,' said Neelkanth.

'A peace that permeates the hearts of all those who observe you. Look at the branches of the trees.'

Neelkanth looked up and saw the branches lined with birds. All their heads were bowed in his direction.

'Even the birds are mesmerized by your presence,' the king said.

'I am the servant of the poor, the meek, and the holy. The Lord appears on Earth to destroy evil and to protect the righteous. Trust in him always and all your wishes will be granted.'

The king pointed at the Shaligram sitting on a bed of roses. 'I have wanted a Shaligram like yours for years,' he said.

'I would give you mine, but I only have one. It – He – has accompanied me every step of my journey and protected me from evil glares.'

'I will make sure I get one,' the king said. He stood up. 'I shall visit again. I am sure my family will be eager to meet you.'

Jairam reached for the clay pot as soon as the king and his entourage left.

'Is it still hot?' Neelkanth asked, touching the pot. He felt its warmth.

'The sambhar is hot,' Jairam said.

Neelkanth took a little and offered the rest to Jairam.

The king visited the next day with his family. The queen's heart succumbed to Neelkanth's austere nature, his sacrifice at such a tender age. 'How is it that your mother let you go? A soul so pure at heart and gentle,' she asked like so many mothers before.

Neelkanth bowed to her maternal tenderness. 'Mother, I would not have been able to leave had she been alive.'

'How long have you been wandering?'

'Since I was eleven. I am sixteen now.'

'A mere child, still.'

Neelkanth saw the tears in her eyes. 'Do not cry for me, mother. I travel in search of the pure in heart, to protect them, to show them the path to God. I have no other desire. What you see is what I have. It is all I need.'

'A true ascetic is very difficult to find,' the king said. 'Stay here for as long as you wish. We will look after you as our son.'

'You are very kind.' Neelkanth blessed the family. The king got up. 'Have you secured a Shaligram?' Neelkanth asked, looking up.

'Sadly, no. I asked the leader of the monks to give me one, but he got angry and said I would not know how to worship them.'

'He has a bag full of Shaligrams and treats them like stones,' the gardener said.

The following day, Neelkanth asked Jairam to go to the leader to ask for a Shaligram for the king. Jairam hesitated, afraid of how the leader might react, but went anyway. He came running back moments later with the leader behind him, a trident in hand. Jairam hid behind Neelkanth.

'How dare your servant ask for a Shaligram?'

Neelkanth calmed him. 'They are not mere stones but possess the power of God if worshipped by the pure. I hear you have a bagful and treat them like stones.'

'Yes. What is it to you? You are just a child. What would you know about worship?' The leader stomped off.

He stood in front of Neelkanth menacingly early next morning after the visit of the king and his family, his trident pointing at him again.

'Where are my Shaligrams? Where have you hidden them?'

'You will not find the Shaligrams with me. I have not taken them, nor has the king.'

'Where are they then?'

'Are they not found on the shores of lakes, oceans, and rivers?'

'Where is your servant? Has he stolen them and run away?'

'Jairam is not a servant. He is my friend who would not pick a flower without asking the owners.' Neelkanth closed his eyes.

The leader returned with his disciples and started pelting stones at Neelkanth. The stones bounced an invisible wall and fell to the ground. The leader stomped his trident on the ground and ordered his disciples to surround Neelkanth and hit him with stones from all sides. The stones fell to the ground without touching Neelkanth. After a while, a wall of stones surrounded Neelkanth. Neelkanth sat still, silent, deep in meditation, throughout their attack.

When Jairam returned, he could not find Neelkanth anywhere. He ran to the palace and informed the king, who came with the soldiers.

'There is your child yogi,' the leader said, pointing at a heap of stones where Neelkanth sat. The monks pointed their tridents, spears, and swords at the soldiers when they stepped forward to grab them. The soldiers pushed them back with their swords.

'Kill them all,' the king ordered. 'They are a stain on the pure soil of Manaspur.'

While the soldiers and monks fought, some soldiers helped the king and Jairam remove the stones. They found Neelkanth deep in meditation until the last stone was removed and every monk fell dead to the ground.

Neelkanth stared at the monks lying still on the ground, blood pouring out of their wounds. He shook his head in sorrow. 'The unrighteous will never learn. Their souls are mired by greed, arrogance, and cruelty.' He glanced at Jairam. 'Please gather your things, Jairam.'

'Will you not stay a few days more?' the king knelt before Neelkanth.

'Please clear the dead and cremate them with respect. I will pray for their soul to find a better life in the next birth. Many are blameless, misguided by those who should know better.'

The queen came in a carriage with her children. They rushed to Neelkanth and fell at his feet.

'Mother, teach them well,' said Neelkanth. He got up and glanced at Jairam who followed him out of the garden. They walked quietly until they were far away from Manaspur, Jairam more alert than ever to the perils of traveling with Neelkanth, and Neelkanth in silent prayer for the dead monks.

'My parents will be pining for my return,' Jairam said when they approached a quiet and secluded spot near the shore. Neelkanth sat down on a large stone and watched the many birds riding the warm air currents above the sea. 'The birds look happy playing in the warm air,' he said. 'You too could be happy, Jairam. I know you wish me to return to your home, but you know I cannot.'

Jairam turned to the sea and watched the birds. 'They look happy because they do not know any better. They cannot think like us. It is good that they cannot because otherwise, they would feel the futility of their existence.'

Neelkanth smiled. 'At least you have learned something. I have enjoyed our time together. You must decide whether you wish to join me or return home.'

'You know I cannot come,' Jairam said. 'If I stay with you, I will worry about my family. If I go home, I will worry about you.'

Neelkanth thought about his parents and family. He knew the pain his parents would have suffered had he left when they were alive. 'I understand, Jairam.' Neelkanth took Jairam's hand. 'Do not worry about me. I will be fine, but you must return home. You will not be happy until you do.'

Jairam knelt and bowed, tears streaming down his cheeks.

Neelkanth wiped the tears with his fingers. 'You will forever sing the glory of God because your name says so. Continue to trust in Him always. Serve your parents. If you ever feel the need to see me again, think of me, and you will see me as I am and where I am.'

'As you are?' Jairam cried, unable to believe that he would always know where Neelkanth was. They fell into an embrace.

'I will be in Kathiawar at the end of my pilgrimage. Join me if you wish in a few years.'

'Kathiawar is a large state. How will I find you there?'

'I will be known as Sahajanand,' said Neelkanth without hesitation.

'You know the future and you know the past. How is that possible?'

Neelkanth smiled without replying.

'Since you know, Neelkanthji,' Jairam asked. 'Be kind and tell me where I will find you without searching the whole state.'

'Trust me, Jairam, you will find me.'

Jairam bowed. He had stopped being surprised by Neelkanth. Neelkanth watched him until he reached the top of a hill. Jairam stopped and turned. He waved when Neelkanth waved. Neelkanth watched him until he disappeared behind the hill, then took the route south.

11

Rameshwaram

The thought of Ram hastened Neelkanth's pace to Rameshwaram. He had heard from his father about the bridge that Ram had built to reach Lanka and was keen to see if it still existed, even if only a small trace of it. He stopped after many hours of walking on the edge of a dense forest. They had always been an enormous challenge, but he had crossed enough of them by now to feel confident that he would come out alive at the other end. Going around these forests was not an option he had ever contemplated because of the extra miles it added to his journey.

A dense tropical forest closed around him as he gradually made his way. The light grew dim until it became pitch dark deep in the forest. Unable to see clearly, he felt the smarting of branches and thorns. The chirping of crickets pierced through the roars of tigers, and leaves rustled uneasily in the breeze.

He stopped after many hours of walking when he heard a loud snore but quickly dismissed it as a snore of a sleeping wild animal and followed a faint light penetrating through the umbrella of leaves. His feet touched something hard. He stopped and felt the obstruction with his hands, the smooth scaly skin. He patted it with his hands as it woke up and rose, hissing wildly. Neelkanth stepped back and raised his right arm as it slid forward. The python fell at his feet and raised his head. Neelkanth sensed its pain. He gazed at it with kindness. He wanted to know his story. He blessed the creature with the power of speech with his yogic powers.

The python hissed with relief as it heard the sound of his voice. His head bowed in gratitude. 'I was once a good king of the Telangana region. Long ago, I was asked to sit in judgment of a dispute between two wise Brahmins, Jaidev and Mukundev, whose children were engaged when they were mere infants. Unfortunately, Mukundev's boy developed smallpox and became blind. Jaidev, therefore, broke off the engagement of his daughter to the boy, returning all clothes, gifts, and jewelry. This made Mukundev very angry and he came to me for justice. I sought advice from my ministers and pronounced that Jaidev was well within his rights to call off the engagement. Mukundev became very angry. He said that my judgment was flawed and cursed me, saying that I would die in a few days and be born as a python. Although Jaidev came, apologetic for having put me in this situation, he said he could not reverse the curse of a Brahmin but promised me that, one day, God himself would come to lift the curse. I have lived this wretched life for longer than I care to remember. In that time, many false Gods have blessed me, but none have been able to lift me from this curse.

They have broken my heart with false promises. Yet, I feel sure that today you will lift the curse because never before have I found the voice to express my thoughts until now.'

Neelkanth gazed at the python, his head still with anxiety as it waited for Neelkanth to respond. 'Did you not once kill a Brahmin to satisfy your hunger?' asked Neelkanth to test the python's sincerity.

The python hissed. 'I cannot hide anything from the one who knows all. I had not eaten for a whole week. The only son of a father with two daughters. It is the reason I have been lying here like a wretch.'

'God is all-forgiving,' said Neelkanth. He placed his hand on the head of the python. 'You will soon die and will be reborn in Kathiawar where you will be called Rato Bashiya. You will then have the chance to redeem yourself.'

The python hissed with relief. His head dropped at Neelkanth's feet. Neelkanth again placed his hand on his head as it hissed its last breath and proceeded on his journey.

The sun had just crept up the eastern horizon when Neelkanth reached the edge of the forest. He stopped to absorb the warmth of the rays. As the mist cleared, his eyes fell on a farmer taking water from a well to water his crops. Neelkanth approached him and saw that the water was being brought up with a leather bucket.

The man stopped and stared at the emaciated body of Neelkanth. Neelkanth bowed and smiled. 'Father,' he said, 'Have you got a string so that I can collect some water in my gourd?'

The man pointed at the leather bucket. 'There is plenty of water in the bucket.'

'I cannot drink water brought up in a leather bucket because it is from a dead animal. I have taken the vow of non-violence.'

'That is all I have,' the man said. 'You should carry a string if you are so fussy!'

Neelkanth felt the harshness in his voice and decided to teach the farmer a lesson in looking after visitors. He picked up his empty gourd and sat on the wall surrounding the well. A sudden burst of water rose to the mouth of the well. Neelkanth filled the gourd, drank a little, and refilled it.

The man saw the water drop to the floor of the well as quickly as it had risen. 'Oh, please show me how you did that,' the man asked, bowing at Neelkanth's feet in regret.

Neelkanth got up. 'Do not be harsh to the meek and the gentle. Even the water spirit comes to quench the thirst of those who are pure of heart,' he said, before walking away, eager to get to Rameshwararam.

As he entered the dirt road out of the village, a pristine voice reached his ears. He stopped and listened to the singer pining for his beloved Sri Krishna.

This Vruja land of ours, oh Krishna, has always been rich,
For Lakshmi is here because of your birth,
When all the people are happy, we the Gopis who love you,
Search for you in all places,
so be pleased to come before us,
Oh darling Krishna...

Neelkanth followed it like a child following the voice of his mother and saw a monk sitting underneath a tree. He quietly approached him, mindful not to disturb him. The monk opened his eyes. Neelkanth smiled but saw the pain in his eyes. 'Lord Krishna has blessed you with a beautiful voice,' said Neelkanth.

'I am Sevakram,' the monk said. He curiously stared at Neelkanth's emaciated body for a long time. The face looked familiar, but the body was unrecognizable.

'I am Neelkanth. I am on a pilgrimage of all the holy sites,' he said before Sevakram said anything.

Sevakram shook his head. 'They are the songs of the Gopis, pining for their beloved Krishna. Alas, I sing, but there is no one to listen to my supplication.'

'Why do you say that? If He had not listened, He would not have sent me. What is that you wish me to do?'

Sevakram reached for a heavy bag he carried. 'My body is weak from diarrhea, but there is no one to look after me.'

'Is that all? I shall look after you,' said Neelkanth. He stepped forward.

'You look weak. Your body is thin. I can see every bone in your body. How will you be able to look after me, let alone carry this heavy load?'

Neelkanth grinned brightly. 'Do not be deceived by the sight of this emaciated body. I have traveled long, through the unforgiving Himalayas, to the Ashram of

Gopal Yogi and Kapil Muni, to Puri. I shall gladly look after you until you are well.'

Sevakram sighed at having found a willing person to nurse him back to health. 'I have not eaten for days. Please go to the village and buy some vegetables, jaggery, ghee, and flour.' He gave Neelkanth a gold coin. 'Be sure to bring back the change.'

Neelkanth's eyes fell on a banana plantation behind the tree. 'Let me make you comfortable first.' He cut a heap of banana leaves and placed them under the shade of the tree. He piled them on top of each other until a soft bed, a foot-high, spread on the floor.

Sevakram felt it with his hands and sat down. 'God knows I need to rest on a comfortable bed after months of sleeping on hard ground.'

'Rest until I return,' said Neelkanth, smiling to reassure Sevakram.

When Neelkanth returned, he prepared a meal of sweets, vegetable curry, lentil soup, rice, and chapattis. He served Sevakram until he rubbed his stomach with delight. 'Where did you learn to cook such delicious food?'

'I have been on the road for five years,' said Neelkanth, looking at the leftover food.

'Yes, put that away for the evening,' Sevakram said.

Neelkanth glanced at Sevakram with surprise because he had not offered it to him after his effort to cook the food for him. He had not eaten for days. He thought Sevakram must have forgotten as he was ill. When Sevakram fell asleep, Neelkanth went back to the village and begged for food. It was afternoon, so he had not expected anyone to open the door. It was hot and everyone would have been asleep, resting after a long morning of working on the farms. He was surprised when a girl appeared at the door of the house with a bowl of rice and a few leftover chapattis. He found some shade near a well outside the village and ate after offering it to the Shaligram on a banana leaf. In the evening, he warmed the leftover food and served it to Sevakram, who finished all of it without offering some to Neelkanth.

Neelkanth hoped Sevakram would realize the error of his neglect. As the day before, Neelkanth went to the village and bought whatever was requested. After cooking it, he served it to Sevakram, who, once again, ate without offering anything to him. Neelkanth could not understand how someone could be so cruel and not share the food. He again begged alms from the village and ate whatever was offered to him without ever complaining to Sevakram.

He continued to cook, serve, and wash Sevakram's dirty clothes, often stained with blood due to his illness, in the hope that he would change his ways. One day, he sat down in front of Sevakram after he had cooked the meal and served it to him. He had decided that if he did not offer him anything today, he would leave him.

'It seems you are fully recovered now,' said Neelkanth, studying him keenly.

'Yes. I am beginning to regain my strength.'

'Good.' Neelkanth wanted to tell him how cruel he had been for not sharing the food that he had cooked but felt there was little point in telling an old dog to change his ways. They are wretched of the Earth, and though they walk around chanting the name of God, they have not learned the first lesson of the godly to serve the poor and the meek. It was yet another confirmation of how the purity of India was awash with greed and deception, and he vowed to wash the stain from India's soil.

Sevakram laid down on the bed of banana leaves. Soon, he was snoring. Neelkanth wrapped the Shaligram in a cloth and tied it around his neck. Then he tucked his pouch with the notebook to his waist, picked up the gourd, and walked away.

'Why can they not honor the rich heritage of the sages?' Neelkanth cried out in pain, frightening the many birds nestled in the trees on either side of the dirt road.

The land opened into farmland a little ahead. Neelkanth crossed the fields, watching whole families crouched, picking the harvest. They stared at him as he passed. Many stood up in respect and bowed, seeing his emaciated body. A girl came to him as he crossed a canal of water with a bunch of bananas. Neelkanth took one and ate it.

'Please take some with you,' her father said.

'The Lord has always provided when I have been hungry,' said Neelkanth. He thanked them and walked on, his faith restored somewhat.

The sun was directly above him when he reached the edge of a village. It was hot, so he sat down under the shade of a tree to drink some water. A cool breeze blew at him as he rested. He wondered how that was possible in the middle of the day when the sun was at its hottest. He looked around and saw a man walking away.

'Bhagwandas!' shouted Neelkanth.

Bhagwandas turned, surprised to hear his name. Neelkanth raised his hand and shouted his name again. Bhagwandas approached him, curious to discover how Neelkanth knew his name. He bowed and asked.

Neelkanth studied him keenly. 'You appear to be in a rush to go somewhere.'

'Yes. My mother has sent me to search for God.'

'Search for God?' asked Neelkanth. 'How will you know him when you find him?'

Bhagwandas sat on the ground. 'Oh, that's easy. God has nine unique marks on the sole of his right foot and seven more on the left.' Bhagwandas took out a piece of paper his mother had given to him from a pouch and showed it to Neelkanth. Neelkanth studied them with interest.

'Yes, this is correct. But how are you going to check everyone's feet? Do you think people will allow you to do so? They will think you are mad.'

'Ah, but I will be able to check if they have a shadow or not during the day,' Bhagwandas said with a beaming smile.

'Your mother has prepared you well. Anyway, I called you to remove a thorn from my foot. It will be a huge favor if you would kindly do so.'

'My mother would never forgive me if I did not help a learned yogi, especially someone so young. Please stretch out your foot and let me check.'

Neelkanth stretched out his right leg and placed it on the lap of Bhagwandas. 'They are dirty. I can't see anything.' He poured some water on a napkin from a jug and wiped his foot. His eyes opened wide when he checked. He counted the marks. 'There is no thorn on this foot, young yogi. Perhaps it is on the left foot,' he said, keen to check if it had the other seven marks.

'Yes, it may be on this foot.' Neelkanth stretched out his left leg and placed it on his lap. Bhagwandas wiped it and saw the remaining seven marks. 'There is no thorn on this foot either,' he said. Unable to believe what he saw, he looked for Neelkanth's shadow but couldn't find it under the shade of the tree. Neelkanth helped him by stepping out of the shade.

Bhagwandas bounced with joy. He put his palms together and bowed his head at Neelkanth's feet. 'Please come and visit our home,' he said, pleading.

Neelkanth placed his hand on his head. 'I would like to meet your mother,' he said.

'Please allow me to carry your gourd.' Bhagwandas took it from Neelkanth even before Neelkanth could reply. They walked to the river a few miles away and crossed it in a boat. It was dark when they reached home.

Bhagwandas knocked on the door. His wife opened the door with a lamp in her hand. 'Back already,' she said as she saw her husband.

'Did I not tell you I would not have to search far if the heart of our mother is pure?' He stepped aside.

Neelkanth bowed.

'A boy,' his wife said.

'Raise the lamp higher,' her mother-in-law said from behind.

As the lamp rose, they both saw the shadow of Bhagwandas on the ground behind him but nothing for Neelkanth. The light of the lamp miraculously appeared to pass through the body of Neelkanth.

'God in the form of a boy,' the mother said, her old heart racing with joy. 'Oh, I am getting too old for all this excitement.' She clutched her chest as she stepped forward, took Neelkanth's hand, and led him inside. 'Somehow, my heart knew you would come,' she said.

'The heart always speaks the truth,' said Neelkanth, 'because God always resides in the pure of heart.'

'Oh, look at you, just skin and bones.' She felt the ribs on Neelkanth's chest.

'It is only because of your love that I have come.' Neelkanth gazed into her eyes.

'You must be starving. Bhagwan, please get some warm water ready so that our beloved Neelkanth can wash while we cook the food.'

They presented Neelkanth with a rich variety of dishes spread on a large steel plate. Neelkanth served the food to the Shaligram, then took some in a bowl, lovingly served by Bhagwandas.

Bhagwandas prepared a soft mattress after dinner. He massaged Neelkanth's legs until he fell asleep. Afterward, he went to invite all the villagers to their house. 'Come early,' he said to everyone. 'You will never get a chance like this again.'

Bhagwandas was ready with a bucket of warm water when Neelkanth woke up. He asked Neelkanth to sit down on a stone in the courtyard and poured the water over his head while Neelkanth scrubbed and washed. He offered him a new loincloth in exchange for the one Neelkanth wore. 'It is wet and needs to dry,' he said.

Neelkanth took it, wiped his body with it, and then wrapped it around his waist while he rinsed the old loincloth. 'Why waste a good cloth that has kept me clothed for almost five years?' He wrapped the old loincloth around his tiny waist.

'But it needs to dry,' Bhagwandas cried.

'It is warm and it will soon dry.' Neelkanth sat down in meditation. Bhagwandas was expecting all the villagers to come and had chosen the most visible part of the veranda for Neelkanth's prayers. With the matted hair tied in a bun, Neelkanth radiated like a young Shiva in deep meditation. Bhagwandas sat near him, still unsure if the villagers would come.

The sun had still not risen when the courtyard began to fill with the villagers who all came with their oil lamps. They gasped at the sight of Neelkanth, glowing brighter with the light from the lamp of each visiting villager. Cries of 'Bhagwan…Bhagwan' echoed over the courtyard as they observed the rays pass straight through Neelkanth's body.

Soon there was standing room only as news traveled to the villages nearby of a divine child. Bhagwandas grinned brightly, unable to believe what was unfolding in his home. A sudden flash of light filled the courtyard when Neelkanth opened his eyes. A glowing image of Sri Krishna stood where he sat. A melodious tune from a flute filled the courtyard with a soft, soothing sound. Everyone stared with folded hands as if in a trance, unable to believe what they were witnessing. After a while, the image merged into Neelkanth's body.

Bhagwandas invited everyone to come forward. Neelkanth stretched out his legs. The auspicious marks on the sole of his feet glowed red as they touched them. While the women bowed their heads at his feet, the men touched his feet to their chests in reverence. Bhagwandas insisted everyone stay for breakfast of idli sambhar and coconut chutney.

'I haven't made enough,' his wife said in a panic.

Neelkanth overheard her. 'Don't worry, continue to serve everyone,' he said.

As visitors continued to come all day with their families, his wife frequently rushed to the pans, only to find that neither the number of steamed rice cakes nor the level of sambhar seemed to go down.

'God has blessed our home with the visit of this child yogi,' the elderly mother said. 'Now I can rest in peace.'

At night, they all sat around Neelkanth. The sun had set, but it was still bright. The wife sighed. 'I have lost all sense of day or night,' she said.

Bhagwandas laughed and knelt in front of his mother. 'It is because of your faith that God has come to our home,' he said and bowed his head.

'You have served everyone well,' said Neelkanth, watching the family lost in joy. 'All three of you will pass away shortly and will be reborn in north Gujarat, where we will meet again.'

The family rejoiced at the thought of another life of devotion and service.

A solitary lamp on a post bathed the courtyard when Neelkanth stepped outside early next morning. His eyes fell on the few flies clinging to the dim light. He watched them circle the post before flying towards him. Some settled near his feet before rising above the garden. Neelkanth followed them with his eyes until he could see them no longer, lost against the dark sky teeming with the stars. He stepped down the veranda, bowed to the sleeping family, and quietly walked out of the courtyard.

The beach was packed with boats preparing to set sail when Neelkanth reached the shore. He inquired if any of the boats were sailing for Rameshwaram.

'Most of the boats here are fishing boats preparing to set sail for their day's catch,' an elderly man said, examining Neelkanth's body from head to toe. He shook his head in sadness.

'Do not worry, father,' said Neelkanth. 'The strength of the body is not found in one's physique but the will of the heart.'

'Who are you?' the man asked, staring at him. 'I come to this shore daily, but I have never seen a yogi who has given me so much peace. I have been a fisherman all my life. I have killed more fish than I can count. Allow me to take you to Rameshwaram. I feel like the sins of killing all the fish will float away from this one selfless journey.'

'The Lord only looks for a small token of our goodwill to forgive,' said Neelkanth grinning.

'Please let me carry your gourd,' the man said. Neelkanth gave it to him. He had been walking on a dirt road for many hours and the sole of his feet hurt, so Neelkanth stepped in the cool waters of the sea as he followed the man.

It was an old boat, patched up with pieces of wood and glue to keep it sea-worthy. 'It has served me well, better than my children serve me,' the old man said.

'And will do so for many years more.' Neelkanth stepped into the boat. The old man held his hand and sat him down on a cushion placed on a wooden plank. He pushed the boat into deeper water and unfurled the sail. Neelkanth examined it for patches but found none to his surprise. The wind soon caught the sail and propelled them forward.

Dolphins surrounded the boat as if to protect it, jumping and riding the sea with ease to match the speed of the boat. Neelkanth crawled to the front of the boat, untied his hair, and let it fall around his face before opening his arms in a crucifix to feel the wind flow through him. The man laughed, seeing the child in Neelkanth share his joy. He thought about his many grandchildren who used to join him before the work on the farm started to demand their time. He had been sailing alone for many years now and was glad for some company. He knew he didn't have to fish anymore but loved the thrill of sailing so much that he still took out his old boat every day.

As the boat sailed closer to Rameshwaram, Neelkanth saw the line of pilgrims bathing in the sea. He stood up and searched for the bridge that Ram had built. 'Will it be possible to go to the bridge?' Neelkanth asked the man.

'There are only small remnants of the bridge, most of them scattered below the sea.' The man directed the boat over the submerged bridge. Neelkanth looked down at the large boulders underwater. He took some water in the bowl of his palms and poured it over his head in reverence. He thought about Ram's devotion to Sita and her sacrifice by joining him in his exile to the forest. He thought about Laxman's selflessness and his devotion to both of them. Truly, there is no wife like Sita anywhere in this world, nor a brother like Laxman.

'Amazing, isn't it? How Ram raised an army to rescue Sita. The construction of the bridge alone would have taken months,' the man said.

'Five days.' Neelkanth corrected the man without hesitation. 'He could have built it in an instant had he wished but wanted to engage the services of all in its construction. Sita was not a mere wife but an incarnation of Goddess Laxmi. She was his strength, his wealth, his peace, his love, but above all else, the purity of every woman. She proved it when she decided to sacrifice everything for him when he was exiled, insisting that a wife's place is always by the side of her husband. That is the glory, the sacrifice of all wives, daughters, and mothers of India. They give without asking for anything in return.'

The old man gazed at Neelkanth for a long time, listening to the wisdom of his words that belied his young age. 'Child, you have taught me that wisdom is not determined by age or wealth, nor the position one holds in society but by the humility of the heart.' The man bent low and tried to touch Neelkanth's feet.

Neelkanth stepped back. 'You are old enough to be my grandfather. It is I who should be bowing at your feet. Please take me to the beach.'

The man turned the oar to sail towards the beach. Neelkanth jumped out as soon as the bottom of the boat touched the soft sand. The man folded the sail and tied it to the mast. He pushed the boat onto the beach.

'Thank you so much,' said Neelkanth. 'God will liberate you of all the sins.'

'My child, I have been blessed many times before, but never have I felt so sure about a blessing.' Neelkanth put his palms together and left.

189

A small group of people followed him to the Shiva temple of a thousand pillars in the center of Rameshwaram. Neelkanth did not notice them. His eyes were fixed ahead to see the pillar of lights, the Linga as it was known, representing Lord Shiva. He had visited the Linga in Badrinath and Jagannath Puri. This was the third of the four chief pilgrim sites. He thought about the last in Dwarka. He hoped to visit it at the end of his pilgrimage to Kathiawar.

As soon as he entered the long corridor, monks surrounded him to shield him from the gathering crowd. 'It is as if child Shiva has come in person to bless us all,' the chief monk said, looking at Neelkanth's slender frame and matted hair.

Neelkanth accepted their help without replying, his gaze fixed on the large double doors that stood at the end of the corridor. He fell to his knees as soon as he saw the Linga shining like a golden sun. 'May you grant peace to all the pilgrims,' he prayed.

'Oh, please,' the monk said and laid a rug on the ground.

Neelkanth declined the offer. 'It is the dust of the feet of the pilgrims I wish to touch,' he said and laid face down on the ground, arms stretched in front in an apex, feet stretched behind him.

'Observe how to prostrate before the Lord,' the chief monk said to his young disciples.

Neelkanth stood up and touched the feet of all the monks. 'Will you stay in our ashram?' the chief monk asked.

Neelkanth pressed his palms together. 'Thank you for your kind offer, but my heart craves the open skies and the sound of the waves in the sea. I shall stay near the sea.'

'Will you at least take food with us? Our young disciples can learn a lot from your company.'

'I am sure they have wise leaders,' said Neelkanth and excused himself. He walked around the perimeter of the temple before returning to the beach. There, he found a secluded tree on a hill away from the crowd and sat down in meditation. Again, he thought about Ram and his determination to find Sita. He thought about the sacrifice of Sita, about Laxman's selfless service to both Ram and Sita, and the army of brave monkeys led by Hanuman packed on the same beach many thousands of years before.

'My Lord,' Hanuman appeared, kneeling before him.

Neelkanth opened his eyes and smiled. 'Thank you for coming. You were present with Ram, devoted Laxman, and the army.'

'I still remember everything as vividly,' Hanuman bowed.

'Ram saw nothing but your love for him in your heart.' Neelkanth gazed at his broad chest.

'And still, it is the same,' Hanuman said. 'I meditate on our beloved Ram and Sita daily.'

'Please tell me about what happened here.'

Hanuman bowed, his voice choking, humbled that Neelkanth should choose him to tell the story. 'Is it not time to tell the world about –'

'Everything will happen in its own time,' Neelkanth stopped him.

Hanuman sat down and made himself comfortable. Neelkanth got up. 'The pupil must always sit below the teacher,' he said.

'Even though he is Ram in a different avatar?'

'The pupil must always honor the teacher.'

Hanuman got up and reluctantly sat down on the seat Neelkanth vacated. Neelkanth remembered his many visits to the temple in Ayodhya to listen to the recital of the Ramayan. Now he had a chance to listen to the story from someone who was the key player.

'Sita was Ram's strength, his power,' Hanuman began. 'Losing her was like losing his limbs. She had given up the life of a princess to keep him company in the forest because a wife must be by the side of her husband, in good health or in illness, in good fortune or bad, and in richness or poverty.'

'What about the husband's duty?' asked Neelkanth.

Hanuman contemplated for a while. 'The husband must protect his wife, love her, and keep her honor. Ravan had taken her away like a coward – stolen Sita when she was at her most vulnerable. How could he allow him to get away with it?'

'And you rose to the challenge.'

'I was living a life of a monkey in the forest, completely unaware of what I must do.'

'Until Lord Ram entered your heart and woke you up.'

'I saw the injustice in it all.'

'Did you know about your strength?'

Hanuman closed his eyes. 'It was not my strength. It was the strength given to me by Lord Ram.' Hanuman laughed. 'Have you ever seen a monkey fly? The best we can do is leap from branch to branch. Grow in size and lift whole mountains? They are due to the grace of Ram.'

Neelkanth laughed. 'Your strength comes from your devotion to Ram. What about the bridge to Lanka?'

'Skeptical people question its construction in five days. Yet, remember, we had gathered an army of thousands, each soldier with the strength of an elephant. We were inspired and worked night and day with one purpose – to save Princess Sita from the clutches of Ravan. Every hour was an hour of pain for her. We all saw the pain on Lord Ram's face daily. So, every hour was a pain for us. I once saw him get up in the middle of the night, walk to the shore, and cry Sita. It was not a love of this world.' Hanuman's face dropped.

Neelkanth saw the tears in his eyes. He hugged him. 'That will be enough for today.'

'Let me get some fruits,' Hanuman said.

'I have eaten at the temple. One meal per day is enough.'

'Thank you for giving me the honor of your company again.' Hanuman bowed and leaped in the air. Neelkanth saw him disappear in a flash.

He came daily with fruits for Neelkanth and served him while he spoke about his time with Ram. Neelkanth enjoyed the stories and observed how they sounded so much more real when they were told by someone who was there at the time.

'I sense that you are going to be leaving tonight,' Hanuman said one day.

'I have already spent too long in Rameshwaram. People are suffering everywhere. I hear their cries every day.'

'It is the age of Kalyug,' Hanuman said.

'Superstition and exploitation of the poor are on the rise and the purity of our land is under threat. It is being stained with the blood of the poor, the meek, and the holy. Priests are sacrificing animals to appease the Gods. How can violence appease a non-violent God? I must stop it before it is too late.'

'Will this be the last I will see you?' Hanuman asked with his palms pressed in reverence.

'Oh, my beloved Hanuman. How can you even say that? You have watched over me since I was a baby. There are no goodbyes between us. I am sure to need your help again.'

'Please think of me always.' Hanuman put his palms together.

'It was a joy,' Neelkanth whispered after Hanuman disappeared. There was a feeling of emptiness in his heart as he laid down to rest for the night. He took the rosary in his hand and started chanting until he fell asleep.

12

Forgiveness

Neelkanth woke up in the middle of the night. The air was still and he felt a little warm. He sat up and meditated while listening to the soothing sound of the ocean waves before bathing.

Dawn had not yet broken when he got up to take the dirt road to Madurai, away from the shore. There were still many temples he wanted to visit in the area. The humid night meant a hot day ahead and he expected it to be a long and arduous journey but was pleasantly surprised by the fertile land, tropical forest, and paddy fields. Crouching farmers looked up as he passed. Many stared at his emaciated body and shook their heads. Neelkanth always acknowledged them by gently bowing his head in admiration of their daily toil on the farms.

He discovered the source of the fertile land when he entered the valley of the Vaigai River and laughed loudly when he thought about it because he should have expected nothing less from the land that had once been touched by the feet of Ram, Laxman, and Hanuman.

On the morning of the fourth day, he sighted the many domes of the Meenakshi temple in the distance, bathed in the orange glow of the rising sun. He had already been walking for hours to ensure he reached the temple before the start of the morning prayers.

He entered the long-pillared corridor with the many statues of gods just when the bell tolled to summon people to prayers. As he approached the shrine of Shiva, a bright ball of light rose from the matted hair on the head of Shiva and entered Neelkanth. The priest saw the ball of light enter Neelkanth and rushed to Neelkanth to offer him the golden pond with five burning candles.

As the corridor echoed with song to the accompaniment of drums and bells, Neelkanth waved the candles in front of Shiva. He sang at the top of his voice, which echoed loudly above everyone. There was love, there was devotion, and there was reverence. Mesmerized by the purity of his sweet voice, everyone stopped singing and listened to him. A divine aura embraced their hearts and touched their souls.

When the last drum beat sounded the end of the prayer, everyone converged towards Neelkanth. He pressed his palms together as they bent down and bowed. They followed him to the temple pool, where Neelkanth took some water in the bowl of his hands and threw it over his head in reverence. He walked around the entire temple complex to pay his respects, stopping only at the end to pay his respects to the shrine of Parvati on the south side of the temple.

It was the convenient beginning for his journey south, where he again entered a dense tropical forest. Neelkanth had heard a lot about Swami Ramanuja from his father and was keen to pay a visit to his ashram in Srirangam. He followed a trail left by a herd of elephants for hours until it turned right in front of a steep hill. The faint rays of the sun penetrating the tall trees pointed south up the hill. He knew he had no choice but to climb. He brushed aside a few shrubs and stepped forward. His feet felt the sharp stings of the thorns. He cringed but worked his way through the bushes for hours, resting every so often to gather his breath.

His stomach groaned, but there were no fruit trees to relieve the hunger pangs. He shook the gourd and drank the last trickle of water before stepping forward. When pitch darkness descended on the forest, he cleared the ground, laid down, and fell asleep within moments of his head resting on his arm. The roar of the wild, nature's many wonders, were not able to perturb his rest after an exhausting day of walking.

On the third day, he encountered a hill of red stone, an obstruction that, at first, seemed too difficult, but was overcome by the thought of his many adventures in the mighty Himalayas. As he stepped forward, he felt the heat of the stone that had been baking in the sun. He sensed the burning but found that it felt fine if he kept moving. In heat and cold, in rain and sun, and in thirst and hunger, Neelkanth had vowed to move forward no matter what the obstacle. What was heat when he had survived the glaciers of the Himalayas barefoot and a thin loincloth? He willed himself up the stone hill. It was like walking on burning coal. He had seen it in Ayodhya with some monks, eager to show the power of the mind and the resilience of the human body. He reminded himself that the will of his mind was stronger than the pain of the body and his intellect even greater. He needed a lesson from neither. Gopal Yogi had taught him that the power of the human spirit was more incredible than anything in the material world.

Though not steep, the hill seemed to go on and on, sinking in a wave in places as if to declare the edge, only to rise higher. The sun sapped what little energy he had left. His skin burned. His feet scalded. Neelkanth slumped to the ground and crawled to a welcome shade under an arching stone.

A tiger raised his head and growled as if to alert Neelkanth of his presence. Neelkanth fearlessly met his eyes as it stepped closer. He stroked his forehead. It lazily circled Neelkanth before settling near him. Neelkanth rested his head on his arm and fell asleep.

The tiger was not there when Neelkanth woke up. The sun had dipped below what looked like the summit. Neelkanth willed himself up and walked to the top. A forest stretched out invitingly below him, a chance for some shade and water. Neelkanth tied his empty gourd around his waist and stepped sideways to make his way down by holding the shrubs, which clung to the rocks, down to the forest, pulling hard on each of them to check that they were not loose. His legs gave way when he reached near the end. He slid and fell to the ground. Exhausted, he closed his eyes and fell asleep.

The mating chirps of crickets filled the air when he woke up. His head hurt, but he willed himself up. Tears filled his eyes when he thought about the Shaligram. He had not been able to offer any food or water for days.

When dawn broke, he came across an old deserted well. A reflection of the faint light peered back at him when he cleared the weeds and reeds. He pulled the string from around his waist, tied it to the gourd, and threw it in. The splash was meek, but he knew there was enough water to bathe and drink. He had not washed for many days, so he pulled up several gourdfuls and poured it over his head, each shower more refreshing than the one before.

The Shaligram waited its turn on a stone seat. He pulled up one more gourd and slowly poured the water. The water spread over the surface of the Shaligram and disappeared below it. Surprised by the disappearance of the water, he pulled one more gourd and poured it over the Shaligram, only to see it disappear again. It had never happened before, so he picked up the Shaligram to check if there was a hole in the stone. He laughed at his skepticism. 'You must be very thirsty, my Lord,' he said aloud and pulled one more gourd and poured it over the Shaligram. Again, the water disappeared. It took two more gourds before the Shaligram left some water on the stone. 'Please forgive me for not offering any food.' He glanced around for a fruit tree but found none. Instead, his eyes fell on a couple sitting on a bull. It was a dense forest, so he was not expecting anyone.

They approached closer. Neelkanth stood up and stared at the man, who looked like an older version of himself with dark matted hair and a lean physique. The woman wore an old sari and held a silver plate covered with a napkin. Neelkanth stared at the eye on the forehead. 'You are not by any chance Shiva and Parvati?' he asked.

The third eye opened and a beam of intense bright light flashed from it, blinding Neelkanth. The woman smiled and nodded. 'You haven't eaten for days and we thought you might like some cooked food.' She raised the napkin to reveal a heap of sweets.

'You came at the right time. I was looking for some fruits. The Shaligram has not eaten for days.' Neelkanth took the plate from Parvati.

With his throat now moist with the water, he opened his voice with joy and sang at the top of his voice. 'Salutations to thee, my Lord. Forgive this boy for not offering any food. Please accept this humble offering, which has been cooked by your beloved Parvati and blessed by Lord Shiva himself. Salutations to thee, my Lord.' As he sang, the forest came alive with tweets, whistles, and roars.

Parvati stepped forward when Neelkanth stopped. 'You sing like a child I know.'

'Mother, you remind me of a mother I left behind,' said Neelkanth.

Parvati placed a cloth on the ground. 'Please sit down here.'

Neelkanth hesitated, unaware of what she had in mind.

'If I am like your mother, you must then do as I say,' Parvati said.

'If I was you, I would do as she says,' Shiva said, grinning.

Neelkanth smiled and sat down. Parvati sat down in front of him, took the plate of sweets, and fed them to him until he said enough. 'They are delicious, but you will know that it isn't good to eat too much on an empty stomach.'

Shiva laughed. Parvati glowered at him. 'Tell me about it. Our Lord here has been performing penance since the beginning of time, but you have a physical body to sustain. It has withered away since we last saw you in Haridwar. You must eat if you are to finish what you have come to do.'

Neelkanth saw tears in her eyes. He opened the bowl of his hands. 'I will take them with me since you have made them with such love.'

Shiva tenderly placed his hand on Parvati's shoulder. 'I think Neelkanth is keen to get started.' The bull raised his head and mooed as if to agree.

Neelkanth laughed. Parvati wrapped the sweets in a napkin and gave them to Neelkanth before hugging him like a mother does when her son is leaving the sanctuary of the home for the first time. 'Go well, my son,' she said.

Shiva placed his hand on Neelkanth's head. 'You may call on us anytime you wish and we will be there in an instant.' They mounted the bull. Neelkanth watched them until they disappeared. He dropped his face and sighed.

Energy returned in him after the divine meal. There was still no end in sight, so he threw the gourd into the well to refill it with water, unsure of when he would next see water.

The walk was easier under the shade of tall trees. Beautiful peafowls opened their feathers and cried to catch his attention while great hornbills watched from the branches of Mesua trees in envy. Neelkanth stopped as one peafowl ambled towards him. He took a sweet and offered it to the fowl and watched with glee as it picked up the crumbs and gave a cry for more.

'Too much is not good for you,' said Neelkanth. He opened his voice and sang, 'Lord Hanuman has walked this land. I am honored to walk in his steps, for he has served Ram with devotion. Lord Hanuman has walked this land...'

The birds sang their tunes around him as if to put music to his lyrics. Some followed, leaping from branch to branch to keep up with him until the soothing sound of flowing water caught Neelkanth's ear. He followed it to a river.

Thirsty animals raised their heads in fear. 'Drink without fear,' said Neelkanth to reassure them. He took some water in the bowl of his palms and washed his face before immersing his feet in the cool water. The flowing water eased the tiredness out of his feet while he ate the sweets and enjoyed the calm around him.

He got up when he saw a group of monks in the distance sitting under a tree. He approached them and bowed. 'Jai Narayan,' he said.

'What are you doing here?' the monks snapped in alarm.

Neelkanth realized all was not as it appeared.

'It is evening and it is not safe for anyone to stay here,' the monk said.

'Tigers come to drink water at night,' another said.

'There are ghosts here. It is not safe for anyone except a great yogi. Go to the village, boy. It is not far away.' They all pointed him in the direction of the village.

Neelkanth sensed the sharpness of their tone and their eagerness to get rid of him. What were they hiding? Curiosity gripped his heart. 'The village is far. It is evening, so I shall spend the night here. The river will be good to bathe in the morning. I will not disturb you.' He picked a spot not far away from them and sat down in meditation. As night fell, he rested his head on his arm and fell asleep.

The scent of spices woke him up. He observed the monks eating, chatting, and joking about how foolish the villagers were to donate generously and how careless they were in leaving their valuables lying in their courtyards for them to steal.

The elder monk glanced in Neelkanth's direction when they finished eating. Neelkanth closed his eyes and pretended to be asleep until he felt a nudge. 'We have prepared some food for you,' a monk said.

Neelkanth thought about their deception of the naïve villagers. 'I am not hungry,' he said. He watched them wash their pots and pans, lift the seat where the elder monk sat, and put all the utensils away in the bunker.

'This is all we could gather today,' one monk said afterward. He placed a pile of jewelry in front of the elder monk. Neelkanth saw them wrap their loot in a cloth and place it in the bunker. He got up when they all went to sleep and quietly sneaked out, unwilling to associate with the pretense any longer than he had to. 'I will expose them all,' he cried when he was far away, frightening the birds resting in the nests.

It was late morning when he entered the village. There was a large crowd on either side of the main thoroughfare. Neelkanth thought there was some festival. Curious to discover what was happening, he found a spot behind the crowd, which was hurling abusive words at someone. His eyes fell on an approaching donkey, a man sitting on the donkey, facing the tail. He thought it odd and knew something was up. As the donkey came near, Neelkanth recognized the older monk. His head was shaven and his eyes bowed down. Women hurled abuses at him as he passed while children picked up little stones and threw them in his direction.

Neelkanth held the hand of one boy. 'You will hurt him,' he said. It was enough to force the boy to drop the stones, prompting other children to do the same.

His eyes met the painful gaze of the monk. Confident that the monk would learn his lesson after this insult and be good, Neelkanth forgave him, his compassionate heart unable to watch the suffering of any being. He crossed the thoroughfare on his way south.

A few days later, Neelkanth arrived at the edge of Srirangam. The thought of visiting the ashram of Swami Ramanuja had been on his mind ever since his father had alerted him about it during their many lessons. He wanted to pay homage to the simplicity and devotion of the monks. Living in the north of India, his parents had not been able to visit the south and had hoped that Neelkanth would one day complete the pilgrimage for them.

'All I know is due to your devotion,' Neelkanth whispered and bowed his head in the direction of the setting sun in honor of his parents.

As the bells tolled in the distance, his eyes fell on a flock of birds rising from a dome. Eager to reach the temple before the start of the evening prayers, Neelkanth walked with haste. Families joined him as he neared the dome. Many glanced at him, bowed, and gave way. Neelkanth bowed to thank them, his gaze fixed on the rising dome, intricately carved with statues of deities. Majestic stone pillars to match the dome led him to the inner sanctum where the many-headed python, Shesh, stood over the head of Lord Vishnu. Neelkanth's eyes fell on the serene face of Vishnu. They blurred with tears as he thought about his parents and fell to his knees. 'This is for you,' he whispered and prostrated. He lay there for a long time, contemplating the long journey.

'I am Jeer Swami. Welcome to the ashram,' a monk said when he got up. He took Neelkanth's hand and led him to the shrine. Neelkanth sensed the peace, the humble devotion, and the recognition of the glory of God as he stared at the Swami, his eyes full of love. 'It was my parents' wish that I should visit the ashram,' he said after a while.

'You honor them by fulfilling their wish. You will, of course, stay with us.'

'I am keen to learn about the philosophy of the great Acharya,' said Neelkanth.

'There will be no better place to master it than in the ashram that propagates the Ramanuja philosophy of complete surrender to God together with the realization of his true glory.'

'The strength of the Acharya's philosophy lies in its simplicity,' said Neelkanth.

They walked to the shrine of Vishnu. Neelkanth pressed his palms together and prayed with a fixed gaze unshaken by the noise around him. Jeer Swami studied Neelkanth keenly. The emaciated appearance of a yogi who had put his body through relentless penance, the gaunt abdomen that must only have eaten to survive, the raised green veins crisscrossing the body like hills on a stressed terrain, and the matted dark hair of young Shiva. Here is a child worthy of this seat, but will he stay? Jeer Swami contemplated. Will the child even want the seat of Ramanuja? Never had he seen anyone so singularly engaged in prayer. He decided there and then to keep Neelkanth in the ashram for as long as he could.

'This is no mere stone statue,' said Neelkanth when he returned. 'Serve him well, for he listens to all who pray with pure heart and love.'

Jeer Swami nodded. 'Don't I know it.' They entered the kitchen, where a line of monks sat for the evening meal. He led Neelkanth to a seat near him. A monk placed a steel plate in front of them. Others followed and served a curry of peas and potatoes, spinach, dal, rice, yogurt, and sweets. Neelkanth emptied the bowl of rice on the plate and took a little of everything in it. He mixed it with his fingers and ate.

Jeer Swami observed what Neelkanth did and stood up. He called everyone to attention. 'A monk must subjugate their sense of taste. We have, since the time of Acharya Ramanuja, enjoyed our food. Some of us enjoy it more than others.' He patted his pot belly to a ripple of laughter. 'From today, I too will eat like this teenage yogi.' Everyone turned to Neelkanth and saw the mixture of all the foods in one bowl.

Neelkanth nodded in approval when Jeer Swami sat down. As Swami emptied his bowl of rice, others followed and did the same. Jeer Swami ate a morsel and chewed to absorb the mixture of flavors. 'It is surprisingly more delicious than when eaten separately,' he said to a ripple of laughter. He watched everyone eat a morsel.

'It will all be mixed in the stomach anyway,' said Neelkanth. He remembered that Gopal Yogi used to add water to kill the flavors. 'Add a little water,' he said to Swami.

Ever ready to take on a challenge, Jeer Swami poured some water into his bowl and mixed it before eating. 'The flavors are a little diluted,' he said.

Neelkanth nodded and ate in silence. Inspired by the demonstration at dinner, the monks gathered around him in the evening in their ashram. They asked him to tell the story of his life. Neelkanth refused because he did not want to dent their devotion to Ramanuja. It was the purest form of what he wanted to create in the future. Yet, persistent pleas every evening forced him to think hard about what he should reveal. He thought about his visit to Badrivan, the meeting with Rishi Narayan, and the visits to Lake Mansarovar and Mount Kedarnath. But he decided to tell them about his one year with Gopal Yogi. He had mastered the highest form of Raja Yoga and attained a state of Samadhi – a transcendence that few achieved. He felt compelled to teach them the aspects of his experience. 'If Swamiji will permit me, I can teach you some of the postures of yoga I learned from Gopal Yogi.'

He sat down, cross-legged, and took a deep breath before rotating his stomach to demonstrate. Jeer Swami looked at him in admiration at the ease with which he accomplished the posture. 'You are indeed a yogi without equal, so accomplished at such a tender age.'

'It is due to the grace of Acharyas like you,' Neelkanth bowed. He had absorbed the best of all the wise seers he had met on his pilgrimage.

'Teach them all you know. This body is far too old for such challenges,' Jeer Swami said to the amusement of all the monks. Neelkanth liked his jolly manner.

'Rise early tomorrow and join me in the garden,' he said to the monks. 'The discipline of each posture must begin with the discipline of the body, mind, intellect, and the soul.'

Next morning, five young monks sat in front of Neelkanth in the garden. He began with simple stretching exercises before he demonstrated the sun salutation. He lay flat on his front, then raised his upper body with his arms until the arms stood like pillars, supporting the arc of the upper body, the head tilted back, staring at the crest of the rising sun. Neelkanth held the position until the white disk of the fiery sun stood above the horizon.

The young monks tried to replicate the posture but soon gave way and fell flat to the floor as the muscles they had not used stretched with pain.

'Raise the head, close your eyes, and feel the warmth of the morning sun. There is nothing like it after a cool night,' Neelkanth encouraged them.

The monks closed their eyes. Neelkanth stood on the side and observed the strain on their faces as they held the position of the sun salutation but soon saw it transformed into a smile as the warmth of the sun touched their bare upper bodies. Neelkanth smiled when he heard their voices hum with joy.

He told them to stand upright with their arms in a crucifix. 'Close your eyes and feel the warmth.'

He showed them the *Tadasana,* the *Utkatasana,* the *Uttana Shishosana,* the *Adho Mukha Svanasana,* the *Virabhadrasana II,* the *Trikonasana*...amongst many other yoga poses, twisting and bending their young bodies in ways they had never done before. 'There is beauty in our ancient scriptures,' he told them, 'that has been forgotten for far too long. It is time to revive it. It is up to the youth of Mother India to revive it.'

Though much older than him, they followed him like obedient pupils of a wise master. Neelkanth was not surprised when the next day, all twenty young monks of the ashram joined them with a beaming smile.

'It would be too much for anyone who is doing it for the first time,' he said. 'Do it gently. Stretch, but don't strain. You don't want to tear any muscle. We embrace spirituality to become awake so that we can transform our minds and abandon the undesirable elements of greed, hatred, and ignorance, and cultivate a spirit of love, generosity, and wisdom. That is the discipline given by yoga.'

The impressionable young monks gathered around Neelkanth after each session, eager to learn from the like-minded teenage yogi. 'You are young. Your bodies are supple and you will be able to learn the postures with ease if you practice after the lessons. Yoga is a challenging skill, but like all things, it can be mastered with perseverance, dedication, and devotion.'

As news traveled of this new awakening, young male disciples of the ashram began to join them. When young women started to join, Neelkanth felt it was time to hold separate lessons for them. He did not feel it was appropriate for monks who had taken the vows of celibacy to mix with women. He had observed it since he arrived at the ashram but never felt comfortable with it because of the natural attraction each felt for the other. It was bound to compromise their vows because of the desires that inevitably surface in youth. If they wanted to associate with women, it was better to marry and serve God as householders.

Unable to put the thought of this association out of his mind, Neelkanth tentatively approached Jeer Swami. He sat down on the floor and bowed.

'Swami, you are a respected monk in the area and honor the memory of Swami Ramanuja, who highlights the importance of sacrifice. Our scriptures specify the rules of conduct for monks. They particularly emphasize the sacrifice of wealth, women, taste, and addictions. You are a model monk who has renounced the world in the service of God and people. I have loved many things I have observed in the ashram. You have looked after me like a son. And yet, one question burns in my heart. Please permit me to ask.'

Jeer Swami sat up on his seat, intrigued by the question that Neelkanth wanted to ask. 'You have transformed the energy of the ashram, young yogi. There is a buzz around the place I have not witnessed before. People are enamored by you, your simplicity, and your mastery of our ancient wisdom at such a tender age.'

Neelkanth bowed gently. 'Swami, I am the servant of the poor, the meek, and the holy.'

'Please ask the question,' Jeer Swami pressed him.

'Swami, the bondage of women has driven many celibates to break their vows. They have captivated even Brahma and many wise seers. Please permit me to ask what vows a monk should uphold?'

Neelkanth stared at Jeer Swami as the joy on his face faded. He summoned the nearest monk. 'Get this boy out of my sight,' he shouted. 'Drive him out of the ashram. Though only a child, he questions the conduct of an Acharya. Take him from me. I shall not eat or drink till then.'

As other monks came running, Neelkanth stood up. 'Respected Swami, it is not proper for a guru to display anger.'

'Take him away from my sight instantly,' Jeer Swami shouted.

The monks grabbed Neelkanth by the shoulders and pushed him out of the gates of the ashram. Neelkanth fell to the ground. He got up, dusted himself, and spent the night opposite the temple before leaving in the early morning. 'I will not rest until I restore the purity of the monks,' he said loudly, looking at the ashram.

Undaunted by the rejection, Neelkanth's voice opened with songs as he made his way south. He walked for many days in quiet contemplation.

The sun had not peered above the horizon when he stepped onto the soft sand of the beach at Kanyakumari, the southern-most tip of the sub-continent. He placed the gourd on the sand and bathed in the water before sitting in meditation.

As the faint warmth of the rising sun reached his face, he stood on one leg, raised his arms above his head, and chanted Narayan with each turn of the bead of the rosary. The untainted view of the rising sun above the Indian Ocean brought many villagers to gather on the beach and offer prayers at sunrise. Their eyes fell on the emaciated body of Neelkanth, standing still, eyes closed, hands aloft, turning a rosary, one bead at a time, with a whisper of Narayan on his lips. They felt peace in their warming hearts, and instead of bowing to the rising sun, they stepped forward, bowed to Neelkanth, and sat down in front of him in reverence. The beauty of the horizon of the rising sun rediscovered in the vision of the child yogi, glowing brightly like the sun.

Neelkanth stood in prayers until the white disk of the sun burnt the mist from the ocean. A flash of light filled the beach when he opened his eyes. He smiled, placed the rosary around his neck, then pressed his palms together and bowed.

The crowd reciprocated. Neelkanth took particular care to look at everyone, one at a time. 'You are all very blessed to live in such a beautiful place,' he said.

An elderly man in the front row stood up. 'Child, who are you? Where do you come from? Who are your parents? Why have you sacrificed the world at such a young age?'

'Father, the whole world is my home,' said Neelkanth, his face beaming with joy. 'I come from nowhere and everywhere. God is my father and my mother. I have sacrificed nothing and everything, and I am in search of those who are themselves in search of God.'

'It seems penance has withered your body like a tree deprived of water. Will you take some food?' the old man asked.

'I will take some milk if you will bring some,' Neelkanth bowed.

Eager to feed the young yogi, several people in the crowd stood up and ran. Neelkanth watched them and laughed. 'And so generous,' he said.

'The Lord gives and takes,' the old man said.

'Indeed, he is the ultimate provider.'

Everyone looked up as a seagull flew above them. Neelkanth raised his arm and held it up. The seagull spiraled above the crowd as it flew down and settled on Neelkanth's arm. Neelkanth whispered something as he brushed its feathers before letting it go. 'It will be born in one young family and bring immense joy to his parents,' he said.

Everyone watched the seagull play with the warm air currents until the people returned with jugs of milk. Neelkanth glanced at their eager faces. 'I will take a little from each jug. Serve the rest to everyone.' He collected a little from each jug in a glass and took a long sip. 'The sweetest milk I have drunk in many months,' he smiled. He stood up while the milk was being distributed. 'Keep God in your hearts, trust in him always, and everything you wish for will be fulfilled.'

The old man bowed his head at Neelkanth's feet. It encouraged many others to do the same.

As the crowd dispersed, the old man did not let go. His trembling hands reached for Neelkanth's hand.

'I must go now,' said Neelkanth. 'There are many other places I want to visit.'

'I will see you to the edge of the village,' the old man said. They walked quietly together, hand-in-hand like grandfather and grandson, until they reached a dirt road. 'This will take you north. Go safely, my child.'

Neelkanth's opened his arms and embraced the old man. 'God will come to take you at the time of your death,' he whispered.

'I have met many holy men, but none have filled my heart with peace like you,' the old man said, his eyes misting.

'Your faith will be your salvation,' said Neelkanth. He turned and took the dirt road. As the road curved, Neelkanth glanced back and saw that the old man was still there. He waved. 'I will come for you,' a voice echoed from the sky.

Neelkanth saw the old man kneel to the ground and prostrate in his direction. He raised his hand and blessed him before moving on.

After many hours of walking, he crossed River Kritamala and arrived at the city of Trivandrum, where, in the richly carved pyramid temple, he paid his respects to the sleeping statue of Lord Vishnu under the canopy of Shesh. His eyes fell on the statue of Brahma rising from the navel of Lord Vishnu and, for a long time, reflected on the fragility of life, the impermanence of earth, the sun, the planets, and the universe. We toil for wealth, for bigger and better houses, seldom remembering that time will destroy it all one day, and everything will be dissolved. 'May you guide them all,' Neelkanth whispered.

He watched the people from the steps of the temple, the stall holders and shopkeepers, lining either side of the dirt road. He blessed them all by raising his right hand, thinking about how they toiled daily to live a good life before stepping down the steps, eager to make his way north. There was an urgency in his stride he did not understand.

After many days of walking, he came across River Tapti in full flow. There were a lot of people waiting on the bank for a river boat to take them across. Neelkanth learned that the boat would not arrive for several hours. Keen to get to the opposite bank, he contemplated swimming as he thought about how the Saryu had carried him in its bowl when he left Ayodhya, and perhaps, the Tapti would do the same.

He contemplated on Goddess Tapti, the daughter of the Sun God. Neelkanth remembered how the Sun God had appeared in person to bless him after his penance in the Himalayas. 'Bless me,' he whispered before stepping near the edge.

'The water is too deep!' people shouted from behind.

Neelkanth ignored them and placed his first step on the water, fixed his gaze ahead, and started walking until his feet touched the firm ground of the opposite bank. He turned and saw the heads of the people on the opposite bank bowing in reverence at the miracle of walking on water.

After a few days, Neelkanth arrived at the bank of River Narmada. He sensed he was nearing the end of his pilgrimage. The river ran rapidly through a gorge, so Neelkanth followed it west until it grew wide and the rapids slowed in a valley. It was morning, so there were a lot of women with children. While the women washed the clothes, the children played in the river. There was an innocent joy in their play that Neelkanth liked. He watched them for a while before moving on to find a secluded spot to bathe.

He followed the river until it opened into an estuary, flowing into the Arabian sea. The rapids slowed to a serene lethargic stroll. Neelkanth followed the river, paddling in the shallow bank whenever he could to ease the tiredness of his legs. Above him, eagles soared and occasionally swept down and rose with a fish in their talons. He watched them for a while – their singular determination to catch a fish. If only we had the same determination to become Brahman and worship Para-Brahman, he thought.

He arrived in Vadodara in the late evening and, for some odd reason, felt compelled to enter the city. The streets were busy with traders as he made his way to the center, where, in a large square, he found a twelve-gated pergola. It seemed like a good place to rest for the night.

Watching his glowing teenage face sitting serenely in meditation, the emaciated body withered by penance, the passing public felt compelled to pay their respects. Several gathered around him, crouched, and bowed their heads at his feet.

Neelkanth opened his eyes when he heard the familiar cry of a young mother. 'Who are you? Where do you come from?'

'I am the servant of the poor, the meek, and the holy,' said Neelkanth.

The mother waved her hand, gazing at his body. 'How will you serve them with a body that looks as if it is about to give up on life?'

Neelkanth looked at the mother with kindness, his heart melting with her selfless love. 'Mother, I will eat if you will bring some food.'

The woman rushed into the merchant's shop on the edge of the square. She boiled some rice and lentils, lightly spiced with turmeric and salt. She served it in a bowl, put some ghee in a smaller bowl, and was about to take it to Neelkanth when her husband appeared in the kitchen.

'I know,' she said, grinning even before he had the chance to say anything.

'Savita, you have read my mind,' her husband said.

Savita placed a glass of warm milk on the plate and covered her head with the edge of her sari before stepping out of the shop. It was dark outside, so her husband picked up a lantern and a low stool and guided her to the pergola.

The small crowd made way as the couple arrived and placed the plate in front of Neelkanth. Neelkanth unwrapped the Shaligram from around his neck, folded the cloth, and placed the Shaligram on it. His pristine voice opened with a song as he served the food to the Shaligram. The crowds started to clap, filling the square, which usually echoed with the calls of traders, with rare prayers.

Neelkanth ate a little and gave the plate to the couple. 'What are your names?'

'I am Amichand and this is my wife Savita.'

'Please come and rest in our house for the night,' Amichand said.

'I have been resting under the sky for years,' said Neelkanth. 'This pergola will be fine.' He laid down, placed his head on his arm, and fell asleep.

In the morning, Amichand came rushing to Neelkanth when he saw him preparing to leave. 'Please come and bless our home,' he begged again.

Neelkanth looked into his eyes and observed his eagerness to serve. 'I will come in the future,' he said.

'What chance is there that I will be alive when you come?' Amichand asked with folded hands.

Neelkanth smiled. 'Oh, you will be,' he said. 'There are statues of Goddess Lakshmi and Narayan buried in your house. I will need them to install in a temple. I will send my monks for them when I need them.'

Amichand gazed at Neelkanth in surprise. 'Only I know of these statues that my father has buried in the house,' he said and fell at the feet of Neelkanth.

Neelkanth blessed him and stepped down the pergola. Savita came running to Amichand. 'Did you not invite him for breakfast?' she asked.

'He is from another world and told me something that only I knew. He said he would send his monks in the future. How can I disobey someone who knows everything?'

They watched Neelkanth with folded hands until he disappeared behind some buildings.

13
Gujarat

Neelkanth reached the banks of River Mahi in the middle of the morning. The rays of the sun curled in the gentle ripples of the clear waters of the river. He sat down on the soft sand, took some water in the bowl of his palms, and offered it in prayers before bathing. As he sat down to meditate, his eyes fell on the festivities on the opposite bank. He curiously watched them for a while before closing his eyes.

At midday, he got up and crossed the river. A man came running towards him. 'Bless you, young yogi. You came at the right time,' the man said and fell to his feet. 'I am Laldas. Lunch is being served. So, please do join us.'

Neelkanth sensed the sincerity of his request and followed him without saying a word. Brahmins rose in awe as Neelkanth approached. It was as if Lord Shiva had arrived in person to honor them. They made way and laid a rug for Neelkanth. Laldas sat down in front of him and served Neelkanth with sweets and lentil soup. As always, Neelkanth mixed both in a wooden bowl and took a little.

'The young yogi is an incarnation of Shiva whose joy lays in meditation and sacrifice,' the Brahmin sitting next to him said.

'You look so thin,' Laldas said and insisted that he eat more.

'It is not good to eat too much on an empty stomach,' said Neelkanth but took a little more to please Laldas. He stood up when he finished, keen to be on his way.

The Brahmins gathered around him. 'Laldas is blessed with many daughters like Goddess Lakshmi but no sons,' one Brahmin alerted Neelkanth.

Neelkanth raised his arm. 'Your family will be blessed with a virtuous son. His name will be Kashi,' he said.

Laldas bowed his head humbly without saying anything. He had been blessed many times by traveling monks, but each time, his hopes of a son were quashed after his wife failed to deliver a boy. After many such blessings, he had given up any hope of fathering a son. He took joy in pampering his daughters, spoiled them, and prayed that they would find husbands worthy of their beauty and noble character. Yet, today, he felt so sure of the blessings because for the first time, not only had he been blessed with a son, but he had also been told what name he would give him. Laldas thanked Neelkanth and accompanied him to the dirt road to the next village.

After passing through several more villages without stopping, Neelkanth arrived at Vadtal, a small village with a maze of small farms surrounding it. It was early morning, so he bathed with water from a well and sat down in meditation near a small temple of Hanuman. His eyes fell on a man sitting a few paces away from him when dawn broke.

'Joban!' Neelkanth summoned him.

Joban stepped forward with folded hands, convinced that Neelkanth was no ordinary yogi, otherwise he could not have known his name. He bowed. 'Young yogi, my house is not far. Please come and bless my family and take some food.'

'I am on a pilgrimage to the holy sites, so I will not be able to visit today, but I promise you I will surely come in the future,' said Neelkanth.

Joban's heart sunk. 'When will I have a chance to honor a yogi like you? You must surely come again but please do not leave without food today. I have committed great sins, killed and stolen to provide for my family, but I also have immense love for yogis. So, please come.' Joban knelt and bowed his head at Neelkanth's feet.

Neelkanth sensed the sincerity of his plea. He stood up and followed Joban to his house. After eating, he stayed the night at the house of Joban's brother, Devkaran, before leaving early the next morning.

He arrived at Bochasan and rested near the lake. Judging from the large number of people in the village, there appeared to be a festival in the village. Neelkanth sat in meditation but was soon forced to move once a group of women came to bathe near the Ram temple on the banks. He went inside the temple and prostrated in front of the statue of Ram.

Narsinhdas, the temple priest, gazed at the emaciated body of Neelkanth and came rushing out.

'Yogiraj, who are you? Where do you come from? Who are your parents? Why have you abandoned normal life at such a tender age?'

Neelkanth gave his usual response. He inquired about the festivities in the village and discovered that Kandas, the village chief, had organized a feast for everyone. 'He is a devoted disciple of Ram and every so often kindly arranges a feast for the villagers.'

Neelkanth realized the purpose of his visit and sat in meditation. Narsinhdas sent a child to fetch the village chief. Kandas sent his son Kasidas to invite Neelkanth.

A peace exuded from Kasidas' heart when his eyes fell on the radiant face of Neelkanth, sitting in deep meditation. He fell to his knees. Villagers gasped as they saw Kasidas bow. Never had they seen him so humbled.

'You are a yogi like none other I have met before,' Kasidas said. 'Who are you? Where do you come from?'

'I am Neelkanth. I am a servant of the poor, the meek, and the holy.'

Kasidas stared at the matted hair, the emaciated body that exposed every bone, the thin legs, and the old loincloth. 'It appears to me you are a young Shiva in disguise?'

Neelkanth bowed gently. 'People know me by many names.'

'Your arrival today is indeed propitious for the village, perhaps the fruits of our good deeds, for my father has arranged a feast for all the villagers. My father will be very pleased if you join us for a meal.'

Neelkanth told Kasidas to call him when the food was ready and closed his eyes to the curious crowd growing around him.

It was evening when Kasidas returned. News had traveled far and wide of Neelkanth's presence in the village and the crowd had grown in size. They made way as Neelkanth got up; many tried to touch his feet as he passed, having never seen an illustrious young yogi of such stature and aura. All followed him to the house of the village chief. After all, they, too, had been invited to the feast.

Kandas was waiting for him with a garland of rose and jasmine flowers when Neelkanth arrived. He placed it around his neck. Neelkanth immediately took it off and placed it around the neck of Kandas.

'It appears as if you have brought the entire village,' Kandas said, glancing at the crowd in the courtyard. He asked Neelkanth to sit on a mat in the courtyard.

Kandas' mother came out of the house. 'You invite a prince to visit our home but don't even invite him into the house,' she said, glowering at Kandas.

'This is my mother, Nanibai,' Kandas introduced her.

Neelkanth bowed, ever alert to the selfless love of a mother. 'Mother, what is a house when the whole world is my home,' he said.

Embarrassed by his mother, Kandas held out his hand and led Neelkanth into the house.

Nanibai observed that Neelkanth ate very little of the sweet and dal served to him. She stepped forward. 'You have hardly touched the food,' she said. 'Perhaps we can make something else.'

Neelkanth's eyes fell on the cow in the courtyard. Nanibai took the hint but knew that the cow had been milked and never offered milk twice in a day. Yet convinced by Neelkanth's divinity, she took a jug to the cow and placed it under the udders. She was overjoyed when streams of milk poured into the jug from all the udders at the same time. Never had she witnessed anything like it. While Kandas served the villagers, Nanibai joyfully served the sweet milk with rice to Neelkanth.

Eager to return to the temple, Neelkanth got up as soon as he finished. Nanibai pleaded with him to stay.

'Mother, there will be time enough for that in the future. I shall certainly come several times and happily stay in your house.'

Nanibai gazed at him in confusion.

'I promise you I will return again,' said Neelkanth again.

Nanibai bowed, feeling reassured.

After the evening prayers, Neelkanth bowed to the statues of Ram, Laxman, and Sita. 'One day, these same statues will be housed in a magnificent temple in the village,' he said to the priest. The priest felt confident that Neelkanth's prophesies would come true. There was a divinity in this child yogi he had not witnessed in anyone before.

Dawn had not yet broken when Neelkanth got up and left quietly. It was a long walk to the next village, but Neelkanth liked the green and fertile land interspersed with rivers and lakes. He liked the devotion of the people, their faith in God, and their reverence for holy men and women. It reminded him of the day in Ayodhya when he climbed a tree while playing with his friends and looked west and knew even then that one day he would touch its soil.

He arrived in Budhej in the evening and approached a shopkeeper engrossed in his accounts. 'Where is the alms house?' asked Neelkanth.

The shopkeeper, preoccupied with the account showing a loss, dismissively raised his hand without looking up and waved him forward. Neelkanth entered a courtyard a few houses ahead and called out 'Jai Narayan' several times to summon someone.

'Wait in the adjacent room. I am busy at present,' a woman shouted from inside a room.

Neelkanth did as asked and walked around the room several times. After seven rounds, he stopped and held a chain hanging from the ceiling to rest. The woman appeared shortly with a bowl of grains.

Neelkanth examined the grains. 'How will I cook them? Please bring me something cooked.'

The eyes of the woman narrowed. 'I am Dasi. We get many visitors like you asking for cooked food,' she said sharply. 'It is practically impossible to serve cooked food to everyone.'

Neelkanth sensed her impatience. 'Mother, you may have had many people asking for alms, but I assure you, you will not have met a person like me.'

Dasi studied Neelkanth's bare-footed emaciated frame, the bun of matted hair, the sharp features of his radiant face. 'Yogiraj, you should know that we have many yogis greater than you visiting the almshouse. You are thin, your hair is dark, and you are not even old enough for a beard. I have seen many with thick matted hair, long enough to touch the ground if unwound, with long white beards to match, taller and fatter than you.'

Neelkanth sensed the anger in her tone and grinned. He held out the bowl of his hand to accept the grains. As he left, he heard the pigeons in the trees gurgling in hunger. He ate a few grains to acknowledge the reluctant generosity of the woman and threw the rest on the ground. Pigeons flew down and started pecking at them. Neelkanth watched them in joy and walked on, disappointed with the nature of the villagers.

It was late afternoon when he came to a well on the outskirts of the village of Gorad to quench his thirst. A man was drawing water with two bullocks. Neelkanth sat down under the shade of a tree and observed the bullocks trudge with pain. He saw that the ropes around the bullocks had cut through the skin underneath. Unable to tolerate the slightest pain of helpless farm animals that were often worked to death, Neelkanth approached the farmer.

'Brother, what is your name?' he asked.

'Bijal,' the man said without looking up.

'If I may ask, is it possible for you to give me some water to quench my thirst?'

Bijal pointed at the leather bucket. 'Drink as much as you like when I draw the water,' he said.

Neelkanth remembered his previous similar encounter. 'Brother, your bucket is made of leather. I don't drink water from a leather bucket.'

Bijal glowered at Neelkanth. 'The water is deep. The drought has diminished our water supplies. The water level is very low and I haven't got anything else to draw the water up.'

Sensing the frustration, Neelkanth stepped to the edge of the well. 'Don't worry, I don't need anything to pull the water up.' He held his gourd at the mouth of the well. The water from the well burst through the well like a geyser and sent a shower around the well. Bijal rushed to the well and saw the water settle at its mouth, bubbling like boiling water. Neelkanth filled his gourd and saw the water sink to the bottom of the well.

'How did you do that?' Bijal asked, looking into the well. 'It has never done that before.'

Neelkanth smiled without saying a word. Bijal realized his mistake, crouched, and bowed his head on the ground. 'Oh, please, please, will you not give my tired bullocks some rest and keep the well filled to the brim?'

Neelkanth stared at the bullock. 'You drive the bullock to draw the water without any thought for their pain.'

'What can I do? There is a drought and the crops need water,' Bijal cried.

'Can you not cushion the coarse rope with a soft cloth?'

Bijal bowed. Neelkanth looked inside the well and the water again rose to the mouth of the well. 'It will remain so until the lacerations on the neck of the bullock are healed,' he said and left. Bijal tried to stop him, but Neelkanth did not look back.

The shore along the Gulf of Khambhat was lined with fishing boats. Dry dust swirled above the land because of the drought. Neelkanth followed the beach curving west, walking in the water to keep his feet cool, when his eyes fell on a man in rags. The man stopped and placed his bag in the water before touching Neelkanth's feet in reverence.

'What it is that you have in the bag? Will it not get wet?' asked Neelkanth, concerned.

The man waved. 'There is only dead fish in the bag. The saltwater will do it good,' he said.

'Oh,' cried Neelkanth, his heart melting at the thought of death. 'What is your name?'

'Lakho.'

'Lakho, why eat dead fish when the land gives grains in abundance. Indeed, why kill the creatures of God who do no harm.'

Lakho looked down guiltily. 'What can I do? The drought has robbed us of a good harvest. The well is dry and there are no grains in the store. It is either fish or we die of hunger.'

Neelkanth placed his hand on his shoulder. 'Lakho, don't the other farmers help? Don't they share their harvest?'

'They have reserves, but only enough for their families. What we grow, we sell and eat what is left.'

Neelkanth sensed Lakho's pain. 'Do not worry. Go, return to your farm and start planting the crops. The well will provide enough water for a good harvest. But do one thing before you go. Return the fish to the sea.'

'Yogiraj, allow me to eat this last catch. The fish is dead and they will only go to waste.'

Neelkanth placed his hand on the bag. 'Go, return them.'

Lakho walked to deeper water, opened the bag, and emptied it into the sea. He gasped when the fish jumped up and swam away. He ran to Neelkanth and fell at his feet. 'You have given life to the dead. You are a yogi without equal,' Lakho said, bowing repeatedly.

'Lakho, it is God who gives life, and God who takes it away,' said Neelkanth, unwilling to claim the credit for the fish coming alive.

'Please stay with us,' Lakho said. 'It will soon be evening and the roads are deserted. Where will you stay? Where will you spend the night?'

'Lakho, you are very kind, but I am in a hurry to reach my destination.'

'Yogiraj, you will not be able to cross the confluence of Rivers Mahi and Sabarmati at this time. The water will be very deep there and impossible to cross. And even if you somehow manage to cross the river, the forest on the opposite bank is full of wild animals.'

'I have been traveling for almost seven years, Lakho. I have crossed many difficult rivers along the way.'

'Seven years?' Lakho said, gasping. 'How old are you now?'

'I am nearly eighteen.'

Lakho stared at Neelkanth in surprise. 'That means you have been traveling since you were eleven, a mere child. Were you not afraid of traveling alone at such a young age?'

'Lakho, what is there to fear? The soul is eternal. It was never born and it will never die. Even when this body dies, the soul will live on.'

'I am a simple farmer. I do not understand these things,' Lakho said, confessing his ignorance.

'They are the most intelligent who claim to know nothing,' said Neelkanth, smiling. 'I crave the dangerous and isolated places. Please show me the way to the confluence.'

Lakho led Neelkanth to the confluence. The setting sun painted the sky with a burst of red and orange. As they approached the confluence, the thrust of waters joining the two rivers filled the air with an eerie danger, made worse by the setting sun. Lakho jumped when they heard a roar from the opposite bank.

'Even the sound of water is frightening,' Lakho said. 'I beg you to wait until the tide ebbs. Let us light a fire and make camp here.'

'Lakho, will your family not worry about your whereabouts?'

'They will but –'

'It is not right that they should worry because of me. Allow me to cross now so that you can go home. I will wave once I reach the opposite bank.' Neelkanth placed his hand on Lakho's head and blessed him before stepping in the water.

'Go safely,' Lakho said from behind.

A trail of sparks burst from Neelkanth's feet with each step as he walked to the opposite bank. 'Go peacefully, my dear Lakho,' he waved. Lakho heard the echo of his words from the sky.

The roar of a tiger welcomed Neelkanth when he turned his back to the confluence. He grinned at the sound of the familiar. He arrived at the edge of Vagad just as the bells of the temple tolled for the last prayers. He sat down on the outskirts of the village until the bells stopped ringing and made his way to a potter's home, carefully selecting it as the place he wanted to spend the night from among the many huts in the village. There was a large heap of clay in the courtyard. 'Jai Narayan,' Neelkanth called out to draw the family's attention.

A man came running out of the hut and welcomed Neelkanth with joy. 'I am Rana.' He pointed Neelkanth to a mat while he went inside the house and brought some hotchpotch of rice and lentils. While Neelkanth ate, Rana went inside the hut and prepared a mattress.

When Neelkanth finished eating, he glanced at the heap of soil, stepped on it, and laid down. 'This will be fine,' he said. He placed his palms behind his head to serve as a pillow and rested. Once the lamps went out, it was pitch dark. Neelkanth stared at the dark umbrella of the sky teeming with stars and fell asleep.

He woke up early and left quietly to bathe in the river. He reached the village of Polarpur and felt compelled to enter the courtyard of a house on the edge of the village.

'Welcome, welcome, young yogi. You have withered your body to the bones. My name is Jetha Banani. Today is the eleventh day after the passing of our beloved mother. It will give her soul peace if you take some food. Yogis like you are rare. It is her good fortune that you should honor her with your presence today. Please.' Jetha invited Neelkanth into the house.

Neelkanth raised his hand. 'I will not come in but do bring something.'

Jetha rushed inside the house and brought a plate of sweets. Neelkanth accepted the sweets in a napkin. 'May

God bless her soul,' he said and went to a well nearby. He filled his gourd with water and washed his hands and feet before offering the sweets to the Shaligram. He sat down in meditation after eating the sweets.

Neelkanth opened his eyes when cows mooed, pulling carts laden with fruits and crops, followed by the farmers. Some farmers stopped and bowed. Neelkanth blessed them before getting up. He walked to Jetha's house and sat down on the wide seat in front of the courtyard. The passing public gathered around him, curious to discover his identity.

The noise drew Jetha's wife to check. Her eyes fell on Neelkanth. 'I am Jetha's wife, Lalita, Yogiraj. Monks who come to the village go to the temple in the village square and stay there. So, go there. This seat belongs to us.'

'Mother, the village square is packed with shops, traders, and people. Men are smoking and my young lungs cannot tolerate the stench of smoke, so please allow me to sit here. I will not disturb anyone.'

Lalita stared at him for a while and felt her heart warm. 'Okay. Stay,' she said.

At sunset, more herds of cows passed Neelkanth, raising a cloud of dust. Neelkanth opened the door and sat down in the corner of the courtyard.

Lalita saw him. 'Yogiraj, you've entered the courtyard because I let you sit on our stone seat outside.'

'Mother, the farmers are returning with their cattle and the dust is flying everywhere. I just want to sit quietly and meditate, so please allow me to sit here.'

A little later, she saw him sitting at the entrance of a room. 'Yogiraj, it seems there is no place that is suitable for you. Every time I gracefully allow you to sit where you want, you keep on moving.'

'Mother, there are animals in the courtyard. I will need to bathe if they touch me, so please allow me to sit here.'

'Allow him to sit. He is not disturbing anyone,' Jetha shouted from inside a room. 'We are fortunate to have the boy in our home when we are celebrating our mother's life. He is not asking for a mattress and pillow.'

As night fell, Neelkanth's stomach groaned. He got up and knocked on the door of a room where the guests were resting after dinner. 'Mother, I am hungry. You fed everyone, but you didn't give me anything. Please give me something to eat.'

'Yogiraj, all the food is finished. We have fed everyone and washed the utensils.'

'Mother, why are you speaking untruthfully? There is a hotchpotch of boiled rice and lentil on the burning coal.'

'Yogiraj, there is nothing in it except hot water. I placed it there because the coal was still hot.'

'Mother, please check. I am sure it is there.'

Lalita got up and looked inside the pan. She scratched her head when she saw the hotchpotch.

'Please give the boy something if you have anything. He is hungry,' Jetha said.

She pulled out a plate, poured some hotchpotch on the plate, and served it to Neelkanth.

Neelkanth glanced at it. 'Mother, it will be easier to swallow if you could add some ghee.'

Lalita was beginning to like being called 'mother'. She went inside and brought out a bowl of ghee and generously added a large spoonful to the hotchpotch. Neelkanth looked up. 'Mother, you wouldn't have any milk by any chance, would you?'

'All the milk is finished. It is the end of the day, and we have already milked the cow once, so you will have to do without any milk.'

'Mother, please try. Go to the cow. I am sure it will give you some milk. Let me touch the jug before you take it.'

Lalita was beginning to believe in the power of Neelkanth after discovering the hotchpotch when she was sure she had placed water to heat. She picked up a jug and took it to Neelkanth. Neelkanth touched it. Lalita went to the cow and washed the udders before placing the jug under them. She gasped when streams of milk poured from all the udders. She poured the milk into a glass and gave it to Neelkanth.

'Mother, I cannot drink unfiltered milk.'

'Yogiraj, the milk will lose all its goodness if you filter it,' Jetha said.

'It does not matter. I cannot drink unfiltered milk.'

Lalita went inside and filtered the milk and offered it to Neelkanth.

Neelkanth ate the meal with immense satisfaction. He woke up early in the morning and left after blessing the family. He was sure he would meet Lalita again. (1)

14

A Promise to Jasu

Neelkanth followed the shore to the Mahadev temple in Gopinath. The statue of Lord Shiva in meditation reminded him of his time in the Himalayas, the difficult circumambulation of Mount Kedarnath, and his meetings with Shiva and Parvati. He gazed at the statue in prayers without blinking, thankful that he had survived so far without any illness.

The head of the temple was waiting for him when he stepped away. Neelkanth bowed. His eyes fell on his scarlet dhoti, the golden bangles on the wrists, the golden chain around the neck, a smaller chain wrapped around a tuft of hair on his head, and the studs on both his ears. There was an instant clash in Neelkanth's heart because the materialism of the gold jewelry did not sit well with the sacrifice of the scarlet dhoti.

'Welcome, young yogi. I am Nrusinhanand. You have performed intense penance to wither your body so much. It is our good fortune that you should honor us with your visit. Who are you? Where do you come from?'

Neelkanth gave his usual cryptic response to the questions as the monk led him to a seat. Nrusinhanand offered Neelkanth some food. Neelkanth declined the food but asked if there was any milk.

'Yogiraj, there is plenty of milk in our dairy. You will certainly receive it, but we are all about to sit for lunch. So please join us.' Nrusinhanand pressed his palms together in humility.

Neelkanth observed the sincerity of his plea and bowed. He shared a rich lunch of sweets, soups, and curries. After lunch, Nrusinhanand offered him a mattress to rest. Neelkanth decided to sit in mediation instead to shake the lethargy of a rich meal.

When Nrusinhanand returned to check on him in the late afternoon, Neelkanth expressed an interest to bathe in the sea.

'We will all go,' Nrusinhanand said with joy. 'It has been a hot day. The tide is low, so the waters will be kind. You should know that during high tide, the waters rise to the edge of the temple compound.' He summoned the younger monks, and together, they accompanied Neelkanth to the sea. They bathed and played in the cooling waters while Neelkanth dug a bowl in the soft sand and sat in meditation. When the sun sunk below the horizon, Nrusinhanand alerted him to the call for the evening prayers.

Neelkanth looked up. 'When will I get a chance to come here again? If you don't mind, I will meditate here for the evening.'

'Yogiraj, it will soon be dark, and it will get cold.'

'Please allow me to meditate in this peaceful place,' Neelkanth put his palms together and asked.

'Yogiraj, you will catch a cold.'

'Please send some burning cow dung.'

'Yogiraj, the high tide will soon arrive and you will not be able to sit here.'

'When the pure sit in meditation, the water spirit comes to protect them,' said Neelkanth and closed his eyes.

Nrusinhanand returned to the temple and sent his disciples back with the burning cow dung. Neelkanth remained in meditation when the high tide came. The water surrounded him but stopped at the edge of the bowl he had dug, creating a wall of water. The burning dung continued to provide heat for the entire night.

Worried about Neelkanth, Nrusinhanand tossed and turned in his bed all night. He woke up early in the morning and went to the highest point in the temple to check on Neelkanth. He saw a flame rising from the sea. 'How can a flame remain lit in high tide?' he mumbled, doubting what he saw.

As soon as the tide receded, he asked his disciples to light a lantern. They walked to the place where they had left Neelkanth and found him in meditation. Nrusinhanand saw the bowl was dry and the flame was still burning. He saw the rays of light emanate from the body of Neelkanth and form into a radiant image of a boy. The image took Nrusinhanand to a beautiful palace of crystals with the brightness of a thousand suns. 'What? Where?' he gasped.

He entered the palace and saw the smiling, radiant image sitting on a throne, served by maids and servants on either side. Nrusinhanand studied the face keenly and saw that it was Neelkanth's. 'You had earlier asked me where I came from,' said Neelkanth. 'This is my divine home.'

Nrusinhanand fell to his knees and bowed his head, unable to believe what he saw. When he returned, he saw the same Neelkanth on the beach. 'You are indeed the Mahadev of Gopinath, who has come to bless us for our service. Please, please stay with us. My work is done now and I beg you to look after the temple. Yogiraj, stay with us.'

Neelkanth thought about the heartfelt plea of Nrusinhanand. 'I have come because of your selfless devotion. Continue to guide the young. I have many other places to visit, but I will stay for a few days because of your love.'

Nrusinhanand got up and danced with joy. 'Jai Yogiraj, Jai Narayan, Jai Mahadev!' he cried. The young monks joined him in the dance.

After keeping his promise to stay for a few days, Neelkanth walked to the sea in the early morning, bathed, and sat in meditation until the warmth of the rising sun touched his face. He stood up and opened his arms to absorb the rays of the sun for a while before leaving, walking with some urgency, his gaze on the ground.

He stopped when he heard a cry of a woman. 'Maharaj, oh, Maharaj. Please stop.' It was the first time anyone had called him 'Maharaj'. There was devotion in the voice of the woman. He looked behind and saw the woman rushing towards him.

'Young Maharaj, please accept this milk.' The woman offered him a jug. 'My name is Janbai and I live in the village nearby. I take a jug of milk to Mahadev every morning, but I have one rule. If I meet anyone on the

239

way, I offer the milk to the person without discrimination. Please take the milk. It is cow's milk, milked early today, filtered and pure.'

Neelkanth took the jug. 'Mother, you should know that Mahadev Himself has come in person to drink your milk.' A tall figure of Lord Shiva rose from Neelkanth's body. Janbai saw Lord Shiva drink the milk. She knelt before him and bowed her head on the ground.

'It is because of your love and devotion. Remember this image always,' said Neelkanth and went on his way.

Neelkanth arrived at the banks of River Malan near the village of Mahuva at noon, bathed, and sat in meditation on the soft sand until a man greeted him with a polite 'Jai Narayan'.

'Yogiraj, it would give us immense pleasure if you accept some food.'

Neelkanth could not refuse the offer of food when offered with such grace. He asked the man to bring whatever he had. The man went to his oxen cart and brought slices of coconut and sugar crystals in a napkin. Neelkanth served it to the Shaligram, ate a little and offered the rest to the man.

'What is your name?' asked Neelkanth.

'Yogiraj, I am Pitambar. I have a store in Kalsar and I am on my way back after buying some goods from Mahuva.'

Neelkanth reflected for a while. 'Why do you keep a store in a small village? You will never be happy by trading in a small village.'

'Yogiraj, it is true that I have been trading for more than twenty years and have little to show for it.'

'Stay and trade in Mahuva,' said Neelkanth.

Pitambar thought for a while. He had learned from his parents to listen to the words of the pure and selfless. 'Yogiraj, I will do as you ask.' He placed his head at Neelkanth's feet for his blessings. (2)

After spending three nights in Mahuva, Neelkanth arrived outside the village of Patvadar. He met a farmer outside the village of Patvadar, who was tilling the soil with a hoe with two wheels, and thought it a good idea. 'I have been traveling all over India for years, but I have never come across a hoe on wheels,' he commended the farmer and asked him to guide him to an almshouse.

'There is the house of Nagpal Varu where you will surely receive something.' The farmer pointed him in the direction of the house.

'Will you please show me?' Neelkanth bowed.

The farmer tied his cattle to a branch of a tree and led Neelkanth to the house. The house was surrounded by a high wall with a wooden door. Neelkanth thanked the farmer and knocked on the door handle. A young girl opened the door. 'Is Nagpal Bapu at home?' asked Neelkanth.

'My father is not at home at present,' the girl said.

'Jasu, who is it?' a woman shouted from inside the house. She came out.

'This is my mother,' Jasu said.

Observing the radiance on Neelkanth's face, the woman immediately put her palms together and bowed. 'Welcome. Welcome, Yogiraj,' she said with delight. She led Neelkanth into the shade of the veranda. 'Please sit here. I will soon get some food ready,' she said and went inside the house.

Neelkanth sat in meditation. Soon, the woman brought a warm glass of sweet milk and offered it to him. Neelkanth took a sip and glanced at Jasu sitting curiously near him, intrigued by the strangest visitor she had welcomed to their home. 'You look so thin,' Jasu giggled when Neelkanth put the glass down.

'I have been traveling for seven years. How old are you, Jasu?'

'I am six,' Jasu said, 'but now that I have told you my age, it is only fair that you should tell me yours.'

Neelkanth grinned at the quick intelligence of the girl. 'I am eighteen,' he said.

'That means you left home when you were eleven.'

'Yes. You are very smart, Jasu.'

'Were you not afraid to travel alone?'

'What is there to fear, Jasu?'

'I don't know,' Jasu said, waving her little hand uncertainly. 'My parents wouldn't have let me go. They would worry about me all the time.'

'So would mine,' said Neelkanth, just as a man entered the courtyard.

'Bapu,' Jasu cried and jumped to her feet. Her father picked her up and hugged her. His eyes fell on Neelkanth. 'Welcome, Yogiraj, welcome.' He fell to his knees. 'It is evening and soon it will be dark, so please stay here for the night and have dinner with us.'

Neelkanth bowed to accept the invitation. After dinner, Neelkanth told them about his many years of traveling around India. Jasu listened to the stories with interest until late. Neelkanth stopped when Jasu yawned. 'I will be leaving early tomorrow,' he said, not wishing to leave without letting the family know. 'You have looked after me like a son. What shall I give you in return?'

Nagpal glanced at his wife for help. 'Yogiraj, it is every parent's wish that their daughter should find a good husband,' she said. 'So if you must grant a wish, bless Jasu with a good husband.'

Neelkanth gazed at Jasu and smiled. He observed the innocence of her heart. 'Mother, I shall do better than that. I will find her husband for you. She is a special girl and deserves a special husband. I promise you I will return one day with a proposal.'

The couple glanced at each other with joy, not knowing what to think. They bowed at Neelkanth's feet. Jasu followed them. 'Promise me that you will come again,' Jasu pleaded.

'I promise, Jasu. How can I not come when you have looked after me so well?' Neelkanth affectionately placed his hand on her head. Jasu got up and fell into her mother's embrace.

'You have quashed all our doubts,' Nagpal said.

'It is because of your selfless service that I have come. I promise I will return,' said Neelkanth. (3)

15

God with Form

The family was fast asleep when Neelkanth woke up. He picked up the gourd and quietly walked out to follow the coast west. After passing through several villages near the coast, he arrived at a well outside the village of Timur. There, he bathed. The village was small, and the atmosphere peaceful. So, Neelkanth decided to stay the night in the ashram in the village. He woke up early and, as was his habit, sat in meditation near the well after bathing.

As dawn broke, passing farmers stopped and stared at Neelkanth's radiant body, youthful face, crowned with matted hair. An inner peace hugged their hearts and melted their fears, including the burden of the daily grind and providing for the family. They rushed forward to touch Neelkanth's feet when he opened his eyes to acknowledge them.

One man sat down in front of Neelkanth. 'Yogiraj, I am Lala and I live in the village. It appears as if you have performed intense penance. Our house is nearby. It will be an honor to serve you lunch. Your body needs nourishment and we will prepare a scrumptious meal.'

Neelkanth felt the deep love in his request. He put his palms together and bowed. 'Call me when the meal is ready,' he said.

At noon, Lala appeared at the door of the ashram. Neelkanth followed him. Rarely had he come across anyone who had such a deep desire to offer him food. He stopped at a well, pulled some water, and filtered it into his gourd. As they entered the village square, a rare calm filled the square as everyone stopped whatever they were doing and stared at Neelkanth – the downcast eyes, the bare feet, the gourd in his left hand and a rosary in another, and an old loincloth wrapped around the waist that exposed the bones of his skeleton. They saw the bounce in Lala's feet. Never had they seen him so excited to take someone to his house.

The entire Lala family stood in a line when Neelkanth entered the courtyard. Lala's son knelt and washed Neelkanth's feet. His daughters placed a garland around his neck. Lala showed Neelkanth to the shade of the veranda and placed a low stool in front of him as a man brought a steel plate with bowls of sweet milk and an assortment of vegetable curries, pickles, rice, dal, and fried bread. 'Yogiraj, you need to put some flesh on your body,' Lala said. 'Today, you should eat like a maharaja.'

Neelkanth offered the food to the Shaligram before taking some in his wooden bowl. The man served him, compelled by Lala, until every bowl in the steel plate was empty. Neelkanth smiled, placed his hand on his stomach, and rubbed it to show that he had enjoyed the meal. 'May God bless your family, may he grant peace and happiness to all,' he said in blessing.

Lala stepped forward and folded his hands. 'Yogiraj, did you enjoy the meal?'

Neelkanth nodded. 'I did.'

'Please be kind,' Lala said.

'But I came here because of kindness,' Neelkanth said to remind Lala. He was beginning to suspect an ulterior motive.

'Yogiraj, if you are happy, make me happy by blessing me with wealth.'

Neelkanth smiled, sensing Lala's motive for his exuberant welcome.

'Yogiraj, why are you smiling? Bless me, so that I may acquire gold and wealth.'

'Lala,' Neelkanth said. 'Lala, show me a person in the village who is happier than you?'

'Yogiraj, this is a small village. There is no one happier in the village than me because I am the wealthiest. Yet, there are so many people in the world who are so much wealthier.'

'Lala, understand this from a person who has nothing but what you see in front of you that there is no joy in wealth.'

'Yogiraj, where there is wealth, there is respect, fame, and praise. All joy is in wealth. Everything we wish for in life is found in wealth.'

'But Lala, you are the wealthiest in the village.'

'Yogiraj, this is a small village. At least give me enough wealth so that I become the wealthiest in Gujarat. Please be kind.'

'Lala, you have misunderstood the reason for your birth. It is not to accumulate material things but to liberate your soul from the cycle of birth and death. So, be happy with what you have. Abandon this foolish desire for wealth but develop a desire for God.'

'Yogiraj, you are learned in our scriptures and will know that Sri Krishna received little respect when he looked after the cows of Vrindavan but gained the glory of the world when he became the king of Dwarka.'

'Lala, Krishna is God. He is generous while you are a miser. Even if I bless you with wealth, it will not benefit others because you will keep it all in your incessant desire to accumulate more. The greatest peace is found in having little. Lala, you came with empty hands and you will leave with empty hands. So, give up this foolish desire for wealth. Take joy in what God has already given you.'

Lala kept on asking for wealth. Neelkanth realized there was no changing Lala's mind and left. Lala followed Neelkanth to the edge of the village. 'Yogiraj, please, please bless me with wealth.'

Neelkanth stopped and turned. 'Lala, will it please you if I say that you will never lose your wealth and that what you have, you will always keep?'

'It will,' Lala said.

'So be it.' Neelkanth placed his hand on Lala's head and went on his way.

Neelkanth sighed with joy as he entered the forest of Gir. Teak and acacia trees lived happily in the woods. He inhaled deeply to smell the air – a strong scent of warm honey and spice. He liked the scent. It warmed his heart that craved silence and solitude after many months of traveling through villages and meeting people. He smiled when the lions roared as if to welcome him to the forest. Peafowls sang in joy while woodpeckers leaped from branch to branch to keep him company. The rustle of leaves fanned a breeze and the ripple of streams opened their voices into a song. In the afternoon, Neelkanth sat down in meditation on the edge of a lake, often lost for many hours in prayer. At night, owls gently hooted to ease him to sleep.

Despite having not eaten for days, there was a bounce in Neelkanth's steps when he emerged to the west. It was late afternoon when he arrived on the outskirts of Una. There, he bathed in the reservoir before sitting down under the shade of a tree in meditation.

It was only broken hours later with a 'Jai Narayan'. His eyes fell on two merchants kneeling before him, dressed in fine clothes. They introduced themselves as Ganesh and Hansraj.

'It seems you have performed intense penance at such a young age,' Ganesh said and invited Neelkanth to their home for food.

'I do not go where there are crowds,' said Neelkanth, reluctant to enter any house after his experience with Lala.

'If not in our home, Yogiraj, will you at least take some food here?' Hansraj asked.

The two men rushed home as soon as Neelkanth nodded. They returned not long after with a pot of hotchpotch but, in their eagerness to feed Neelkanth, forgot to bring a bowl. They apologized for their oversight. 'Yogiraj, how will you eat this?' Ganesh asked, hoping Neelkanth would offer a solution.

Neelkanth looked around and found a flat stone. He picked it up and washed it. 'Please put some here,' he said.

Hansraj laughed at Neelkanth's quick solution. Ganesh placed the hotchpotch on the stone. Neelkanth unwrapped the Shaligram from around his neck and placed it on the side of the stone. As his sweet voice opened with a song, the merchants started clapping, filling the cool evening air with prayers.

The love for the enigmatic teenage yogi grew as they watched Neelkanth eat from the stone plate. They could not hold the tears in their eyes and fell at his feet, bowing repeatedly, the pride of their wealth melting away like ice on a hot day.

Neelkanth raised his hand and stopped them. 'If you must serve, serve the meek and the poor. God has given you more than enough, but it will all go to waste if you don't use it to serve those with little.'

'Yogiraj,' Ganesh said. 'We will do as you ask but promise us that this will not be the last we will see of you.'

Neelkanth sensed their compassion. 'We shall certainly meet again, not once but many times,' he said. 'Remember this image always.'

Neelkanth told them about his long pilgrimage. The merchants listened with interest, their admiration for the young yogi growing with each tale of his pilgrimage.

It was dark when the merchants asked for permission to leave. Neelkanth blessed them and watched them disappear into the dark. (4)

After leaving Una, Neelkanth arrived at a shepherd's settlement on the outskirts of the village of Dholera early next morning. There was a straw and mud hut in the corner of the settlement with a fence surrounding it. The shepherd was busy pouring water into a large bowl cut into the trunk of a tree. Neelkanth waited patiently to catch the eye of the shepherd.

The bucket fell from the shepherd's hands as soon as he saw Neelkanth. He rushed to him and invited him into the courtyard, where he offered him a stone seat under the shade of a teak tree. The shepherd ran his eyes down the emaciated body of Neelkanth and offered to serve him food.

Neelkanth gazed at a couple of grazing cows in the corner of the courtyard. 'I will not eat today,' he said.

The shepherd put his palms together and bowed. 'Yogiraj, I have the rule to serve all who visit my farm. I have not allowed anyone to leave without food so far. You will be the first if you leave without taking any food.'

Neelkanth sensed the sincerity of his plea. 'What is your name?'

'I am Bhola.'

Neelkanth recognized the shepherd's gentle nature. 'I will take some milk if you have some.'

Bhola went into the hut and brought out a jug of milk. 'It is fresh from the cows milked only this morning.' Neelkanth took some in a bowl and drank it.

In the evening, a monk visited the shepherd to fill the settlement with songs in praise of God. Neelkanth sat down in the corner and listened with love, rocking from side to side with each clap of his hands. As tiredness crept into the monk's voice, Bhola offered him a mattress to sleep. The monk invited Neelkanth to share the mattress.

Neelkanth accepted the offer but heard the monk say 'Hey Ram' every time he turned in his sleep. Each time, Neelkanth responded to his call.

The monk got up. 'You reply every time I say, Hey Ram. Yogiraj, please tell me, are you Ram?' the monk asked.

Neelkanth got up and put his palms together. 'Gurudev, only He who is Ram can reply to the name.' An oblong bowl of light rose from the body of Neelkanth and formed into an image of Ram.

The monk folded his hands and fell at Neelkanth's feet. 'Yogiraj, the reason for which I left home, the reason for which I sing devotional songs, and, indeed, the reason for which I have been wandering the length and breadth of Mother India, has been fulfilled today.' He shouted to call Bhola, unwilling to allow Bhola to miss this rarest of visions.

Bhola came running out of his hut and saw the glowing image of Ram where Neelkanth stood. He fell to his knees in reverence. Neelkanth reassumed his original form.

'Who are you?' the monk asked.

'I am the servant of the poor, the meek, and the holy. I have come because I see all three in this courtyard.'

Bhola and the monk sat down and listened to Neelkanth's many stories about his pilgrimage. Neelkanth sneaked out in the morning, having realized that Bhola and the monk would not let him go otherwise.

He followed the edge of a reservoir, shielded by tall shrubs, bushes, and trees. He arrived at Lodhwa and purposefully walked to a farmhouse. A woman greeted him with folded hands. 'I am Lakhu,' she introduced herself. 'This almshouse has been built for yogis like you.'

Neelkanth entered a central courtyard. He glanced at the cleanliness of the place and decided to stay at the house. Lakhu offered Neelkanth a cushion to sit on while she sat down on the side.

'Son, what have you done to your body? You look weak and famished. There is no flesh on your body. I can see every vein. Your abdomen has shrunk. There are only bones and skin. How many years have you been doing this? It is not right for a young boy to punish his body as you have done. A growing boy needs all the nourishment. How will you serve God with a weak body?'

Neelkanth sensed Lakhu's compassionate nature. It was a quality he had observed in many mothers he had met during his long pilgrimage. 'Mother,' he said, 'if God wishes me to serve, he will sustain me with air.'

'He may decide to sustain you with air, but you will eat well while you live in my home.' Lakhu got up and went to the kitchen and reappeared shortly after with a glass of warm sweet milk. 'Drink this for now. It is the cream of the best milk from our buffaloes sweetened with sugar.'

Neelkanth served the milk to the Shaligram and drank a little. 'You have certainly created a beautiful almshouse,' he said.

'It is due to the blessings of my Guru that I serve the godly.'

'He must have been a guru of deep faith,' Neelkanth asked gazing at Lakhu with interest.

'Atmanand Swami was my guru.' Lakhu bowed her head in sadness. 'He had an ashram in Tramba village near Girnar. His words were his legacy. An enlightened soul in life, whatever he said always came true. He taught me that God is formless, a bowl of divine light like no other. He initiated me, along with Vithalanand and Balanand, into the philosophy of a formless God. Vithal and Bala have been living with me ever since, helping my son Viru to look after the cows on the farm. Swami Atmanand is like God to us.'

The men entered the courtyard just as their names were mentioned. 'Here they come,' Lakhu said. She went to the kitchen while the men washed and sat down with Neelkanth. Lakhu brought a tray of bowls filled to the brim with steaming hot foods. Neelkanth observed the devotion of Lakhu to the men. 'Will you not eat?' he asked.

'I will eat later,' she said and served them until every bowl in the tray was empty. After a tiring day at the farm, the men went to sleep early. Neelkanth sat in mediation, quietly turning the rosary until he felt sleepy.

He woke up early in the morning and went with the men to the farm. While they worked, he sat under the shade of a banyan tree, lost in meditation, often for hours. Vithal, Bala, and Viru felt drawn to his gentle nature. They liked Neelkanth's simplicity, his ability to meditate for long hours without feeling agitated. They had only ever witnessed it in Guru Atmanand before, yet he had had a lifetime of experience of finding that rare peace, a stillness that finds one when one has attained a state of pure enlightenment. Neelkanth was still a boy. It raised many questions because it was to find that same rare peace that they had served Atmanand.

Neelkanth sensed their desire to learn. So, when they sat together in prayers in the morning, he asked Bala, the youngest amongst the men, who or what he mediated on if he believed in a God without a form.

'I meditate on myself,' Bala said.

Neelkanth chuckled at the response Bala gave and felt compelled to teach them about the true path to God because of their compassionate natures.

Lakhu, always alert to Neelkanth's slightest change of heart, noted that Neelkanth had not liked the response. 'Yogiraj, there was one instruction Swami Atmanand gave to all his disciples before leaving. That we should all become the disciples of Swami Ramanand.'

'Swami Ramanand,' asked Neelkanth, intrigued. He had heard the name before but could not remember when. He sensed the name would give meaning to his life. 'Tell me about him.'

Lakhu sensed Neelkanth's sudden interest, his desire to learn more about Swami Ramanand, and like a good storyteller, she decided to hold the story for the evening when they would have more time. 'The animals on the farm will be hungry and need feeding,' she said. 'We will speak in the evening.'

Unable to put the name out of his mind all day, Neelkanth reminded Lakhu about Swami Ramanand at the first opportunity after dinner.

Lakhu gazed at him with glee. 'Swami Ramanand was also a disciple of Guru Atmanand,' she said, 'but he left because he did not agree with the philosophy of a formless God. He had a deep inner desire to have the vision of Sri Krishna.'

Neelkanth felt a deep desire to meet this Swami Ramanand because it was the philosophy of God with a form he wanted to spread and was at the core of his heart. 'If Swami Atmanand told you to become the disciples of Swami Ramanand, why don't you follow his instructions? Is it not the duty of a disciple to follow the instructions of a guru without question?'

Lakhu looked down. 'There is no greater duty,' she said, 'but we are so attached to Guru Atmanand that we cannot abandon him.'

'Tell me about Swami Ramanand,' asked Neelkanth.

'He was born in Ayodhya to Ajayprasad and mother Sarmani. He holds the honor of being born on the same day as Sri Krishna. They named him Ram Sharma. After studying under the guidance of his father, he left home at twelve in search of God, traveling from one holy place to another in search of a guru who would bless him with a vision of Sri Krishna. He visited Dwarka after many years of travel, and there, a monk told him to find Swami Atmanand at the foot of Girnar.

'Swami Atmanand promised him that he would show him God, but said that he could only do so if he initiated as his disciple. I remember they used to debate almost daily about whether God has a form or not. Our guru did not believe in the worship of stone statues. Ramanand could not accept that. To him, the worship of God in statues was an important part of the devotion and service of God.

'I used to tell him. Why do you persist in this futile search for a God with a form when Guru Atmanand tells us otherwise? He always said that he would not rest until he had seen Sri Krishna as real as you and I.'

Ayodhya, the birth on the same day as Sri Krishna, the name Ramanand – all aroused Neelkanth's interest even more. Then he remembered that his father had mentioned the name to him once and had asked him to find Swami Ramanand if he ever felt lost. 'Where is Swami Ramanand?' he asked Lakhu.

'I believe he has an ashram in Kathiawar in a village...'

'In Loj,' Vithal helped her.

'Yes, in Loj. Ramanand visited us afterward and told us that the late great Acharya Ramanuja had appeared in his dreams and initiated him into the fold. While he was here, I often used to sit near him when he sat in prayers. I have seen how the food he served to Sri Krishna disappeared from the plate.'

'And yet you remain unconvinced.'

'Yogiraj, it is difficult to abandon Guru Atmanand even though he has told us that what Ramanand says is true.'

Vithal cleared his throat. 'I have heard that Swami Ramanand often tells his disciples that he is a mere drum player preparing the stage for the arrival of the real hero, God himself.'

Neelkanth smiled. 'I must find this Swami Ramanand.'

'How can you have faith in someone who says God has already taken birth?' Lakhu said.

'Taken birth? Does he not send his choicest seers to prepare the stage before his arrival?' asked Neelkanth.

'We are living in Kalyug,' Lakhu said skeptically. 'God is unlikely to take birth now.'

'Swami Ramanand has been telling his disciples that God has already taken birth and is currently visiting all the holy places,' Vithal said.

'Yogiraj, we cannot ever abandon our Guru Atmanand,' Lakhu said.

Neelkanth made a mental note to teach them about God with a form. They were good people and deserved a chance to know the truth. Over the next few months, he sat down with them every evening and told them about his many experiences on his travels until they were convinced.

On the evening before his departure, he told Lakhu to ask for anything she wished for in return for looking after him so well.

Lakhu thought for a while. She was convinced about the capacity of the teenage yogi to fulfill any wish that she requested. 'Yogiraj, please bless me so that my son Viru, my sixty buffaloes, and my fields become immortal.'

Neelkanth grinned at her request and the futility of it because that which was made of matter, stained by materialism, could not possibly hope to survive forever. 'Mother,' he said. 'Everything that is born must one day grow old, die, and decay. Even when Sri Krishna took birth, he had to abandon his body eventually. It is the law of nature that that which is born must die. Even the sun will die one day. This home that we call earth and the solar system as we know it will all perish. The stars that you see in the night sky go through the same cycle of birth and death. Mother, nothing can escape death. So, ask for something else.'

Lakhu did not relent and persisted with her request. Neelkanth realized the hopelessness of her plea but blessed her still, 'Lakhu, if immortality is what you seek, then I will grant you Akshardham. Once you reach there, you will indeed be immortal.'

'Akshardham,' Lakhu frowned. 'What is that?'

'It is a place like none other,' said Neelkanth with a broad grin.

16

Girnar

The thought of Lakhu's futile request to become immortal in the same body played on Neelkanth's mind when he went to bathe in the reservoir the next morning and sat in meditation. Many great seers had strived for the same, but all had failed. Nothing that is born, nothing that is part of this material universe can ever hope to exist for eternity. It is impossible to achieve the divine without sacrificing the material body. He hoped that she would embrace the wisdom of what he had taught her and achieve immortality in a divine body.

He got up when he felt the warmth of the sun's rays on his face and followed the coastline to Prabhaspatan, where he visited several temples in Somnath and Damodar before making his way north to the hills of Girnar. Neelkanth only rested at night outside villages before starting early again the next morning.

The green hills of Girnar were shaded by the dark clouds of the monsoon when Neelkanth reached the foothills in the middle of the morning. He had enjoyed the walk under the shade of the clouds. Crowds had gathered at the bottom of the long corridor of steps leading to the top, mustering the courage to start on the long walk up. Neelkanth surveyed the crowd on the periphery before working his way through, his eyes downcast. People easily gave way when they saw him, with some Jain elders even holding a line to allow him through as if he was Swami Mahavir passing through. Neelkanth was not surprised because he had experienced the same reverence enough times through the holy sites of Mother India. While the hearts of its people had been stained by centuries of violence, their souls craved the touch of the pure. It pleased Neelkanth that they clung to their roots despite the adversities of life.

He stopped at the bottom of the corridor and bowed to the image of his parents in his heart. 'This is for you,' he said softly, before starting the long arduous climb. He remembered they had always spoken about visiting the holy hills.

Parents stopped and bowed as he climbed the steps while their children knelt and tried to touch his feet. Stopping only momentarily to bless the children, Neelkanth continued to climb. It was afternoon when he reached the sacred pond of Gaumukhi and felt compelled to bathe. He placed his few belongings to the side without thinking twice and stepped inside.

'Eh, boy,' he heard someone shout from behind. 'This is our pond. We don't allow anyone to bathe in it.'

Neelkanth turned and saw a band of monks. He stared at them and sent them into a trance where they saw an image of the dwarf God Vamanji. The monks rushed to him when Neelkanth released them and plunged into the pond with him. Neelkanth pressed his palms and closed his eyes. They took his hand, surrounded him, rinsed his loincloth then wiped his body before sitting him down on a stone pedestal.

The elder monks came forward with bowls of sandalwood paste and anointed his body in worship. Others brought rose garlands and placed them around his neck before serving a variety of sweets and savories. Neelkanth ate a little while they sang in reverence in his honor and asked the rest to be distributed.

The monks bowed at his feet when Neelkanth stood up to leave and re-entered the corridor of steps to the top. Pilgrims coming down stepped aside, bowed as before. He tried to keep a steady pace but felt the heaviness of his legs higher up. It had been a long time since he had climbed such a high mountain.

It was late afternoon when he reached the top, five hours later, exhausted. He was glad that the monsoon clouds had shielded him from the harsh sun. He rested awhile before entering the temple to pay his respects to the deities.

The dark clouds of the monsoon had cleared when he came out and walked around the temple several times in reverence, stopping in different directions to survey the terrain below. With a clear sky, he could see far into the distance, a jigsaw of farms separated by shrubs and bushes below the deep green of the forest on the slopes, dirt lanes linking villages on the plains as if to highlight their interdependence. His heart rejoiced when his eyes fell on the many temple domes rising like pinnacles of hope in the middle of the villages. He listened carefully for the call of the wild before marking out his journey ahead.

A man stepped forward and bowed while he was enjoying the scenery. 'Yogiraj, who are you? Where do you come from? I have been climbing these steps for years in the hope that one day our Lord Dattatreya will bless me with his vision.'

Neelkanth gazed into his eyes without saying a word and sent him into a trance. Lord Dattatreya rose from the emaciated body of Neelkanth and blessed him.

The man fell to his feet. Neelkanth placed his hand on his head. 'Lord Dattatreya himself will come to take you when your time comes,' he said and went inside the temple to meditate. He spent the night on the top.

A mist cloaked the hills when Neelkanth started his descent early next morning. The coolness of the morning and the absence of pilgrims on the deserted corridor of steps made the early descent easier. It only became busier lower down with pilgrims stopping Neelkanth every so often for blessings.

It was late morning when he stepped down the last stone step. Pilgrims rushed to him as if God himself had descended from the mountains to bless them at the start of their climb. Neelkanth patiently waited before making his way to a pond. Lunch was being served, so he joined a line of monks.

'Brother, move from here and sit elsewhere,' a monk said just as Neelkanth was about to sit down. Neelkanth sat down where he was directed. 'Not, here. Find another place.' Again Neelkanth got up and prepared to sit down where he was told. 'Not here…not here…not here… not here.' He was moved six times. Each time Neelkanth smiled and did as he was told, but when he was asked to move for the seventh time, he picked up his gourd and left, even though he had not eaten for days.

He made his way to the shrine of Hatkeshwar Mahadev, where, after paying respects to Lord Shiva, he sat down in meditation under the shade of a tree in the courtyard until he was summoned with a 'Jai Narayan'. He gazed at the man standing in front of him with pressed palms. Neelkanth reciprocated.

'Yogiraj, I am the priest of the temple. Looking at your matted hair, the bare upper body emaciated with penance, the simple loincloth, and the rosary in one hand, I feel as if young Shiva has come to bless me for my years of service. Yogiraj, will you please take some food?'

Neelkanth nodded after sensing the love of his devotion. The priest leaped to his feet and rushed home. He appeared after a while with a plate of sweets, curries, and fried bread. Neelkanth offered them to the Shaligram and ate a little before calling an ascetic sitting on the steps of the temple. He asked the ascetic for his bowl and served a portion of the food to him.

'You have a kind and generous heart, Yogiraj,' the ascetic said 'Forgive me, but I have been following you since you were asked to get up seven times in the almshouse. It seems you haven't eaten for days and yet take only a little and offer the rest to us. How is it that you maintain such detachment at such a tender age?'

'A yogi should not indulge in too much of anything. Complete detachment to all the joys of our senses and total attachment to the joy of God is the only way to liberation from the cycle of birth and death.'

'I am from a small village in the Himalayas and have been on a pilgrimage for years, yet I have not met a yogi like you anywhere. So young, yet with the wisdom of our ancient seers. My heart rejoices by merely looking at you. Today, you have offered me sweets, curry, and fried bread for my salvation, but please do me the honor with this same vision at the time of my death.'

Neelkanth raised his right hand in blessing and promised that he would be there for him at the time of his death. (5)

Neelkanth left early in the morning and arrived at the Mahadev temple in Bhutnath. After prayers, he walked to Vanthali, where he washed the tiredness out of his limbs by bathing in the Suryakund pond. It was evening by the time he finished eating at an almshouse, so he decided to spend the night there.

A morning mist engulfed the village when he left. Dawn had not yet broken, so it was still quite cool. But Neelkanth liked the quiet solitude of early mornings, the flowers opening their petals and the chirps, the whistles, and the tweets of the birds, broken only by an occasional roar of the wild animals.

He took the dirt road south, crossing a jigsaw of farms before arriving at Piplana just as the sun crept up the horizon. His abdomen groaned with pain as he entered the village square. He found it odd that it did because he had only eaten at the almshouse the evening before. He put it down to his habit of eating little and asked a man if there was an almshouse in the village.

'There is no almshouse in the village, but I am sure you will find some food at the house of Narsinh Mehta,' the man said, pointing at the house near the square.

Neelkanth gazed at the door to the courtyard and knew exactly why he felt hungry. He knocked on the door and said 'Jai Narayan'.

A girl appeared at the door with a bowl of flour. Neelkanth glanced at it. 'What will I do with the flour? Please give me something cooked.'

'Our mother will make you some food if you wait for a while,' the girl said.

'I am in a hurry,' said Neelkanth and left, walking in haste to the river outside the village.

'Yogiraj, eh, Yogiraj,' a boy came running behind him. He stopped to catch his breath. 'Yogiraj, I am Kalyan. My father has sent me to call you back. Please return to our home to eat.'

'I am in a hurry, so I will not return,' said Neelkanth.

The boy put his palms together. 'Yogiraj, please come. I will not return home without you. My father would never forgive me.'

Neelkanth stared at the boy's eyes, saw the love in his heart, and followed him. Kalyan's father came rushing towards him when Neelkanth entered the courtyard. He bowed at his feet and offered him a rug under a tree.

'I am Narsinh.' Narsinh sat down a few paces away while the girl and their mother sat down on the veranda. Their eyes were filled with tears as they stared at Neelkanth's ribs, the shrunken abdomen, the sticklike legs, a body withered with intense austerities yet radiating an aura that contradicted everything they saw.

Kalyan placed a large bowl of sweet milk and rice in front of Neelkanth. Neelkanth offered the sweet milk to the Shaligram, then dipped his hand in the milk to crush the rice to a pulp.

'Yogiraj, you must have performed some intense penance,' Narsinh said. 'If I may ask, are you doing this penance to please God or for other reasons?'

Neelkanth looked up. 'I am doing it to please God.'

'Yogiraj, you will not find God through penance even if you die,' Narsinh said. 'You will only find God through our Guru Ramanand.'

Neelkanth's face lit up when he heard the name. He looked up. 'Please tell me about him.'

'He is our Guru with an ashram in the village of Loj. It is his wish that we should run this almshouse. He is the incarnation of Uddhavji and only he can offer you the vision of God.'

Neelkanth remembered the story of Uddhavji, an ardent devotee of Sri Krishna who, at the time of his passing, had told Uddhavji to go to Badrivan and stay there until his rebirth on earth. That's why I did not see him in Badrivan during my visit there, Neelkanth thought. He smiled as he drank the mixture of sweet milk and rice and washed it down with a sip of water. His desire to meet Swami Ramanand grew. He got up as soon as he finished. 'Thank you. May God bless your family,' he said.

'We would love you to stay for one day, rest, and regain your strength,' Narsinh bowed.

'I am eager to get on with my pilgrimage,' said Neelkanth.

Narsinh took the gourd from Neelkanth. 'I have the rule to walk all the visitors to our house to the opposite bank of River Odhav.' They walked silently to the river and paddled through its shallow waters.

'You must go back now,' said Neelkanth when they reached the opposite bank. He glanced at Narsinh as he stepped away and put him into a trance. A divine glow engulfed Neelkanth. Narsinh knelt and pressed his palms together in wonder as he saw previous incarnations of God emerge from Neelkanth's body and hover around him for a while before merging back.

Narsinh remembered the boon he had received in Girnar when, as a young man, he had decided to kill himself in frustration after not getting a vision of God despite years of prayers and devotion. 'Today, you have fulfilled the boon I received in Girnar that one day – God will visit our home in person. Please return to our home so that we can serve you for a few more days.'

Neelkanth placed his hand on Narsinh's head. 'This will not be the last time I shall visit your house, so don't worry,' he said. 'I must get on with my pilgrimage for now.'

As Neelkanth walked away, Narsinh bowed his head toward the spot where Neelkanth had stood. He watched him until he disappeared behind a hill. (6)

It was the middle of the afternoon when a cluster of tamarind trees attracted Neelkanth's attention near the village of Akha. The rustle of leaves blew a cool breeze. Neelkanth sat down in the shade of the trees, drank some water, and rested for a while before passing the village in his eagerness to reach the village of Madhada.

There, he walked straight to a house and knocked on the knob of the wooden gate. A man shortly opened the door and gazed at Neelkanth. 'Ohhhh, welcome, welcome, Yogiraj,' he said. 'How fortunate we are that a yogi of your aura should honor us with a visit to our home.' He led Neelkanth to a room.

Neelkanth sat down on the mud and dung floor. A woman came rushing in with a cushion. 'Yogiraj, welcome. Please sit on the cushion,' she said.

'Yogiraj, I am Jetha Mer and this is my wife, Samu. What intense penance you have performed. Please stay for a meal. We will summon a Brahmin to prepare the food.'

'Jetha, I will gladly take food,' said Neelkanth.

Samu got up as soon as Neelkanth agreed.

'Where are you going?' asked Neelkanth.

'To call a Brahmin.'

'No, mother, today I will only eat food prepared with your hands.'

'Yogiraj, it will be no trouble to summon a Brahmin,' Jetha said.

'I will not take food prepared by anyone else,' Neelkanth insisted. 'Go and help your wife,' he told Jetha.

Neelkanth closed his eyes and sat in meditation while the couple prepared the food. They placed the tray of steaming hot food on a stool in front of him. Neelkanth pleasingly glanced at the array of dishes, untied the

Shaligram from around his neck, and placed him on the stool. His pristine voice opened in a song as he offered the food to the Shaligram. Samu smiled at her husband as they listened and watched the devotion of their young visitor. 'Where are your plates?' asked Neelkanth when he stopped.

'Yogiraj, we will eat after you have eaten,' Jetha said.

'No, go and get your plates.' Neelkanth cut a slice of chapatti and dipped it into the curry and dal before eating. 'It reminds me of my mother's cooking,' he said as Samu sat down with the plates. Neelkanth took a spoon and served most of the food from each bowl on their plates.

'Yogiraj, you are the one in need of nourishment,' Samu said. 'We have become fat after a lifetime of eating.'

Neelkanth laughed. He ate until he finished everything on his plate. Samu cleared the plates. 'Wash them later,' Neelkanth told her.

'Yogiraj, they will get dry and will be difficult to clean.'

'Soak them and join us.'

Intrigued by Neelkanth's insistence, Samu hurriedly soaked the dishes in water and returned. Neelkanth spoke about his years of pilgrimage all over India, particularly speaking with immense fondness about his year with Gopal Yogi.

The couple folded their hands in wonder. 'Yogiraj, we would like to ask a question,' Jetha said.

Neelkanth bowed.

'Yogiraj, you could have visited any house you wanted, yet you chose ours. Please tell us to what do we owe this privilege.'

Neelkanth grinned brightly. 'It is late now. Rest and it will all become clear.'

Jetha laid a mattress on the ground for Neelkanth. As Neelkanth laid down and closed his eyes, a divine light rose from his body and flooded the room. Lords Brahma, Vishnu, and Shiva appeared with their respective consorts, Goddesses Saraswati, Laxmi, and Parvati. The couple saw them fanning, feeding, and worshipping Neelkanth.

'Jetha and Samu,' said Brahma. 'You have been following a life of celibacy despite being a couple for millennia and more. Whenever you have been born, wherever you have been born, in whichever family you have been born, you have always found each other and got married, yet followed the path of celibacy. The temptations of the flesh are difficult to resist. It is hard, even for wise seers, to remain celibate. And yet you have accomplished it as a couple. Neelkanth has come to bless you both because of your sacrifices. He is no ordinary yogi. He is the supreme yogi, the master of all that exists in infinite universes. He has come to bless you for what you have accomplished.'

The couple bowed with misty eyes. They sat in front of Neelkanth in silent reverence until they fell asleep. They were already awake when Neelkanth got up in the morning. Jetha had prepared a bucket of warm water, while Samu had prepared sweet milk mixed with grated almonds.

'We know,' Jetha said. 'Thank you for visiting our house.'

Neelkanth simply bowed without saying anything. Jetha watched him in silence while Samu prepared some spicy parathas. She placed them in front of the Shaligram with the sweet milk. Neelkanth took a little after the prayers and shared the rest with the couple.

'Yogiraj, please stay here,' Samu said. 'When will we get a chance like this again?'

'I promise I will visit your house many times,' Neelkanth assured them.

They accompanied Neelkanth to the edge of the village and tearfully watched him walk away, unable to believe their luck. (7)

17

In Loj

After a long morning of walking, a village well attracted Neelkanth's attention near the village of Mangrol. Neelkanth drew some water, filtered it, and drank some. The sun beat down in the clear blue sky. It was too hot to walk, so he found a spot under the shade of a tree and sat down in meditation. Crows cried on the trees, fluttering uneasily from one branch to another in the heat of the noon sun. Flies buzzed around him, some settled on his bare body, but Neelkanth did not open his eyes nor react.

He only opened them when he felt a cooling breeze. His eyes fell on a man sitting in front of him, waving his shawl. The man put his palms together. 'Young Maharaj, the flies are settling on your bare body,' he said. 'I am Gordhan and I live in Mangrol. Maharaj, it seems you have performed intense penance at such a tender age. My heart rejoices by merely looking at you. In all the years of my life, never have I felt so at peace.'

'It is the grace of God that gives peace,' said Neelkanth.

'Maharaj, will you take some food?'

Neelkanth grinned, having anticipated the question. He bowed. 'I will if you bring some.'

'Please do us the honor of visiting our home,' Gordhan requested.

'I do not go into crowded places.'

Gordhan stood up. 'Please don't leave. I will rush home and bring something.'

Neelkanth watched Gordhan run into the village and then closed his eyes.

Gordhan returned shortly after with some savories and sweets. Neelkanth ate a little and returned the rest to Gordhan. 'Gordhan, you came back very quickly,' he asked, curiously.

'Yes, Maharaj, the sweet was ready because today is the eleventh day of my aunt's death.'

Neelkanth stared at Gordhan intently. 'Gordhan, your aunt is suffering.'

'Suffering, Maharaj. How? That is not possible. She was a devoted disciple of Swami Ramanand.'

'Do you want to see her?'

'See her, Maharaj? How is that possible?'

'It is possible if you wish to see her,' said Neelkanth, smiling.

'Please, Maharaj.' Gordhan put his palms together.

Neelkanth stared at Gordhan and put him into a trance. He transported Gordhan to a dark place where he saw his aunt being beaten by demons with horns and large teeth. Fires burned all around them. Screeching cries for help haunted the place.

Gordhan saw his aunt and fell to his knees in pain.

'Help me, Gordhan,' his aunt cried when she saw him. Gordhan crawled forward but immediately stopped in fear when the demons approached him with spears. He found himself in front of Neelkanth when he came out of the trance.

'Oh Maharaj. You are right. My aunt is suffering. She is crying for help.'

'Why did you not rescue her?'

'They came at me with spears.'

'Why didn't you think of me? Go back and think of me.' Neelkanth put Gordhan in a trance. This time Gordhan stood his ground and thought about Neelkanth as he was told. The demons instantly retreated. Yama, the God of Death, appeared and asked Gordhan why he was there. 'Neelkanth sent me,' Gordhan replied. Yama instantly nodded to the demons to release the aunt. She disappeared as Gordhan approached her. Gordhan again found himself in front of Neelkanth.

'She disappeared, Maharaj. She disappeared,' Gordhan cried in panic.

'What did you see?'

'I thought of you as you said. Yama himself came and asked me why I was there. I said that you had sent me and he instantly released her.'

'Don't worry. I have sent her to Badrivan to purify her soul. She will take birth again and have the chance to redeem herself.'

'Maharaj, how is it possible that she went to hell? She was a staunch disciple of Swami Ramanand.'

Neelkanth thought for a while. 'Many years ago, Swami Ramanand had given gold jewelry to your aunt to look after, after a disciple had given it to him as a gift. When

Swami Ramanand asked for the jewelry years later, she said that she had already returned it to him. It is because of her greed and dishonesty that she has been suffering.'

Gordhan's eyes misted with tears. 'Thank you, Maharaj. Thank you.' He bowed his head repeatedly at Neelkanth's feet.

'Gordhan, go now. You are a good soul. Rest assured that we will meet again.'

'Maharaj, it is evening. Where will you sleep? Please come to our house and stay there for the night.'

Neelkanth closed his eyes without replying. Late at night, he got up and found a step in front of a shop in the village square and slept there for the night.

He arrived at Loj a few miles away early in the morning. The sun was a long way from rising, so it was still quite cool. Neelkanth bathed in the stepwell and sat down in meditation on a stone under a tree. Pigeons cooed timidly in the branches and sparrows tweeted as faint traces of light spread over the horizon. Some flew near Neelkanth as if to catch his attention. Neelkanth remained still, in deep meditation.

A divine radiance engulfed his body as faint rays of light warmed him. Women from the village arrived to fill their pots with water. Their tender eyes fell on the divine glow around Neelkanth, the emaciated figure, the shrunken abdomen of a famished body. Tears filled their eyes as they stepped forward and bowed. 'Son, who are you? What is your name? Where do you come from? Who is the mother who has abandoned you?' They implored Neelkanth with their maternal tenderness.

Neelkanth could not resist the love of a mother. He opened his eyes and bowed. 'Mother, I am Neelkanth. I come from nowhere and everywhere. My mother would not have had the heart to abandon me, nor my father. They were the incarnation of Dharma and Bhakti. Nor would I have hurt them by abandoning them had they been alive.'

The women stood up when Neelkanth closed his eyes and went inside the stepwell to fill their pots. A monk arrived when the women came out of the stepwell. They waited on the side as the monk approached Neelkanth. A peace like none before embraced the monk's heart as he knelt and bowed.

'Jai Narayan, Yogiraj. What intense penance you have performed. Who are you? Where do you come from? Please open your eyes so that I may have your blessings.'

Hearing 'Jai Narayan' Neelkanth's eyes instantly opened. He keenly studied the saffron mark on the forehead of the monk, the saffron turban, and the matching robes.

'Swami, my Lord is Sri Krishna, the one who releases us from the cycle of birth and death. He is my mother and my father.'

'Yogiraj, what you say is true. There is no greater truth than that.'

'Swami, what is your name? To which order do you belong? Who is your Guru and where is your ashram?'

'Yogiraj, I am Shukanand. It is my good fortune that I should have the honor of meeting a yogi of your eminence so early in the morning. My Guru is Swami Ramanand, who currently resides in Bhuj. His ashram in the village is under the care of Swami Muktanand. Please come and visit our ashram.'

'I do not go where there are too many people,' said Neelkanth.

'Yogiraj, Swami Muktanand is very kind and will welcome you with immense joy. He is very learned and will answer all your questions. Please come.'

'I do not go where there are too many people,' repeated Neelkanth.

Shukanand bowed. 'Yogiraj, please don't go. I will fill the pot and ask Swami Muktanand to come and meet you.'

Neelkanth watched Shukanand enter the well and closed his eyes.

Shukanand rushed back after delivering the water to the ashram. He knelt and bowed. 'Yogiraj, Swami Muktanand has a fever and requests that you should honor us with your visit. If you will still not come, he will come and visit.'

Neelkanth felt a deep desire to meet Swami Muktanand. 'In that case, I will come.' He picked up the gourd and followed Shukanand. He observed the bounce in Shukanand's steps and smiled.

As they entered, Neelkanth ran his eyes around the ashram and instantly liked the peaceful atmosphere and the divine vibrations of the hymns being recited by the monks. Shukanand took Neelkanth to the room where Swami Muktanand was lying. He laid a mat on the floor of the veranda.

Neelkanth put the mat on the side. 'What need is there for a mat when this whole earth is our mat?'

Swami Muktanand came out when he heard Neelkanth. His eyes fell on his emaciated body and his heart leaped with joy. The lethargy of the fever instantly lifted. He put his palms together and welcomed Neelkanth to the ashram. All the monks came running to the room when they heard about Neelkanth. They surrounded him with folded hands. Neelkanth bowed at the feet of Swami Muktanand.

'Yogiraj, thank you for honoring us with a visit to our humble ashram,' Muktanand said. 'You have performed intense penance.'

Neelkanth put his palms together. 'Swami, wherever I go, I ask five questions. If you will allow me, I would like to ask them.'

Muktanand bowed.

'Please define the qualities of Jiva, Ishwar, Maya, Brahman, and Para-Brahman.'

Muktanand smiled. 'Yogiraj, your question is very probing at such a tender age. It highlights your profound intelligence. I am forty-two years old and no one has ever asked me such a probing question.' Muktanand closed his eyes and reflected on the image of Swami Ramanand. 'I will answer them as best as I can, as explained by our Guru Ramanand, although only he can give a more succinct response because your question is very difficult to answer.'

Neelkanth sensed the humility of Swami Muktanand and his apparent devotion to Guru Ramanand.

'The Jiva resides in the heart,' Muktanand said. 'It is eternal and by virtue of its sense of feeling, it pervades the entire body. It cannot be pierced, nor can it be divided.

Maya has three qualities. At times it is pure, at times full of passion, and at other times, it can be ignorant. It is the energy of God responsible for creating attachment to the body and its relations. And, as for Ishwar, know that there is more than one Ishwar. They are conscious spiritual beings, responsible for performing various duties for the sustenance, dissolution, and creation of the universe. Brahman or Akshar is superior to the Jiva, Ishwar, and Maya. It is infinite, eternal, and all-pervading. He is the abode of Para-Brahman, and subservient to him. Para-Brahman on the other hand is the supreme God himself. He is beyond Brahman, Jiva, Ishwar, and Maya, and is the cause of all that exists. He is omnipresent, omniscient, and omnipotent. He resides in the Jiva through these qualities. He is independent and the giver of benefits and consequences according to one's actions. He is to be worshiped for ultimate redemption.'

Neelkanth put his palms together with joy. 'At last,' he sighed. 'Swami, I have asked this question to numerous people in seven years of my pilgrimage to every part of India. I have not received a reply as succinct as yours. You truly have the blessings of Guru Ramanand.'

Muktanand bowed. 'I have replied as has been explained by my Guru.'

'Swami, I have a deep desire to see Sri Krishna in person. I have met many yogis, but none have shown what I seek.'

Muktanand bowed. 'Yogiraj, Sri Krishna himself visits Guru Ramanand during his prayers. Only he can show you what you seek. Please stay with us until he returns.'

Neelkanth thought about what his father had once said to him. 'Swami, my parents had told me that if at any time, I should feel the pangs of detachment, I should go to Guru Ramanand. When I was in the Himalayas, even Gopal Yogi had told me that I would find a true Guru in the cradle of Girnar. Swami, will you keep me in your ashram?'

'Yogiraj, you have impressed us all and filled the ashram with peace. We are all attracted to you like iron is attracted to a magnet. How can we not keep you?'

Neelkanth did not sleep well at night after the excitement of the day. Wondering whether this was the end of his pilgrimage, he got up a long time before anyone and made his way to the stepwell to bathe. After meditating, he returned with a large pot of water to refill the tank in the ashram. He returned to the stepwell several more times until the tank was full. Then, thinking that the monks would be hungry when they woke up, he fired up the wood, sliced some vegetables, and mixed them with rice. He put the mixture to a boil.

He was sweeping the compound when Swami Muktanand came out of his room. It was still only twilight. Neelkanth saw him and bowed. Muktanand gazed at him curiously. 'Yogiraj, what time did you get up?'

'Swami, I have a habit of waking up very early so that I can avoid the hottest part of the day when walking,' said Neelkanth.

Muktanand prepared to go to the well for bathing. 'Swami, I have already collected enough water in the tank for you to wash. He led Muktanand to the stone near the tank and asked him to sit down. 'Allow me to pour water over your head while you rub.'

Muktanand smiled and washed with joy while Neelkanth poured the water over him. 'This is the most refreshing bath I have ever had,' he said when he got up.

'You are the most senior monk in the ashram and I am the most junior, so allow me to serve you. There is no need for you to go to the well anymore. I will get the water ready for you every day.'

Neelkanth went back to sweeping the compound. Muktanand gazed at him and shook his head. 'There is much we can all learn from you,' he whispered before going back to his room to do his prayers.

All the monks were sitting in a line in the shade of the veranda when Muktanand came out. Neelkanth took his hand and led him to a cushion he had kept ready for him. While Muktanand sang 'Ram-Krishna Govinda, Jai Jai Govinda' and the monks followed, Neelkanth served the steaming hot rice and vegetable hotchpotch to everyone.

'We will all grow fat and lazy, Yogiraj, if you continue to spoil us like this,' Muktanand said when Neelkanth placed a large ladle full of the hotchpotch in his bowl.

'Swami, forgive me, but I would not feel comfortable if I did not do my duty around the ashram while I stayed here.'

It was mid-morning by the time Neelkanth and the monks cleared everything. After breakfast, Neelkanth tied two baskets made from pieces of cloth and hung them on either side of a rod. He thrust the rod on the back of his shoulder and went into the village. Calling 'Jai Narayan, Jai Krishna', he summoned the residents to give alms. Women and children rushed to him as he passed their houses and poured whatever they had. Neelkanth returned to the ashram with full baskets to the joy of all the monks. They surrounded him and took the weight of alms from his slender shoulders.

Muktanand came out to discover the reason for the commotion. The monks walked to him with the baskets and showed him the alms Neelkanth had collected. While the monks went to the kitchen to prepare the lunch, Muktanand summoned Neelkanth to sit down next to him on the veranda. He served him a glass of water.

'Who are you?' Muktanand gazed at him with affection.

'I am the servant of the poor, the meek, and the holy,' said Neelkanth, giving a response he had given countless times to curious observers.

Muktanand gazed at his body. 'Your body is skin and bones. You have performed intense penance. How will you meet Guru Ramanand if you continue to put so much strain on your already weak body? Rest, recover your strength, and let us serve you until Swami returns.'

Neelkanth bowed and joined the monks in the kitchen. There, he saw a monk give a burning piece of wood to a woman through a window to the adjoining house. 'We help each other with fire,' the monk said.

The monks have taken the vows of celibacy. They have renounced wealth, women, and family. They can therefore not be seen to associate with either. Neelkanth thought of telling the monks about what he thought of the window in the wall but held back, thinking that they may not receive it well coming from a new arrival to the ashram. After lunch, he led Swami Muktanand to the kitchen with some bricks and mortar.

'Swami, this window in the wall is not just a hole in the wall, but a hole in the code of renunciation the monks have vowed to uphold. 'Please allow me to seal it,' he said, and without waiting for Muktanand to respond, Neelkanth placed the bricks in the window and sealed it.

Muktanand stepped forward and hugged Neelkanth when he finished. 'Who are you?' he gazed at him intently in the hope of a reply this time.

Neelkanth grinned and bowed without replying. He joined all the monks in decorating the ashram with flags, buntings, and flowers the following day for the Janmashtami festival – the birthday of Sri Krishna.

There was joy in Neelkanth's heart when he woke up early and walked to the well to bathe. He saw several young monks from the ashram at the well, filling pots with water. 'We will need a lot of water today and thought we should follow in your footsteps.'

Neelkanth bowed, pleased with their enthusiasm. He bathed and sat in meditation before helping the monks with the water. It was a day of fast, so they spent the rest of the day making flower garlands, decorating the swing, and getting the ashram ready for the festival in the evening.

A statue of child Sri Krishna beautifully adorned in gold jewelry and fine silk garments sat on the swing; monks sat all around singing devotional songs. Drums, harmonium, and sitar accompanied the songs.

Swami Muktanand spoke about the life of Sri Krishna while Neelkanth sat down in front of the swing and pulled the string to set the cradle in motion. At midnight, everyone lit their candles and waved them in front of the statue of child Sri Krishna in celebration. A divine aura engulfed the ashram.

Muktanand saw a glowing image of Neelkanth in the cradle in place of Sri Krishna. Mesmerized by the twin images, his eyes alternated between the Neelkanth on the cradle and the Neelkanth pulling the string. He wondered whether they were the same. Had Sri Krishna come in the guise of the teenage yogi to bless them for their devotion? The image disappeared when the last drum beat reverberated over the ashram and merged into the body of Neelkanth.

Muktanand took Neelkanth's hand and sat him down next to him. The villagers came forward, placed gifts in front of the statue of Sri Krishna, and bowed to Muktanand and Neelkanth before returning home.

'Who are you?' Muktanand asked again when they were alone, only to receive the same reply as before.

18

The Drum Player

Neelkanth kept his promise, never sitting idle, dividing his time between prayers and service. He gathered young monks and taught them the different positions of yoga. He went to collect cow dung, shaped them into cakes, and laid them in the sun to dry for use as fuel for cooking. His sweet voice echoed with songs as he served. Muktanand observed, listened, and learned, his discerning eyes and sharp intellect unable to believe that Neelkanth was just another monk in the ashram. He took joy in the positive influence of Neelkanth on the rest of the monks.

One day, he summoned Neelkanth to his room and gave him two pieces of white cloth. 'We will call you Sarjudas from today because you come from the valley of River Saryu.'

Neelkanth accepted the clothes. 'Swami, I have had this loincloth since I left Ayodhya. By discarding it today, I wash all and every association with the ancient city.'

Muktanand stared at him for a long time and sensed his total detachment from everything associated with his roots. It was a sacrifice that was an example to every ascetic.

A few days later, two farmers from a nearby village of Sheel came to Muktanand to tell him that they had reaped a rich harvest of cucumber and would like to donate a cartload to the ashram. Muktanand asked Shukanand to gather fifteen devotees from the village and accompany the farmers.

'There is no need to waste the time of so many devotees,' said Neelkanth from behind him. 'I will go with Dev Bhakta and bring it all.'

Muktanand glanced at Neelkanth's frail physique. 'Sarjudas, you are still too weak. You will not be able to carry a whole cartload of cucumber. Please take the devotees to help.'

'Don't worry, Swamiji,' Neelkanth assured him and left with Dev Bhakta.

The farmers picked a cartload of cucumbers and offered to help with a cart, but Neelkanth declined. He asked the farmers to tie the cucumbers in two bundles, one large and another small. 'Place the large bundle over my head,' he said.

'How will you carry such a large bundle?' Dev asked, concerned.

When Neelkanth bent low, a group of fifteen farmers raised the large bundle and placed it over his head. The bundle magically hovered over Neelkanth's head. The farmers gasped as the bundle moved with Neelkanth when he stepped forward like it had a life of its own. 'Carry the smaller bundle and follow me,' Neelkanth told Dev.

Neelkanth walked briskly, as if there was nothing on top of his head, his voice singing in joy. He stopped after a mile to check on Dev and saw him struggling behind. He waited and saw Dev soaked in perspiration. 'Dev, climb that slab and place your bundle on top of mine,' Neelkanth told him.

Dev did as he was told, relieved. 'How do you keep so much weight floating over your head?'

'The power of yoga,' said Neelkanth.

Dev shook his head in disbelief, having never witnessed anything like it. Passing villagers gasped and gazed in amazement. Curious children gathered behind them as they entered Loj and followed them to the ashram. Neelkanth stepped aside at the gates of the ashram. The bundles gently floated to the ground. Muktanand and the monks came rushing out to see what the commotion was about. Their eyes fell on the heap of cucumbers.

'You carried all this?' Muktanand gazed at Neelkanth in wonder.

Neelkanth smiled. Dev told everyone what he had seen.

'The power of God,' said Neelkanth, humbly, when Muktanand looked at him. The other monks gathered around Neelkanth and pressed him to teach them. Neelkanth bowed. Muktanand bent low and tried to touch Neelkanth's feet in respect, but Neelkanth stepped back. 'It is I who should be bowing at your feet,' he said.

'Who are you?' Muktanand asked again, his discerning intellect keen to learn the truth.

'I am the servant of the poor, the meek, and the holy,' Neelkanth bowed.

Over the next few months, Muktanand watched Neelkanth immerse himself in the service of everyone in the ashram. No work was too little or too big, nothing was beneath him or above him, personifying the response that he had given to Swami Muktanand each time he had asked him who he was. Muktanand noticed the joy Neelkanth took in serving others, in the sweetness of his singing, in the dance of his feet, in the claps of his hands, and in the way he swayed from side to side whenever he sat in prayers – every action, always in harmony with the other. It was a joy he had never witnessed before. How could someone so young be so engrossed in God, be so faultless?

It was a joy that did not desert Neelkanth until one day. Muktanand saw Neelkanth sitting in the corner singing, his head resting on a pillar. There was a sadness in his voice Muktanand had not heard before.

Ever alert to the welfare of the monks in his charge, Muktanand approached Neelkanth. 'Sarjudas,' he simply said.

He saw Neelkanth's tearful eyes. 'Swami, it has been more than six months, and still Guru Ramanand has not returned.'

Muktanand sat down next to him. 'Sarjudas, please be patient. He is sure to return soon.'

'Swami, I am keen to return to the forest.'

Muktanand gasped. 'Oh, please don't,' he said. 'You will not find a Guru like Swami Ramanand even if you search every corner of the world.' Muktanand paused to reflect, keen to keep Neelkanth in the ashram until Guru Ramanand returned. 'Let us write a letter to him.'

Neelkanth's sadness instantly lifted with Muktanand's assurance. They went to his room and collected two sheets of paper and ink. Neelkanth stepped outside and sat down on the veranda with his back to the wall.

'Swamiji Shree Ramanandji, who is the 'Sun' that has arisen in the form of a true Guru and who is currently presiding at the holy place, Shree Bhujnagar. Accept the prostrations of your devout devotee, Brahmachari Neelkanth, also known as Sarjudas, who remains in your service from the town of Loj.

Moreover, the purpose of writing this letter is that by the will of God, I have arrived here, having traveled through the four great places of pilgrimage. There, I heard your name and heard that you, the living embodiment of a liberated soul, have manifested in the western region. Then, by practicing yoga under the guidance of Gopal Yogiji, I accomplished Ashtang Yoga. At that time, Gopal Yogiji had also told me that I would meet a seer at the base of Girnar. I have spent many days living on air. Still, I did not attain the vision of Sri Krishna in person. Now I have stayed here, considering this place to be pious. Kindly bless me to have a vision with Sri Krishna himself. I have heard that you grant such vision to those who long for that state. Having heard this from Swami Muktanandji, and having known him to be devoid of all deceit, I have stayed here.

Swamiji and Bhattji Mayaram have told me that we will call you here; so, I should stay till then. Bhattji insists that having read both our letters, you will shower such mercy on us. Just as the partridge seeks the moon, I wish that you will give me a chance to meet you at the earliest moment; otherwise, I will come there to be in your service. This letter has been written on 28 February 1800. Show your merciful gaze at the earliest moment after you read this letter. Otherwise, I will not stay here.'

Neelkanth read the letter again, folded it, and gave it to Swami Muktanand, who carefully wrapped both the letters in a piece of cloth and gave them to Bhattji.

Bhattji bowed to Swami Muktanand fourteen days later and presented the reply from Guru Ramanand. Muktanand touched the letters to his head in reverence. Neelkanth came running when he heard that Bhattji had returned with the replies. Muktanand gave Neelkanth his letter. They opened them together and read them in silence.

Muktanand stared at Neelkanth with renewed love. 'Guru Ramanand has given a reply to the question you are not willing to answer,' he said.

'What question, Swamiji?' asked Neelkanth, curiously.

'I have asked you several times who you are,' Muktanand said.

'And I have told you I am the servant of the poor, the meek, and the holy.'

'But you are not, are you?'

'What does the letter say, Swamiji?'

'Guruji has asked me to take care of you. He says I will realize in the future that you are not of this world.' Muktanand grinned. 'I suspected as much.'

'I am still the servant of the poor, the meek, and the holy. Nothing gives me greater joy,' Neelkanth insisted. 'Guruji has asked me to stay here and teach Ashtang Yoga to the monks until he returns.' Neelkanth got up and embraced one of the pillars on the veranda.

'Why are you embracing the pillar?' Muktanand asked.

'Guruji says that if I want to stay in the ashram, I will have to first embrace a pillar.'

Bhattji gazed at Neelkanth and smiled. 'The pillar he refers to is Swami Muktanand. He wants you to stay under his guidance.'

Neelkanth immediately released the pillar, knelt before Swami Muktanand, and bowed his head at his feet. 'You are wise beyond any words,' he said.

Muktanand placed his hand on Neelkanth's head in blessing. But he knew Neelkanth was a special person, his greatness veiled behind his youth. He hoped to discover more from Guru Ramanand when he returned.

One day Neelkanth came to Muktanand, 'Swami, if you do not mind, I shall sit with you during your prayers tomorrow morning.'

'It will be an honor,' Muktanand said but knew there was a purpose to Neelkanth's request.

When Muktanand sat in prayers early in the morning, Neelkanth came and sat beside him. He closed his eyes and linked his mind to Muktanand's mind with his yogic powers. As Muktanand meditated on Guru Ramanand, Neelkanth keenly observed many of his features.

'I have seen Guru Ramanand,' said Neelkanth when they came out of the meditation.

'How, Sarjudas? You haven't even met him.'

Neelkanth grinned. 'Guru Ramanand has a fair complexion, stout body, lotus-shaped eyes, sharp nose, broad forehead, and a deep navel.'

'Sarjudas, you described Guruji perfectly. How did you do that?'

'Through the grace of Gopal Yogiji, I entered your mind while you were meditating on Guru Ramanand and saw him as you meditated on him.'

Muktanand gazed at Neelkanth in stunned silence, not knowing what to make of him. Was he a magician or what? 'I didn't know you could link minds with other people through yoga,' he said. 'Sarjudas, please tell me truthfully, who are you?'

Neelkanth knelt and bowed his head at Muktanand's feet and gave the same response he had given several times before. As instructed by Guru Ramanand, Neelkanth immersed himself in teaching yoga to the monks in the ashram and whatever else Muktanand asked him to do.

A few weeks later, a disciple Kurji Dave arrived late in the evening to see Swami Muktanand with a message from Guru Ramanand. 'Guruji is in Piplana and has asked that all the monks along with Sarjudas should join him there.'

Muktanand presented his turban to Kurji for bringing the good news. Neelkanth danced and clapped with his hands in the air. 'I will give you the gift of my home Akshardham,' he cried.

'Akshardham?' Muktanand asked. He had never heard the word before and wanted to know more.

'Oh, please, Swamiji, can we leave this evening?' Neelkanth asked, deflecting the question.

'You read my mind, Sarjudas.' He glanced at the monks and asked them to get ready. 'Sarjudas, will you ever answer any of my questions? It is not fair that I answer all your questions and you answer none of mine.'

Neelkanth turned to Kurji. 'It will all become clear in time.' He stood ready at the gates of the ashram with his gourd in hand, his old loincloth tied around his waist. Muktanand was not surprised.

They walked briskly in their eagerness to reach Piplana. A light rain fell at sunset. 'It will keep us cool,' Muktanand said, feeling hot after the long walk. Neelkanth struggled to keep up and slowed everyone down.

'When will we reach Piplana if you walk slowly?' Muktanand said. 'Use your yogic powers to keep up.'

Neelkanth sighed deeply and shot ahead, leaving everyone behind. He reached the banks of River Ozat in full flow. Piplana was on the other bank. There was no way of crossing it without being pulled by the current. 'Sarjudas!' Muktanand shouted from behind in concern as Neelkanth stepped on the water. He gasped when he saw Neelkanth walking on water to the opposite bank.

It was early morning, so Neelkanth bathed in the river and sat down in meditation while he waited for everyone. Muktanand and the monks arrived in a boat an hour later. Neelkanth remembered his visit to the house of Narsinh Mehta. He had spoken about Guru Ramanand and guessed that he was sure to be at his house but waited while Muktanand and the monks bathed and got ready. 'We must be pure in heart, body, and mind when meeting our Guru,' Muktanand said.

'Nothing but,' agreed Neelkanth. He requested Muktanand to lead the way since he was the most senior monk.

Narsinh Mehta had received news that Muktanand and the monks were at the river. He sent Kalyan to collect them. It was a humid morning on 19th June 1800.

Guru Ramanand was seated on a decorated seat in the courtyard. He got up as soon as he saw Muktanand.

His eyes fell on Neelkanth, his emaciated body wrapped in an old loincloth, a gourd in hand, and the hair tied in a bun on top of his head. Guru Ramanand's eyes misted as Neelkanth fell to his knees and prostrated. Ramanand raised him from the ground and embraced him like a father meeting his lost son after a long time.

Muktanand knelt and bowed his head at the feet of his guru. Ramanand hugged him when he got up and then took Neelkanth's hand. 'The almshouses we had started in the villages are for this boy? I have been waiting for him to come for a long time.'

Muktanand gazed at his Guru with renewed reverence. 'Swami, you are in constant communion with Sri Krishna, so it is not surprising that you knew about Sarjudas' arrival. Sri Krishna sits in your morning prayers every day and takes all the foods you offer. So, please tell me what you meant when you said in your letter that Sarjudas is not of this world,' Muktanand asked, determined to learn about the true identity of Neelkanth.

'Sarjudas, is that the name you have given to Neelkanth?' Swami Ramanand asked.

'He comes from the valley of River Saryu, so it seemed appropriate.'

'As do I,' Ramanand said. He placed his hand on Muktanand's shoulder as he led him to his seat. Neelkanth, Muktanand, and the rest of the monks sat down around him.

'I have said many times that I am only the drum player for the main performer who is yet to come,' Ramanand said. 'All the avatars are great. Yet, even amongst them,

Sri Krishna is greater than all of them. Each avatar comes with a purpose. Their greatness is defined by the greatness of the tasks they perform. You do not know the full glory of Sarjudas because what you see is a boy in an emaciated body. Yet, know that no words can describe his glory. Only time will allow you to understand his true glory.'

They all returned to Loj to prepare for the Diwali festival. Neelkanth continued to serve under the guidance of Guru Ramanand. A calmness returned to the ashram after the bustle of the festival. Neelkanth's heart craved silence and solitude.

One late afternoon, he tentatively approached Guru Ramanand's room and waited at the door. 'Sarjudas, you appear agitated,' Ramanand said.

Neelkanth bowed. 'Guruji, my heart craves the silence and solitude of the mountains.'

'I know, Sarjudas.' Ramanand took Neelkanth's hands and gazed into his eyes. 'Do you remember you wanted to have the vision of Sri Krishna?'

'It is the only reason I have been so patient and waited for you for so long.'

'You will not see him if you leave. You will not see him, unless you become a monk.'

Neelkanth looked down. 'It means staying here,' he said softly. 'Devote my life to the hectic life of the ashram.'

'It does. I realize it is not what you want,' Ramanand took his hand.

Neelkanth remembered the words of his father that if he ever felt lost, he should search out Guru Ramanand, who would show him the way. He remembered the words of Gopal Yogi that he would find a true seer at the base of Mount Girnar. He had searched the whole of India for an ashram he could call home but had never found one. He thought, where will I find a Guru like Ramanand?

'Guruji,' Neelkanth bowed. 'If becoming a monk is the only way to have the vision of Sri Krishna, please initiate me into the fold.'

Ramanand raised his hand in the air and cried with joy before placing both his hands on Neelkanth's head in blessing. 'Under one condition,' Neelkanth said when he raised his head.

'Sarjudas?' Ramanand gazed at him curiously.

'That Sri Krishna should appear in my prayers as he does in yours and accept whatever I offer him.'

Ramanand smiled. 'Sarjudas, you have always had the capacity to see him at will.' Neelkanth remembered the incident when the Shaligram drank several gourdfuls of water after he was lost in the forest for days. 'Yet, since you impose a condition, you must allow me to do so as well.'

'A disciple must fulfill the wishes of his Guru,' said Neelkanth, bowing.

Ramanand thought for a long time. 'I am old and I will not be able to continue for long.'

'Oh, Guruji, you will, you will.' Neelkanth's clasped his hands. 'I will be lost without you. You are my mother and my father. You are the one true Guru I have searched the whole of India to find. I will not survive without you.'

'Sarjudas, you cannot come where I am going. There is still so much work to do. Mother India has been ravaged for centuries. The land that was once the beacon of love and tolerance has been stained by power, greed, and violence. The true essence of our ancient wisdom has been lost. People are crying for guidance. You are that one true guide.'

'Me, Gurudev?' Neelkanth gasped, sensing what Ramanand was trying to tell him. 'But, Guruji, you have nurtured great monks such as Swami Muktanand, who are so much more worthy. I am only eighteen. No one will even listen to me?'

'If you wish our beloved Sri Krishna to accept whatever you offer, you must accept my condition,' Ramanand insisted.

Neelkanth realized the futility of saying anything else and bowed his head.

Within days, Ramanand organized a huge festival and invited all his disciples to Loj. He asked barbers to shave Neelkanth's head covered with fine hair that had not felt the sharp edge of a blade for seven years and more. Neelkanth arrived on the stage, dressed in white clothes. Ramanand placed a garland of Tulsi beads around his neck. He marked his forehead with a 'U' with sandalwood paste and placed a large vermillion dot in the middle. He smeared his arms and chest with sandalwood paste and then whispered a Guru Mantra in his ear. 'You will be called Sahajanand Swami and Narayan Muni,' he said. 'Uphold the values of our most ancient scriptures and inspire others to do the same so that they can worship the Lord with a realization of his full glory.'

Neelkanth touched the feet of Guru Ramanand for his blessings. He then gazed at Muktanand with love, stepped forward, and bowed his head at his feet. Muktanand instantly raised him from the ground and hugged him.

After the initiation, Ramanand kept Neelkanth with him in all his travels through the villages. He fed Neelkanth nourishing meals to rebuild his strength and put some flesh on his bones. He massaged Neelkanth's body with oil to improve blood circulation and release tension.

'Sacrifice is the best friend of a monk. Massaging the body with oil and eating rich foods are not appropriate for a monk,' said Neelkanth in protest, only to meet the encouraging gaze of Ramanand.

'You will need to rebuild your strength if you are to inspire others,' he said.

A year later, Ramanand held a meeting with Muktanand and his most ardent devotees. 'My time is up and I wish to install someone to take my seat.'

Ever alert to his Guru's wish, Muktanand put his palms together and bowed. 'Gurudev, you have reminded us many times that you are merely a drum player and the main performer is yet to come. Since young Sahajanand is that performer, it is only appropriate that he should be installed on your seat as the Acharya.'

Everyone concurred and echoed what Muktanand had said.

'I worry that people will think he is too young and not accept him,' Ramanand said.

'He is a child for sure, but he has the wisdom of our ancient seers. He has mastered Ashtang Yoga. He can quote our scriptures at will. He is so learned yet humble. When work needs to be done in the ashram, he does it without being told and has done so from the day he walked into the ashram. There is no pretense about any of his actions. Oh, Gurudev, he has won the hearts of everyone like no one before. There is no one better to lead us than Swami Sahajanand.'

Ramanand's eyes misted. He opened his arms and embraced Muktanand. 'I am lucky to have a disciple like you. Thank you for expressing my wish.'

Epilogue

Amid great pomp and ceremony, Neelkanth was installed as the Acharya on 16th November 1801. He was only twenty years old. He grew up to be known as Swaminarayan, an avatar of the supreme God, a great reformer of India who, after the ravages of the Mughal and British Empires, when Maharajas ruled their little kingdoms and filled their treasuries at the expense of their subjects, ushered in the hope for the suffering masses. He gave courage to India's independence movement by resisting violence in any form and reinstated *Ahimsa* – non-violence, as the strongest pillar of Hinduism. He stopped the abhorrent practice of burning widows on the funeral pyre of their husbands and the drowning of newborn girls in milk. He dispelled superstition and social divisions that had marred India for millennia to begin an age of peace, equality, and unity.

Magnificent marble, limestone, and red stone temples have been erected in the name of Swaminarayan, who is worshipped as God, the avatar of all avatars.

Perhaps, the most telling insight into his heart, to his repeated assertion that he was and is the servant of the poor, the meek, and the holy, is best understood in the request he made to Guru Ramanand at the time of his appointment as the Acharya: "If your disciple is to suffer the pain of one scorpion sting, then may the pain of a million scorpion stings befall me on every pore of my body, but no pain should afflict your disciple. And if your disciple is destined to have a begging bowl, then let that begging bowl come to me, but your disciple should not suffer from want of food and clothing. Please grant me these two boons."

Appendix

1. The elderly Lalita met Neelkanth, now popularly known as Bhagwan Swaminarayan or Maharaj, in Loya, unbeknown to her that he was the same Neelkanth who had visited her home until Maharaj reminded her about his visit to their home. Lalita alerted him about the regret she had felt for years after he had left and had longed to put her wrong, right. Maharaj laughed and blessed her.

2. Pitambar did as Neelkanth said. Three boys were born to him, Narsinh, Damji, and Jetha. Pitambar became very happy and a devoted disciple of Maharaj. When the inheritance was shared amongst his sons, Pitambar had accumulated so much money that it had to be weighed.

3. Many years later, Maharaj returned to ask for Jasu's hand in marriage to Dada Khachar, at whose residence in Gadhada he stayed for thirty years.

4. Ganesh Sheth became a devout devotee in the future. He donated funds for the statues of Krishna and Radha in the Junagadh temple. Ganesh did not have a son. Maharaj asked him about the type of son he would like: A son that will eventually die or a son that will live forever. Ganesh replied that he wanted a son who would live forever.

Maharaj asked the monks to bring the statue of Lalji Maharaj and gave it to Ganesh. Ganesh made a will to donate his entire wealth to Lalji upon his death. He had a deep desire to invite Maharaj to Una and parade him on an elephant but failed to fulfill that wish because, by the time he arrived in Gadhada to invite Maharaj, Maharaj had left his earthly body.

Muktanand Swami consoled the distraught Ganesh and gave him the Shaligram that Maharaj had carried with him on his pilgrimage as Neelkanth. The statues of Lalji Maharaj and the Shaligram are, at present, displayed in the temple of Una.

5. Years later, the elderly frail ascetic arrived at the gates of the Dada Khachar's durbar in Gadhada at night and fell to the ground as soon as he entered. Maharaj heard his call and told his disciple Damudar Bhagat to bring a lamp. They rushed to the ascetic lying on the ground and gave him some water. Maharaj sent Damudar to Laduba, a senior woman disciple who often cooked for him, to make some food. 'Tell her, I am hungry,' he said.

Maharaj rushed to Laduba when she came out with a plate. When the ascetic came to his senses, Maharaj raised him from the ground, made him comfortable, and fed him with his own hands, to the surprise of the devotees who had gathered around them.

'Is this not the ashram of Neelkanth Swaminarayan?' the ascetic asked.

'It is his ashram,' said Maharaj.

'Where is he?'

'I am him,' said Maharaj, smiling. 'Did I not promise you that I would come at the time of your death.'

The ascetic gazed at Maharaj. 'You have become very big. When I met you last, you were like a stick. Do you remember you gave me sweets, curry, and fried bread in Hatkeshwar temple?'

'I remember,' Maharaj said.

'You promised you would come at the time of my death.'

'I am here,' Maharaj said.

Relieved by the presence of Maharaj, the ascetic closed his eyes and passed away peacefully.

6. Narsinh Mehta became one of the most devoted disciples of Bhagwan Swaminarayan. Bhagwan Swaminarayan often visited Narsinh's house.

7. With the promise from Neelkanth that he would return, Samu prepared a beautiful shawl and safely put it away in a metal trunk. Neelkanth asked for it when he returned many years later as Bhagwan Swaminarayan, saying, 'I love the worship of devotees who serve selflessly.' Maharaj's body radiated a glow every time he wore the shawl during the morning prayers. Everyone used to rush to watch him.

Brahmanand Swami, one of his senior monks, felt compelled to acquire the shawl and, one day, he said, 'Maharaj, the shawl is too short for you. It doesn't cover your hands or the body fully.'

Maharaj laughed. 'Why are you so interested in the shawl?' Maharaj asked.

While Muktanand Swami was singing, Brahmanand Swami thought for a moment and composed a verse to honor the shawl. When Muktanand Swami stopped singing, Brahmanand Swami sang the verse he had just composed at the top of his voice.

Lucky is the wearer of the shawl
Lucky are the cotton plants that were used to make the shawl
Indeed, lucky are the cotton buds that were used to make the shawl
Lucky are the sparkling beads
Lucky are the colors of the shawl
Indeed, lucky are the people who designed the prints for the shawl
Four hands in length, lucky are the threads that
were used to stitch it
Lucky is the tailor who designed the shawl
Indeed, Lucky is the person who thought of making such a gift
Lucky is the shawl for your wearer is the Lord himself
Indeed, lucky you are because revered saints and
monks meditate on you.

Maharaj laughed when he finished. 'Swami, you are far too big. If it does not fit me, it will certainly not fit you.'

Brahmanand put his palms together. 'Maharaj, I will keep the shawl in my puja. I will meditate on it.'

Maharaj stood up and placed the shawl on Brahmanand Swami. When Brahmanand Swami passed away, he gave the shawl to Devanand Swami, who showed the verse to Poet Dalpatram and gave it to him. The shawl is displayed at Muli Temple at present.

Acknowledgment

Many years ago, I retraced the journey of Neelkanth Varni, visiting many of the places he had visited in his seven-year journey across India. Along the way, I met and keenly observed many pilgrims who told me stories of their search for spirituality, an inner craving that had led them to seek guidance at the feet of the many wise and holy men and women of Mother India. It is a fire that has burnt in the hearts of all Indians since the beginning of civilisation. I am indebted to them all for their inspiration.

Yet, no work, however humble, can be accomplished alone. Many wise and gentle folks, and readers, have held my hand in the long journey of writing and rewriting this book. Notable amongst them are Param Pujya Mahant Swami Maharaj, the Acharyas at Vadtal and Ahmedabad for allowing me access to exhibits; the monks at Bhuj Mandir for their guidance about Bhagwan Swaminarayan's time in Kutch; Pujya Krishnapriyadas Swami from Rajkot Gurukul, whose lectures on Swami Adharanand's stories of Neelkanth Varni have mesmerized me for hours; Pujya Atmaswarup Swami for his encouragement; Pujya Vivekjivandas Swami, Pujya Yogvivekdas Swami, Nirgunpurushdas Swami for their feedback – I bow to them all for their collective wisdom. My heartfelt thanks go to Karan Agarwal at White Falcon, who has so carefully scrutinized every word, every sentence, and every punctuation in the manuscript, to Brijesh Rai, for his patience in staying with me on the long journey of the publication of Neelkanth Varni, and Book layout design by Happy Singh and cover design by Shrikesh Kumar. Lastly, my family, Kanchan, Neil, and Misha, for always being there for me and allowing me to immerse my heart, mind, and soul, for hours on end, into this remarkable tale of Neelkanth Varni.

References

Lectures of Swami Purani Sri Krishnapriyadas on Neelkanth Varni – Rajkot Gurukul

Vachnamrut – Discourses of Bhagwan Swaminarayan

Nilkanth Charitra – BAPS Swaminarayan Aksharpith

The Geeta by Swami Purohit, Faber and Faber Press

From Badrivan to Gangotri BAPS Swami Vivekjivandas and Swami Aksharvatsaldas

CPSIA information can be obtained
at www.ICGtesting.com
Printed in the USA
BVHW010822230123
656717BV00042B/862

9 781636 407814